MW00416835

Addressing
Health Disparities
in the
LGBTQIA+ Community

Sade Kosoko-Lasaki, MD
Mark Duane Goodman, MD
Michael White, MD

ISBN (Print): 978-1-09834-715-4
ISBN (eBook): 978-1-09834-716-1

Table of Contents

Medical Students Write up

Preface

Sade Kosoko-Lasaki, MD, MSPH, MBA

The office of Health Sciences Multicultural and Community Affairs (HS-MACA) at Creighton University was created in 2000. HS-MACA pioneers and synthesizes community, education and research efforts in the development of future health care professionals who are culturally aware and work toward the elimination of health disparities. The mission of the office is *to promote Creighton University as a recognized leader in the training and development of a multicultural health care workforce that serves to reduce health disparities in underserved and diverse communities through research, culturally proficient education, community interaction and engagements through Ignatian values.*

Its vision statement states that *HS-MACA will be recognized and respected as an innovative department that pioneers and synthesizes community, education, research and the development of future healthcare professionals who are culturally aware and work toward the elimination of health disparities.*

The goals of the department include the following:

- To recruit underrepresented or disadvantaged students and faculty in the Health Sciences schools who will promote health and health equality to a diverse population;

- To provide and promote retention activities for culturally competent underrepresented students and faculty;

- To promote, expand and cultivate cultural awareness to campus and community;

- To address health disparities through teaching, research and community advocacy;

- To seek funding opportunities for innovative, integrative and coordinated approaches for the continued and expanded training of diverse health care professionals.

The Medicine Gender and Sexuality Alliance (MedGSA) at Creighton University was created in 2015. The organization aims to establish a safe place for LGBTQIA individuals at Creighton University Medical School. The organization aims to educate about LGBTQIA terminologies and inclusivity. The members hold educational lectures, documentary screenings and informal talks and conversations about topics relating to LGBTQIA issues.

In the same year, 2015, members of the MedGSA organization approached the leadership of HS-MACA to consider designing a course to cover a variety of topics regarding barriers to accessing health care in the LGBTQIA community. Dr Kosoko-Lasaki, the Associate Vice Provost of HSMACA reached out to Dr Mark Goodman, a professor in Family Medicine at Creighton University to help with the design of the course. Members of the MedGSA organizations suggested topics to consider for the course and helped to provide logistical support for the course. The LGBTQIA elective was designed using an existing template of another health disparities elective that Dr Kosoko-Lasaki offers to M4 Medical students. In 2016, Dr Kosoko-Lasaki reached out to Dr Michael White, cardiologist and at that time, Associate Dean for Medical Education at Creighton University, to serve as one of the course directors for the two weeks elective for M4 students.

The LGBTQIA Health Disparities: Issues and Strategies is a two-week course approved by the education committee of the medical school at Creighton University. The course is offered to M4 students and is designed to help students identify the specific health care needs of the LGBTQIA community and the health disparities that affect its members. Students choose their area of focus but are encouraged to choose an area relating to their specialty of interest in residency training. The students also determine the importance of responding respectfully to and preserving the dignity of the LGBTQIA community both within and outside of health and social systems.

The curriculum is attached to this document for the reader's review.

Currently, thirty-eight students have taken this on-going elective. We present the reflections and submission of twenty-eight students in the following chapters in the book. Majority of the students have graduated from medical school. We were able to obtain consent from 19 students to attach their names to the excellent write ups they researched and submitted. The remaining students are described as "anonymous" as we were not able to obtain their consent to attach their names with their work. The names of the "anonymous" student writers are kept on record at Creighton University.

This book will serve as a resource to other medical students, health professions students in Dentistry, Pharmacy, Occupational and Physical Therapy, Nursing, Public Health and the Social Sciences.

Acknowledgement

Sade Kosoko-Lasaki, MD, MSPH, MBA

I thank God the Almighty for his blessings and for giving me the ability to edit this book. My husband, Dr Gbolahan Lasaki, PhD has been a source of encouragement with his unconditional love and support. My children and their families have given me the fortitude and strength both directly and indirectly to continue to give the best of my ability to all God's children even as we address disparities in health care.

Ms Phebe Mercado Jungman, my administrative Specialist at Creighton University has done an excellent job of copyediting and collating the manuscript while Twister Jover is responsible for the cover photograph and design. I appreciate their efforts tremendously.

Finally, I want to thank the leadership at Creighton University, especially the president, Fr. Daniel Hendrickson, PhD and the provost, Thomas Murray, PhD for their true commitment to diversity in all its forms.

The staff of Health Sciences' Multicultural and Community Affairs (HS-MACA) at Creighton University and all the wonderful students, faculty, staff and community that we serve have made this book possible through their comments, challenges and goodwill. The medical students who took the elective that formed this book have done an exceptional job.

My co-authors, Dr Mark Goodman and Dr Michael White are wonderful people to collaborate with. I have enjoyed the experience. Thank you.

Mark Duane Goodman, MD

I honor and thank each of our students, who are creating a better world.

I honor and thank my teachers and mentors, especially Dr. Kosoko-Lasaki for the opportunity to contribute to a kinder and more inclusive world.

I honor and thank my half-side, Rick Shever for being my wingman.

I honor and thank Creator; it has been a wonderful journey thus far.

Michael White, MD, MBA

I am grateful for the support and opportunity of many individuals to allow my participation to edit this book to continue contribute to the growth of knowledge of disparities in healthcare. Specifically, my wife Jolene, who is a constant foundation to build all the success with support and dedication to our families. My daughters Kayli, Emma, and Avery who continue to mature and bring their gifts to their friends and our families.

I recognize the commitment of the healthcare delivery partners; Common Spirit Health with both CHI Health and Dignity Health, Valleywise Health and District Medical Group, that allow Creighton students to be an integral part of care delivery as an essential component of learning. Without these environments, our students would not be able to have the experience to see the direct impact that health disparities have on our patients.

Thank you to Drs. Kosoko-Lasaki and Goodman for allowing me to collaborate on this important work, as well as Ms. Phebe Jungman to coordinate all of these efforts and bring this to fruition.

About the Authors

Sade Kosoko-Lasaki, MD, MSPH, MBA

Sade Kosoko-Lasaki, MD, MSPH, MBA is associate vice provost for Health Sciences, professor of surgery (ophthalmology) and professor of preventive medicine and public health at Creighton University. She is co-founder and co-director of Creighton's Center for Promoting Health and Health Equity (CPHHE) and is a multiple national award winner and an internationally renowned researcher in minority health with a focus on increasing the health care workforce.

Dr. Kosoko-Lasaki has led Creighton University's participation in the training and education of a diverse group of faculty and students at the pre-collegiate and collegiate levels in Nebraska which has resulted in the award of several multi-million-dollar award research initiatives. In addition, her efforts helped achieve the designation of the Creighton School of Medicine as a Center of Excellence in Minority Education from 2005 to 2008.

She leads Creighton's Office of Health Sciences-Multicultural and Community Affairs through programs such as the pre-Medical, pre-Dental and pre-Pharmacy and Health Professions post baccalaureate and pre-matriculation programs;the Health Careers Opportunity Program (HCOP); the Health Professions Pipeline Program; Cultural Proficiency Seminars, Community Outreach Primary Care (COPC) and Health Disparities Initiatives with a focus on community-based participatory research.

As co-founder and co-leader of CPHHE, a community-university collaborative virtual center designed to promote wellness in the Omaha Community, Dr Kosoko-Lasaki and her colleagues have developed a Racial and Ethnic Approach to Community Health (REACH) initiative to reduce chronic disease health disparities in the African American community in Omaha with funding from the U.S. Centers for Disease Control.

Dr. Kosoko-Lasaki has built collaborative relationships locally, nationally and worldwide while serving as a community/academic leader in the Omaha area. She oversees the recruitment of disadvantaged students to Creighton's health science schools, and mentors these students to retain them. Dr. Kosoko-Lasaki has lectured nationally and internationally on cultural proficiency and health disparity issues, focusing on the promotion of "pipeline programs" that prepare and support disadvantaged students from fourth grade through health professional schools, so the students can become successful health care providers.

As an ophthalmologist with a public health degree, Dr. Kosoko-Lasaki is passionate about training and educating individuals in developing countries on blindness prevention, specifically Vitamin A deficiency, which is the leading cause of preventable blindness in children and a major public health problem throughout the world. She is also a specialist in the treatment of glaucoma.

She has served as a consultant to UNICEF, USAID and Helen Keller International in Burkina Faso, Niger, Mauritania, Chad and the Philippines.

Since 1986, Dr. Kosoko-Lasaki, a clinician and surgeon, has researched the prevalence of glaucoma in blacks in St. Lucia, West Indies. With a focus on detecting and treating glaucoma — the most common cause of blindness in African Americans and Hispanics – she has initiated health fairs and screenings throughout the Washington DC metropolitan area, in Nebraska, Iowa, Kansas, the U.S. Virgin Islands and in the Dominican Republic.

In 2001, she created a program for blindness prevention at Creighton University entitled, "Preventing Glaucoma Blindness in Nebraska: A Creighton University Initiative," which targeted individuals at risk for glaucoma blindness in Omaha and surrounding states. Dr. Kosoko-Lasaki had a clinical practice at Creighton University Medical Center from 2000-2015 where she took care of a majority of African Americans and Hispanics: a population with high prevalence of glaucoma. Currently, she practices ophthalmology (Glaucoma) at the Veterans Health Administration in Nebraska and Western Iowa.

Dr. Kosoko-Lasaki has written over a hundred and fifty publications in peer-reviewed journals and has co-authored "Maintaining the Target Intraocular Pressure: African American Glaucoma Specialist", a textbook, "Cultural Proficiency in Addressing Health Disparities" and recently a book, "Diversity and Inclusion in a More Perfect University: HS-MACA Twenty Year History of Success".

Dr Sade Kosoko-Lasaki is married to Dr Gbolahan Lasaki, PhD, a petroleum engineer. She has three children of her own and three stepchildren. They are blessed with four grandchildren.

Mark Duane Goodman, MD

"Enjoy the journey if you can, it's all quite humorous after all!"

That gregarious attitude led Dr. Mark Goodman into a vocation where he would be able to interact with people. Combine that with his desire to find a career that "mattered" and it's no wonder he became a doctor.

The environment at Alegent Creighton Health Clinic plays right into Dr. Goodman's extroverted nature. He has built himself a fine list of consultants that he knows and trusts. The benefits of working as part of a team go directly to the patient.

Dr. Goodman enjoys teaching caregivers of the future so he can leave a legacy for future generations. Research and publications can do only so much but passing the gift of medicine to the students and residents keeps giving.

Dr. Goodman lists yoga, triathlons, travel and dogs as some of his favorite things. He is also passionate about seeking justice, meaning and kindness in his life.

Michael White, MD, MBA

Michael D. White, MD, currently serves as the Executive Vice President and Chief Medical Officer of Valleywise Health in Phoenix, Arizona. Valleywise Health (formerly Maricopa Integrated Health System) has a proud tradition of being both the community safety net health care system, with a mission and commitment to serving the underserved and Arizona's only public teaching hospital.  Valleywise Health consists of Valleywise Health Medical Center, the only Level I Trauma Center in Maricopa County verified by the American College of Surgeons to care for both adults and children, Arizona's only nationally verified Burn Center serving the entire Southwestern United States, the McDowell Healthcare Center, the largest provider of HIV primary care in Arizona, women's and pediatric refugee health services, the Arizona Children's Center, three behavioral health centers, and 12 FQHC sites throughout Maricopa County. Dr. White joined Valleywise Health in August 2019.

Dr. White currently also serves as Associate Dean for Technology and Informatics at the Creighton University School of Medicine. He continually identifies opportunities to enhance the learning environment for healthcare clinicians of the future. Dr. White is an Associate Professor of Medicine in the Division of Cardiology. He joined the faculty of Creighton University School of Medicine in 2008. He previously served as Associate Dean for Medical Education in 2013 and held that role until 2015. In this prior Associate

Dean role, Dr. White oversaw the curriculum for undergraduate medical student education.

Dr. White is a practicing interventional cardiologist. He is board-certified in internal medicine, cardiovascular diseases, and interventional cardiology. He received his Bachelor of Science degree in biology from Creighton University. Dr. White received his medical degree from the Creighton University School of Medicine. He also completed a residency in internal medicine and a fellowship in cardiovascular disease. He completed a fellowship in interventional cardiology at Duke University in Durham, North Carolina. Dr. White earned his MBA degree from Creighton University in 2019.

Contributing Authors

Faculty

1. Dr. Michael Green

2. Dr. Michael White

3. Dr. Mark Duane Goodman

4. Dr. Sade Kosoko-Lasaki

Medical Students

1. Ahmed Tahseen

2. Brianna Bahe

3. Bradley Pfeifer

4. Brittany Simon

5. Christopher Williams

6. Courtney Getchell

7. Hanna Mulder

8. Hannah Van Galder

9. Hussein Safa

10. John Morelli

11. Joseph Saffold

12. Mitchel Kohl

13. Nicholas Giancola

14. Rei Christian Calma

15. Sana Kiblinger

16. Theodore Bosi

17. Tiffany Clark

18. Tyler Badding

19. Zackary Roesch

20. *Anonymous Authors (10)

*These are students who we could not reach to sign a release of their write-ups for publication

Description of the LGBTQIA
Health Disparities Elective

The LGBTQ Health Disparities is an independent study (elective) offered to medical students at Creighton University in the fourth-year curriculum. The course plan and output are described below:

Course Plan

Week 1 – Research

1. Schedule meeting with Dr. Kosoko-Lasaki during week 1.

2. View 10-minute LGBTQIA Healthcare Training Video: "To Treat Me, You Have to Know Who I Am." https://www.youtube.com/watch?v=NUhvJgxgAac

LGBT Healthcare Training Video: 'To Treat Me, You Have to Know Who I Am'

3. Attend one of the three (3) 90-minute GLMA webinars "Quality Healthcare for Lesbian, Gay, Bisexual & Transgender People." http://www.glma.org/index.cfm?fuseaction=Page.viewPage&pageId=1025&grandparentID=534&parentID=940&nodeID=1

4. Read from "Health Disparities and the LGBT Population" – book provided **The importance of sexual orientation disclosure to physicians for women who have sex with women.** Willes, K., & Allen, M. (2014, April). In V. Harvey. & T. Heinz Housel (Eds.), Health Care Disparities and the LGBT Population. Lanham, CT: Lexington Books.

5. **Coming Out Conversations and Gay/Bisexual Health: A Constitutive Model Study.** Manning, Jimmie (2014, April) In V. Harvey. & T. Heinz Housel (Eds.), Health Care Disparities and the LGBT Population. Lanham, CT: Lexington Books.

Part 1: Understanding the Health Needs of LGBT People: An Introduction

Click here to access the archived webinar.

Part 1 of the series, Quality Healthcare for Lesbian, Gay, Bisexual & Transgender People, explores the unique health needs of LGBT people. During this introduction to LGBT health, speakers provide an overview of associated terminology and concepts, describe social issues that impact the health and well-being of LGBT people and discuss specific clinical considerations for LGBT people. Click here to read more about Part 1.

Part 2: Creating a Welcoming and Safe Environment for LGBT People and Families

Click here to access the archived webinar.

Building on the first part of GLMA's cultural competence webinar series exploring the health concerns and healthcare of lesbian, gay, bisexual and transgender (LGBT) people, Part 2 will focus on creating a welcoming and safe healthcare environment. LGBT people face many barriers in accessing healthcare including discrimination, lack of access, misunderstanding and fear. As a consequence, many LGBT people do not regularly access appropriate and timely care. The more informed healthcare professionals are, the more comfortable LGBT patients and clients will feel in an environment that is often alienating, disrespectful and traumatic. In order to create a more welcoming environment, it is essential to look at each aspect from the front desk to the clinical level. Click here to read more about Part 2.

Part 3: Clinical Skills for the Care of Transgender Individuals

Click here to access the archived webinar.

Building on the first two parts of GLMA's cultural competence webinar series exploring the health concerns and healthcare of lesbian, gay, bisexual and transgender (LGBT) people, Part 3 will focus on clinical skills for the care of transgender individuals, including behavioral health. The webinar will be framed using GLMA's Top Ten Things Transgender Persons Should Discuss with their Health Providers, an evidence-based patient education resource. During this 90 minute webinar, the presenters will provide clinical best practices on salient health issues for the transgender population. Click here to read more about Part 3.

This webinar series is a project of GLMA in collaboration with the Hopkins Center for Health Disparities Solutions, Johns Hopkins Bloomberg School of Public Health.

6. Meet with Dr. Kosoko-Lasaki to discuss assignments/progress.

7. Schedule meeting with Dr. Greene the 2-week elective. Dr. Greene will provide advice and counsel to the students as complete LGBTQIA Health Disparities Research. To schedule this meeting email Dr. Greene

(MichaelGreene@creighton.edu) (This meeting must be after final topic is approved by Dr. Kosoko-Lasaki).

8. Identify healthcare disparities facing lesbian, gay, bisexual, and transgender individuals (this topic is used to create final paper)

9. Obtain final paper topic approval from Dr. Kosoko-Lasaki.

10. In addition to meeting Dr. Greene, students must meet with at least one person who is knowledgeable about the Health Disparity topic chosen.

Week 2 – Write Paper

1. Write a 6-page, double-spaced paper on the subject. Paper should be written APA style. Your paper must address the following categories:

   · Introduction

   · Background

   · Public Health

   · Global Perspective

   · Research (interactions)

   · Recommendations

   · Conclusion

2. Paper due date <u>48 hours before final meeting with Dr. Kosoko-Lasaki</u>.

3. Meet with Dr. Kosoko-Lasaki to review paper.

4. Present the paper at a disparity-related forum such as *Common Ground* or other Health Disparity program before graduation from medical school.

Chapter 1.

Introduction

Mark Duane Goodman, MD

Throughout human history there have been individuals who did not sexually conform to the mainstream: and throughout human history these persons have been variously maligned, celebrated, killed, honored, bullied and protected. Perceptions are changing today: but discrimination and misinformation persist. Our book is an attempt to add to the conversation in the pursuit of justice and tolerance especially as it relates to the care of our patients and the education of our students.

"The arc of the moral universe is long, but it bends toward justice." Theodore Parker 1853

Our compilation is a collection of edited submissions from our Creighton medical students over the past few years. To deepen their understanding, we asked the students to attempt to evaluate the medical system from the viewpoint of someone in the LGBTQ (lesbian, gay, bisexual, transgender, queer/questioning) community, and then write about it. Many students discovered injustice, and some identified the "special burdens" that came with being LGBTQ and in need of medical care. Some of the essays reveal how communities and governments also participate in injustice, not just medical caregivers or medical systems.

LGBTQ persons have an interesting history with medical caregivers: recognizing, for example, the deep and extraordinary bonds between a person living with HIV in the 1980's and his or her caregiver, which were often defined as heroic, generous and incredibly kind. Consider also ACT-UP, (AIDS Coalition To Unleash Power) which had a loud voice for fast-tracking potential life-saving treatments at a time when the medical system was moving too slowly.

Despite existing protections, LGBTQ people face disturbing rates of health care discrimination—from harassment and humiliation by providers to being turned away by hospitals, pharmacists, and doctors. The CAP (Center for American Progress) survey data show the types of discrimination that many LGBTQ people face when seeking health care.

Among lesbian, gay, bisexual, and queer (LGBTQ) respondents who had visited a doctor or health care provider in the year before the survey:

- 8 percent said that a doctor or other health care provider refused to see them because of their actual or perceived sexual orientation.

- 6 percent said that a doctor or other health care provider refused to give them health care related to their actual or perceived sexual orientation.

- 7 percent said that a doctor or other health care provider refused to recognize their family, including a child or a same-sex spouse or partner.

- 9 percent said that a doctor or other health care provider used harsh or abusive language when treating them.

- 7 percent said that they experienced unwanted physical contact from a doctor or other health care provider (such as fondling, sexual assault, or rape).

Data from a large observational study suggests that 24% of transgender persons report unequal treatment in health care environments, 19% report refusal of care altogether, and 33% do not seek preventive services.

LGBT youth are at a higher risk for substance use, sexually transmitted diseases (STDs), cancers, cardiovascular diseases, obesity, bullying, isolation, rejection, anxiety, depression, and suicide as compared to the general population. LGBT youth receive poor quality of care due to stigma, lack of healthcare providers' awareness, and insensitivity to the unique needs of this community. Young LGBT individuals find it difficult to report their sexual identity to their clinicians. Some clinicians are not well trained in addressing the concerns of members of this community. A study conducted in Washington DC showed that 68% of sexual minority youth reported about not discussing their sexual orientation, and 90% reported reservations about reporting them to their clinicians.

As with all patient populations, effectively serving LGBT patients requires clinicians to understand the cultural context of their patients' lives, modify practice policies and environments to be inclusive, take detailed and non-judgmental histories, educate themselves about the health issues of importance to their patients, and reflect upon personal attitudes that might prevent them from providing the kind of affirmative care that LGBT people need. By taking these steps, clinicians will ensure that their LGBT patients, and indeed all their patients, attain the highest possible level of health.

The Stonewall riots of June 28, 1969 are considered the starting point of the modern gay liberation movement. Stonewall memorial marches evolved into the PRIDE marches of today. In 2001, the Netherlands became the first country to legalize same-sex marriages. As of November 1, 2019, same-sex marriages are legal in 30 countries. The gay rights movements of the 1970's was overshadowed by the AIDS crisis of the 1980's and beyond: and now resumes with new vigor.

Today, societies around the globe still struggle with gender non-conforming and the same sex relationships, churches, governments and nations are sometimes digging their heels, and sometimes changing: sometimes parting and sometimes reconciling: just like all other human relationships. Thank you for permitting the essays from our students to contribute to the conversation.

References:

1. Shabab Ahmed Mirza & Caitlin Rooney, "Discrimination Prevents LGBTQ People from Accessing Health Care," Center for American Progress, January 18, 2018, https://www.americanprogress.org/issues/lgbt/news/2018/01/18/445130/discrimination-prevents-lgbtq-people-accessing-health-care (accessed June 1, 2018).

2. Grant, IM, Mottett LA, Tanis J, Harrison, J, Herman, JL, Keisling, M. Injustice at every turn: a report of the National Transgender Discrimination survey July 5, 2018

3. Cureus. 2017 Apr; 9(4): e1184 PMCID: PMC5478215, PMID: 28638747 Monitoring Editor: Alexander Muacevic and John R Adler

4. Improving the Health cAre of Lesbian, Gay Bisexual and Transgender (LGBT) People: Understanding and Eliminating Health Disparities, Kevin L Ard MD, MPH, and Harvey J Makadon MD, The National LGBT Health education Center, The Fenway Institue; Brigham and Women's Hospital and harvard Medical School Boston, MA

5. https://www.history.com › topics › gay-rights › the-stonewall-riots

6. https://www.usatoday.com › story › money › 2019/06/13 › countries-wher...

7. https://www.pewforum.org› fact-sheet › gay-marriage-around-the-world

Chapter 2.

The Education of the Medical Students

Michael White, MD, MBA

Introduction

The goal of medical education is to produce physicians who are prepared to serve the fundamental purposes of medicine. To achieve this goal, physicians must possess the attributes that are necessary to meet their individual and collective responsibilities to society. If medical education is to serve the goal of medicine, educational curricula must address learning objectives for programs that reflect an understanding of those attributes. Medical knowledge is accelerating exponentially, and it is essential to train students with the skills related to life-long learning that will allow them to be successful throughout their careers. This allows a learner to progress from undergraduate through medical education (medical school) to graduate medical education (internship and residency) into continuing educational programs after completion of training.

Contemporary medical education is rooted in the fundamentals presented by Dr. Abraham Flexner in his seminal report released in 1910. Flexner promoted a move away from an apprenticeship model of training to an academic model of education which included didactic instruction, research, and ultimately the real-life application. In the late 1990's, due partly to the Institute of Medicine reports[1] on medical errors and the need for better healthcare delivery, medical education professionals began to shift curricular focus to systems-related competencies. The Association of American Medical Colleges (AAMC) has recommended that medical students should accomplish 13 Entrustable Professional Activities (EPAs) prior to graduation and entering residency education. These foundational skills are necessary to build upon to be a successful physician. The Accreditation Council on Graduate Medical Education (ACGME) and American Board of Medical Specialties (ABMS) endorsed the move towards competency-based education in 1999 with approval of the six core competencies which in addition to system-based practice included: patient care, medical knowledge, interpersonal and communication skills, professionalism and practice-based learning and improvement.

In order to achieve a successful career in medicine, a physician must be able to assimilate new and changing information. A key process in this is to develop a process of reflection that will allow maximization of deep learning and professional practice. Initiation of courses within undergraduate medical education curricula that promote a practice of reflection early in the process of professional formation as a skill to be refined throughout a career.

Adult Education

A key step forward improving educational programs in medicine involves appreciating the way adults learn. In order to reach a medical student audience more effectively, educators must understand assumptions regarding adult learners. In 1926, Albert Lindeman identified a series of 5 assumptions regarding adult learners.

1. Adults are motivated to learn as they experience needs and interests arise that require increased knowledge or training. To be successful, learning activities need to be centered around these points.

2. An adult's orientation to learning has foundation in life events. Organizing learning in this way are around situations and not subjects.

3. Experience is the richest source for adult learning and therefore reflection on these experiences are one of the core methodologies for adult learning.

4. A successful educator of adult learners recognize that adults want to direct their own learning. Medical educators serve as a guide and a partner in the inquiries determined by the learner.

5. Differences among adult learners increase with age and therefore educators need to optimize the learning environment by adapting to the style, place, and time of learning.

The motivation to learn must be internal and facilitation must focus on the experiences and needs of the individual learner. Successful medical curricula enhance the skills that help individuals refine their self-structure to guide life-long learning.

As learners age, maturity increases which can lead to increased motivation. Most pedagogical models are rooted in dependency in which the learner expects that the teacher will make all of the decisions about the material to be learned and how it will be taught. This is counter to the way mature adults learn as they require the capacity to be self-directing, identify their readiness to learn, and organize their learning around life experiences. Medical educators are currently in a state of flux in redesigning many of the medical curricula throughout the country to more actively embrace adult learning principles.

Experience suggests that learning occurs in different ways, both within an individual and between learners. While one person may learn by listening to a presentation, another may prefer to learn by reading or finally by participating in an activity. The manner in which an individual most effectively acquires and applies information may be described as their cognitive style. Many learners may use a combination of visualization, listening and verbalization. Design of curricula and experiences encourage learners in material and facilitate a better comprehension.

Building an environment conducive to adult learning is an additional important consideration to facilitate incorporation of the information to enhance patient care. Adults learn best when certain conditions are met, for example when they feel the need to learn and have input into what, why and how they will learn. Additionally, the content and activities of learning have a perceived and meaningful relationship to past experiences. Other factors include what is to be learned as it relates to the learner's individual goals, the climate minimizes anxiety and encourages freedom to new ideas, experiment, and learning styles are accommodated.

Creating experiences within a medical education curriculum for learners to practice these skills is essential to create the next generation of physicians. Most curricula are challenged to better prepare future physicians to address the increasing healthcare needs of culturally racially and inclusively diverse societies. Service-learning is a strategy that will empower learners by immersing them in an environment of authentic experiences that fosters critical thinking, problem solving, and the application of knowledge. The focus on service-learning makes it possible for learners to work in communities of need. In this environment, the learner can discover relationships among the concepts themselves, rather than being a passive recipient of prescriptive information. These activities can be categorized into three broad modalities: education and training, clinic and community-based, with advocacy, policy or outreach. Regardless of the activity, the service must be meaningful and have the learner in a position of ownership, allow for adequate supervision, and be appropriate for the needs being addressed.

Reflection is the key element to connect service and learning to the experience of the learner. These reflections should be continuous, connected to academic and real-life needs, facilitate critical thinking, and involve opportunities for communication. Reflective practice and learning are central to medical education and a successful career in medicine. The drivers for promoting and developing competency in reflection are individual learning and professional competence. Understanding, demonstrating outcomes and promoting a desire for learning is valuable in improving clinical competence and performance.

Our Lesbian, Gay, Bisexual and Transgender (LGBTQ) elective that forms the basis of this book was designed with the guidelines in mind. The elective is taken in the fourth year of medical school. Our students can learn through literature search, webinars, video conferencing and interaction with faculty that care for the LGBTQ population. The students also interact with some members of the LGBTQ population and can learn firsthand the health disparities that this group is experiencing and how to prevent and address such disparities. The students write a reflection paper about their experience and discuss their observation, newly acquired knowledge with core faculty teaching the elective. Medical education requires a diverse group of experiences to foster the development of the next generation of physicians. Active experiences, including service-learning and reflection, are key foundational elements to develop skills that will form the life-long learning skills necessary for a successful care in medicine. These opportunities should begin early in the curriculum and be reinforced at multiple points to facilitate integration for future habits.

References:

1. Flexner A. Medical education in the United States and Canada: a report to the Carnegie Foundation for the Advancement of Teaching. New York: Carnegie Foundation for the Advancement of Teaching, 1910.

2. Institute of Medicine (US). Committee on Quality of Health Care in America. *Crossing the quality chasm: a new health system for the 21st century.* Washington (DC): National Academy Press; 2001.

3. Kohn LT, Corrigan J, Donaldson MS. *To err is human: building a safer health system.* Washington (DC): National Academy Press; 2000.

4. Lindeman, E.C. The Meaning of Adult Education. New York; New Republic. 1926.

5. Knowles, M.S. The Adult Learner (5 ed.). Houston, TX: Gulf Publishing. 1998.

Chapter 3.

Accepting Care of LGBTQIA Patients: A Clinical Perspective

Michael A Greene, MD

Program Director, Creighton University Department of Family Medicine

In the longitudinal care of any patient, there are four principles and one attitude that are helpful in establishing the healing therapeutic provider-patient relationship that is foundational for primary care. These principles acted upon by an experienced clinician -well versed in navigating the sometimes turbulent waters of any committed human relationship, have the capacity to grow both the patient and provider in their respective self-actualization. Having a meaningful relationship with a primary care provider and the opportunities that arise from that can provide healing to person wounded by the inadvertent word or deliberate action. The attitude opens the space for the healing to occur as long as the patient feels safe and motivated to step into it. These four principles together and one attitude together act in synchrony to create a clinical culture that attracts persons seeking release and maintains persons seeking growth. While this culture is of universal benefit to all patients, LGBTQIA patients may especially benefit from the inherent inclusivity

The first principle is that the longitudinal care of the LGBTQIA person (indeed any person) takes time. In order to grow the relationship two people must spend some time together. In this time, they get to know each other, they find common interests and learn through trial and error preferences and dislikes. The healing of the provider-patient relationship often comes over time. The longer the time, the deeper the healing. On the first visit the patient presents with the broken wrist, which is cast. the next visit ends with a cast and some tears. the next visit brings xrays, and some revelations about unhappy relationships. fracture healing is followed by some veiled discussion of domestic violence. further visits culminate in a safe house and introspection. healing begins while health care maintenance is performed and after years, personal growth by both the patient and provider reveal the creation of support groups an blossoming of new relationships and safe spaces. The time of the provider-patient relationship is unique in its brevity. Often taking place in 15-minute intervals, this relationship is the Haiku of structured human relationships. Yet over time, those 15-minute intervals become years of shared experience and mutual reward. Keeping the principle in mind that a commitment to a long-term relationship occurring in fifteen-minute intervals over time is one way to bring health to a LGBTQIA person

The second principle is Trust. For the relationship to grow each party must have a reasonable belief that the other party is trustworthy. As is so often remarked trust must often be earned. of what does this trust consist of? what is trusted by the patient? what is trusted by the provider? To the patient, trust that the provider is beneficent, competent, committed. Beneficent here means that the provider has the patient's best interest at heart as determined by the patient with guidance from the expertise of the provider. While the patient knows ze wants to run the half marathon the provider articulates the training pathway. Competent providers know their craft, study regularly, challenge old opinions with new information for the betterment of the patient and the leveling of the ego. The patient needs to trust the provider is committed to them. After much divulging, expunging, recounting, explaining, grappling and growing with the provider it is difficulty and frankly traumatic to start over. stability is one hallmark of a good primary care provider. For the provider, trust means willingness to move on the path to healing. Willingness is key concept but note that willingness to move on the path, and not actually movement, is sufficient for the provider to build a relationship on. what is conspicuously lacking as an essential requirement for providers to expect of patients in order to grow the provider-patient relationship is Honesty on the part of the patient. Honesty on the part of the provider is always demanded. Honesty is a tricky concept. While trust is building, information may be parceled out by the patient and not fully expounded upon and this is appropriate. The provider, for their part, must be always aware that this is happening and must not fall into the cognitive error of assuming information that has not been share or "read between the lines" of information that has been given out. Some disease states have denial as an essential feature of the illness through no fault of the patient. And in the case of addiction for example, lack of honesty is a gut-wrenching part of the illness and yet does not preclude a meaningful, healing relationship to develop. The patient cannot deliberately deceive the provider and still expect the same level of healing to occur as if the deception was not present, however. Denial, self-deceit is inhibitory to the growth of the patient but not necessarily the relationship.

The third principle is transparency. Transparency is as simple as telling the patient what you are going to do before you do it, and why. It is also revealing why you are asking or going to ask a series of questions in a way that the patient is able to understand why you need to know and how knowing will help the provider take better care of the patient. Most of all transparency is revealing and reassuring over and over that the intent and goal of the provider is to be helpful, beneficial and not to cause harm. Transparency in a relationship is essential in order to build rapport, prevent miscommunication and avoid anxiety. The provider should be transparent about their role as coach and advisor rather than one who will condemn or sit in judgment. In fact, judgement, with its resultant emotion of shame is rarely helpful to individual patient and self-judgment and shame are the cause of many health problems. The transparency about all actions or questions the provider has will help avoid any possible miscommunications. For example, rather than just asking about sexual partners, providers should instead announce the preamble "in order to make recommendations to you about your health its helpful for me to know . . ." Over time, as they get to know one another, less preamble is needed, and the conversation flows more naturally. The more specific the reason the more helpful for the patient to reduce anxiety. Questions should be asked in such a way as to not lead or appear judgmental. Simply asking questions of everyone has the effect of normalizing potentially embarrassing or shameful topics. In the interest of transparency, if what the provider wants to know is if the patient has had to engage in unwelcome sexual intercourse rather than asking "no one has ever forced you to have sex, right?" Ask instead "to the following questions answer always, sometimes, rarely, never. I have been forced to have sex when I did not want to". The provider must at certain intervals, bring the relationship into the light as an object of infection to see what each of them has learned.

The fourth principle is that of trauma informed care. Trauma informed care is care of the individual with special attention the fact that many persons in our society have experienced trauma and the provider, as well as the entire health care team, is making special effort to not re-traumatize the patient. It is a way of conducting the entire health care experience from check in to visit to check out in a way that places the patient in the center and makes special care from the health care team to allow the patient to be safe, secure, cared for and respected. there are many aspects of trauma informed care, some of which have been discussed above.

Imbuing all of the foregoing, it is important the provider conduct themselves with an Attitude of curiosity. Curiosity allows the patient to be placed at center, as important and worthwhile. Curiosity and gentle wondering on the part of the provider fosters an atmosphere of value onto the patient. It acknowledges that every patient is unique, and every person has a backstory that lead them to where they are today. Even patients that the provider knows well should be approached with curiosity always allowing the patient to be the person that they are today and have the values that they have today rather than who they were yesterday. Being curious allows the provider to ask about goals and values over and over rather than assuming them in the case of long-standing patient. This non-judgement culture delights in patients being the person that they are and gives the space for them to express themselves as they are.

These are some of the important principles of the "care" of the LGBTQIA patient. The final piece to discuss is the "taking" part. In English speaking society the phrase "taking care" is often used, as in Taking care of someone. Taking care of any person requires a deliberate action on the part of the Provider, a reaching out to the other person to that which is handed over. For health care providers, Taking is an action that connotes an aggression or invasion. Perhaps a better phrase in English might be accepting care. The life is still that of the patient, the problems remain their own. What then is accepted? In actuality it is the relationship that is accepted. This relationship is a special kind of relationship. It is the healing of open honest and free conversation with a health care expert who is informed in the person of the patient as they stand in relation to their family, their culture, their society, their goals and their dreams.

Chapter 4.
Medical Students Write Up

LGBTQIA Youth: Vulnerabilities within Palliative Care

Badding, Tyler

Introduction

In pediatric medicine, the goals set by patients and their families typically pertain to healing, reassurance, and ensuring healthy growth. Pediatric healthcare professionals are instrumental team members to the completion of these goals. From outpatient clinics to intensive care units, the collective pediatric team strives for each child to flourish and achieve adulthood. Yet, some children tragically are not awarded such fortunate and expected outcomes. It is estimated that over 45,000 infants, children and adolescents, as well as 18,500 young adults aged between 20 to 24 perish each year in the United States of America due to health-related illness, trauma, or congenital disease (Feudtner et al., 2015). These unimaginable consequences faced by families have been met with healthcare teams who solely focus upon pediatric palliative needs. The American Academy of Pediatrics and academic institutions have advanced these needs with educational materials for families and guidelines directed towards pediatric end-of-life care.

While the advances in palliative pediatric medicine have been substantial, a vulnerable population remains largely unresearched in current literature. LGBTQIA youth, a group aged from 13 to 24 who identify as lesbian, gay, bisexual, transgender, queer, intersex, and asexual, represent an at-risk population within pediatrics. Estimated to be quantitatively similar to adults who identify as LGBTQIA (nearly 7.3%), these youth have increased risks of abuse, and lack psychosocial support when compared to their heterosexual counterparts (Baams, 2018; Gates, 2017). Therefore, when LGBTQIA youth require palliative services, the unique challenges present within their sociomedical spheres are intensified with the complexities of end-of-life care. This work will analyze LGBTQIA studies addressing care these youth (aged 13-24), adult palliation to better understand the uniqueness of LGBTQIA disparities, as well as describe why further research and guidelines should be devoted to these young and vulnerable patients.

Background

To better describe these unique palliative needs, it is crucial to investigate current LGBTQIA vulnerabilities in this pediatric population. According to the Centers for Disease Control and Prevention 2017 HIV Surveillance Report, LGBTQIA youth remain at increased risk for HIV infection and conversely are less likely to seek treatment (2017). Further reports show that LGBTQIA youth are more likely to abuse tobacco, alcohol, and prescription opioids (Kann et al. 2016; Girouard, 2018). Kann et al. (2016) has also indicated that LGBTQIA students from grades 9 to 12 are 43% more likely to consider attempting suicide or harming themselves when compared to their heterosexual counterparts. These attempts are 6 times more likely to require intensive care treatment compared to heterosexual studies (CDC, 2016). Serious infections, substance abuse, and suicidal ideation places this population at increased risk for severe health consequences that may require palliation.

Often the first intervening force aimed at mitigating these health concerns falls upon the pediatric healthcare team; unsurprisingly, rates of depression and suicidal ideation decrease dramatically when these teams are included within a pediatric care unit (Hunt, Vennat, & Waters, 2018). Yet, a significant majority of patients describe negative experiences in pediatric clinics and emergency rooms; these negative experiences are described as poor patient-provider communication, disrespect, and a lack or avoidance of sexual health related discussions (Snyder, Burack, & Petrova, 2017). Unfortunately, LGBTQIA youth who have had such negative experiences frequently limit their health-seeking behavior despite the increased life-altering medical risks they often carry (Ard & Makadon, 2012). Furthermore, Meyer (2013) indicates that LGBTQIA youth are several times more likely to experience abuse during childhood. Abusers are more likely to be within the familial unit, often resulting in polyvictimization, a term used to describe a culmination of psychological and physical harm (Baams, 2018; Meyer, 2013). Polyvictimization often results in poor mental health and socioeconomic outcomes (Turner et al., 2015). Forge et al. (2018) argue that LGBTQIA youth are more likely to experience homelessness compared to their heterosexual counterparts; this adverse outcome is often a result of poor familial acceptance complicated with polyvictimization. Poor perception of healthcare complicated by inadequate familial support increases the risk that serious illness, substance abuse, or suicidal ideation may go untreated until it is too late for these vulnerable youth.

The above-mentioned understandings of LGBTQIA pediatric care is important while analyzing the current model of pediatric palliative care. Pediatric palliation is defined as relieving suffering, improving quality of life, facilitating informed decision-making, and assisting in care coordination before, during, and after the untimely death of a child (American Academy of Pediatrics [AAP], 2013). Palliation is a critical asset offered to families during perhaps the most distressing of all healthcare-associated inevitabilities: the death of a child. Thankfully, thorough guidelines are provided to pediatric providers to navigate the intricacies of end-of-life care. The AAP (2013) emphasizes twelve guidelines; the most relevant to the current discussion include the following: collaborative and integrated multimodal care, patient care safety and quality, familial and sibling support, continued research and quality improvement. Briefly, collaboration can be defined as an interdisciplinary approach involving the multitudes of relationships impacting the child; utilizing numerous knowledge bases addresses several facets of pediatric well-being. Patient care safety and quality aim to minimize suffering, allow for bereavement, and provide anticipatory guidance regarding death and dying. Familial and sibling support is described as caring for the familial unit; spiritual, mental, and respite care services are an important conduit for caregivers to remain well both during and after the end-of-life process. Furthermore, bereavement affects siblings of dying patients. The AAP (2013) recommends consistent multimodal therapy aimed at benefitting all ages of siblings. Finally, experimental and observational research should reflect current standards of care as well as support continued advances within palliative medicine. Although these guidelines are instrumental in the care of children, they fail to address the critical differences experienced by LGBTQIA youth. Evaluating current adult LGBTQIA palliative studies globally and domestically, as well as public health issues facing vulnerable youth will justify future research for this group.

Global Perspective and Public Health

Globally, LGBTQIA youth are often met with criminalization. The Human Dignity Trust (2020), a litigation service that defends LGBTQIA rights globally, cites that 73 jurisdictions worldwide criminalize same-sex sexual activity. In palliative medicine, education to health professionals, availability of therapeutic treatments, and implementation of end-of-life care are reflective of governmental policies within these jurisdictions (World Health Organization [WHO], 2014). Health services globally should include prevention, treatment, rehabilitation, and palliative care, especially for those most at risk for discrimination and oppression, namely LGBTQIA youth (WHO, 2014).

Given the disparate health outcomes experienced by LGBTQIA youth summarized by Baams (2018), it is unfortunate that such experiences have yet to be researched via a case-based approach globally, falling drastically behind the adult body of research available. A qualitative study from Hunt et al. (2019) evaluating end-of-life care for LGBTQIA adults in Zimbabwe - a country where same-sex relations are classified as criminal - offers a sobering testimony to these policy-driven complications. A palliative director states, "Isolation comes in, discrimination, and you find many people dying quietly without any family support. They will say you were doing your gay things on your own" (Hunt et al., 2019, p. 690). Such statements command large portions of this study, describing the injustices faced by LGBTQIA patients in countries where discrimination is policy. However, on a global stage, it is important to note that such experiences are not isolated to these specific jurisdictions identified by Human Dignity Trust (2020). According to the Care Quality Commission (2016), discrimination is a reality for healthcare-seeking LGBTQIA individuals on a global scale; the United States of America is not immune to this reality. Nearly 45% of palliative adult patients who identify as LGBTQIA report mistreatment, restriction of visitors, and denial of care within the United States (Justice in Aging, 2015). Further studies have shown that LGBTQIA adults utilizing hospice and palliative services are nearly three times more likely to report having had inadequate, disrespectful, or abusive care when compared to their heterosexual counterparts; these abuses were significantly evident in states without protective statutes (Stein et al., 2020). These startling numbers from adult research demand further investigation into LGBTQIA youth palliative experiences. The mistreatment and discrimination described by Stein et al. (2020) greatly mirrors the disrespect and negative encounters felt by LGBTQIA youth per Snyder, Burack and Petrova (2017).

Despite the 2015 U.S. Supreme Court decision to legalize marriage equality, recent polling has shown increased numbers of hate crimes and discrimination directed towards the LGBTQIA community (GLAAD, 2019). This civil intolerance is mirrored by the current administration's attempts to remove protections of sexual orientation and gender identity under Title VII of the Civil Rights Act of 1964, allowing for discrimination in public accommodations, including healthcare (Greenhouse, 2019). Such intolerance is not limited to quality of care. On January 30th of this year, the Centers for Medicare and Medicaid Services described plans to block grants and per capita cap funding to Medicaid for low-income adults and their young children (Department of Health & Human Services, 2020). Dr. Sally Goza (2020), current President of the AAP reacted to these recent decisions, stating that currently 37 million children utilize these services, a group which is the single largest entity to rely on Medicaid within the United States. Dr. Goza (2020) continues, "It is therefore baffling and alarming that such drastic, harmful changes are being proposed to a program that works so well for such vulnerable groups" (para. 5). While such a decision does not directly imply decreased funding for LGBTQIA youth, research indicates that LGBTQIA adult-aged individuals are nearly two times more likely to utilize Medicaid-based services when compared to their heterosexual counterparts (Rooney, Whittington, & Durso, 2018). Given the vulnerabilities of LGBTQIA youth that demand increased interdisciplinary resources, palliative care opportunities could certainly be restricted for this population given these proposed changes.

Research

Gaps within LGBTQIA pediatric palliation have not gone unnoticed. In Kimberly Acquaviva's (2017) work entitled *LGBTQ-Inclusive Hospice and Palliative Care: A Practical Guide to Transforming Professional Practice*, high-quality inclusive care is described in similar guidelines as exemplified by the AAP, with LGBTQIA adults in mind. Acquaviva (2017) states, "There is no discussion at all of LGBTQ populations in Pediatric Palliative Care" (p. xv). Acknowledging this gap is important, as the numerous objectives within her work both add to existing LGBTQIA palliative understanding as well as demand further research. A brief comparison between the AAP's (2013) guidelines and Acquaviva's (2017) work help to establish the uniqueness of LGBTQIA palliative pediatric patients and the gaps in current care guidelines.

The AAP (2013) emphasizes an integrated interdisciplinary care model that involves medical and familial members. Acquaviva (2017) addresses adult interdisciplinary care with the following thought exercise: 23.9% of LGBTQIA adults smoke cigarettes, compared to 16.6% of heterosexual adults; palliative services may involve oxygen requirements in the home which may pose a safety risk, requiring patient, family and therapy education (CDC 2015). Hunt, Vennat, & Waters (2018) state that LGBTQIA youth have increased rates of risk-taking habits, including cigarette smoking. Palliative providers require guidelines for counseling patients regarding smoking and other LGBTQIA-associated risks, as they do not exist within current pediatric palliative literature. Acquaviva (2017) addresses familial roles by stating that no provider should assume that families of LGBTQIA patients have disowned their relative; equally, the provider should not assume that disownment has not occurred. Given LGBTQIA abuse is often perpetrated by the family (Baams, 2018), and LGBTQIA youth are at increased risk for homeless (Forge et al., 2018), the delicacy of such discussions should be more fully explicit for providers. The AAP (2013) does not address such discussions. Finally, Acquaviva (2017) emphasizes the timeliness and importance of bereavement outcomes, stating that LGBTQIA individuals tend to be reluctant to access care, shortening the traditional bereavement process. LGBTQIA youth often limit their health-seeking behavior due to previous negative encounters (Ard & Makadon, 2012). Palliative providers should be wary of negative associations held by this pediatric population and require tactics to ensure thoughtful communication regarding their services. The AAP (2013) once again does not address such concepts. These three basic yet important differences show that complexity ensnarls pediatric palliation in the context of LGBTQIA health.

Current perspectives from pediatric healthcare teams aid in the discussion of this complexity by offering insight into the frequency of which they encounter LGBTQIA youth in relation to palliative care. While reaching out to area physicians and nurses, several of whom specialize in pediatric palliation, it became increasingly clear that the population of LGBTQIA youth receiving end-of-life care had not garnered much attention. Several physicians gratefully recommended works by academics addressing LGBTQIA literature, while others forwarded the request for insight on to other healthcare workers, frequently leading to dead ends. This sparked this author's attention in two significant ways. First, several physicians had quantities of LGBTQIA focused research to offer, bolstering the literary background of LGBTQIA youth risks and adult LGBTQIA palliative studies within this work. There appeared to be a communal understanding that LGBTQIA studies in general are worthy of merit. Secondly, although the population at hand may be a fraction of the general pediatric palliative cohort, it was overall surprising that not a single provider had acknowledged working with such a patient. Therefore, the thought was brought forward: was there something un-unique about this pediatric population in relation to palliative care? Perhaps LGBTQIA youth navigate the end-of-life journey in a comparable way to heterosexual youth - a way in which their sexual identity does not influence their treatment. Further queries are needed, as the previously documented research suggests that these youth combat complexities largely unknown to their heterosexual counterparts. Such a discrepancy in literature-vs-reality is reflected in the recommendations below.

Recommendations

Upon review of current literature, this work presents four recommendations to better serve LGBTQIA youth. First, quantitative research is required to better categorize deaths for ages 13 to 24 in the LGBTQIA community. Data such as death by suicide are well-documented for this group, yet LGBTQIA youth mortality information is sparse given the multitude of severe health concerns such as HIV-related disease, polyvictimization, and substance abuse. Secondly, qualitative data will give a voice to this currently unstudied group. As evidenced by adult LGBTQIA palliative studies, significant testimony of discrimination exists; this must be explored in the pediatric realm (Justice in Aging, 2015). Thirdly, pediatric healthcare providers should receive LGBTQIA competencies. In doing so, providers are able to identify patients' needs through a guiding lens. This work fully endorses the healthcare workers who provided brief insights into the topic yet identifying patients who may be vulnerable due to their LGBTQIA identities may have been overlooked in palliative encounters. Finally, the AAP should utilize both quantitative and qualitative data to expand their existing pediatric palliative guidelines. As evidenced by Acquaviva's (2017) work, a multitude of differences exist for LGBTQIA adults receiving end-of-life care. The complexities of LGBTQIA youth therefore require unique palliative guidelines to better classify these variations; these guidelines should be available to all members of the pediatric care team.

Conclusion

The untimely death of a child is an unimaginable inevitability in healthcare; thankfully, palliative teams and educational resources dedicated to these young patients and their families have ensured that wholistic care be fully available. While guidelines exist for practicing palliative specialists, an at-risk group has yet to be researched. LGBTQIA youth, a group who frequently fall victim to abuse and sociomedical neglect have unique needs within healthcare, demanding competencies in healthcare training. Studies already show discrimination concerns for end-of-life LGBTQIA adults; therefore, it would not be surprising to see gaps in wholistic care experienced by LGBTQIA youth journeying through palliation. Unfortunately, to date, no detailed quantitative nor qualitative studies have assessed the complexities of this unique population. Until this research is available to clinicians, LGBTQIA youth and their families who experience the diversely emotional and intricate journey through end-of-life care are at risk - a risk of under resourced and under informed palliative practice.

References

1. Acquaviva, K. (2017). *LGBTQ-inclusive hospice and palliative care: A practical guide to transforming professional practice*. Harrington Park Press.

2. American Academy of Pediatrics [AAP]. (2013). Pediatric palliative care and hospice care commitments, guidelines, and recommendations. *Pediatrics, 132*(5), 966-972.

3. Ard K., Makadon H. (2012). Improving the health of LGBT people: Understanding and eliminating health disparities. Fenway Institute. Available at: https://www.lgbthealtheducation.org/wp-content/uploads/Improving-the-Health-of-LGBTPeople.

4. Baams L. (2018). Disparities for LGBTQ and Gender Nonconforming Adolescents. *Pediatrics, 141*(5), e20173004.

5. Care Quality Commission [CQC]. (2016). *A different ending: Addressing inequalities in end of life care*. London: CQC.

6. Centers for Disease Control [CDC]. (2015). *Tips from former smokers: Lesbian, gay (LGBT)*. Accessed February 10, 2020 from http://www.cdc.gov/tobacco/compaign/tips/groups/lgbt.html.

7. Centers for Disease Control [CDC]. (2016). *Sexual identity, sex of sexual contacts, and health-risk behaviors among students in grades 9-12: Youth risk behavior surveillance.* https://www.cdc.gov/mmwr/preview/mmwrhtml/ss6007a1.htm.

8. Centers for Disease Control [CDC]. (2017). *HIV: Youth.* Accessed February 10, 2020 from https://www.cdc.gov/hiv/group/age/youth/index.html

9. Department of Health & Human Services [DHHS]. (2020). *Health Adult Opportunity.* https://www.medicaid.gov/sites/default/files/Federal-Policy-Guidance/Downloads/smd20001.pdf.

10. Feudtner C., Zhong W., Faerber J., Dai D., Feinstein J. (2015). *Dying in America: Improving quality and honoring individual preferences near the end of life.* National Academies Press.

11. Forge N., Hartinger-Saunders R., Wright E., Ruel E. (2018). Out of the system and onto the streets: LGBTQ-identified youth experiencing homelessness with past child welfare system involvement. *Child Welfare, 96*(2), 47-74.Gates G. (2017). *In US, more adults*

12. *identifying as LGBT.* Gallup News. http:// news.gallup.com/poll/201731/lgbt-identification-rises.aspx.

13. Gay & Lesbian Alliance Against Defamation [GLAAD]. (2019). *Accelerating acceptance 2019: A survey of American acceptance and attitudes toward LGBTQ Americans.* New York, NY: GLAAD.

14. Girouard, M. (2018). *Addressing opioid use disorder among LGBTQIA populations.* National LGBT Health Education Center. https://www.lgbthealtheducation.org/wp-content/uploads/2018/06/OpioidUseAmongLGBTQPopulations.pdf

15. Goza, S. (2020). *AAP statement opposing new federal guidance on Medicaid.* American Academy of Pediatrics. https://www.aap.org/en-us/about-the-aap/aap-press-room/Pages/AAP%C2%A0Statement%C2%A0Opposing-New-Federal-Guidance-on-Medicaid.aspx.

16. Greenhouse L. (2019, August). Civil rights turned topsy-turvy. *The New York Times*, Opinion.

17. Justice in Aging. (2015). *LGBT older adults in long-term care facilities: Stories from the field*. Oakland, CA: Justice in Aging.

18. Kann L., Olsen E., McManus T., Harris W., Shanklin S., Flint K., Queen B., Lowry R., Chyen D., Whittle L., Thornton J., Lim C., Yamakawa Y., Brener N., Zaza S. (2016). Sexual identity, sex of sexual contacts, and health-related behaviors amont students in grades 9-12 - United States and selected sites, 2015. *Morbidity and Mortality Weekly Report Surveillance Summary, 65*(9), 1-202.

19. *Map of countries that criminalise LGBT people*. (2020). Human Dignity Trust. Retrieved February 10, 2020 from https://www.humandignitytrust. org/lgbt-the-law/map-of-criminalisation/

20. Hunt J., Bristowe K., Chidyamatare S., Harding R. (2019). 'So isolation comes in, discrimination and you find many people dying quietly without any family support': Accessing palliative care for key populations - an in-depth qualitative study. *Palliative Medicine, 33*(6), 685-692.

21. Hunt L., Vennat M., Waters J. (2018). Health and wellness for LGBTQ. *Advances in Pediatrics, 65*, 41-54.

22. Meyer I. (2003). Prejudice, social stress, and mental health in lesbian, gay, and bisexual populations: Conceptual issues and research evidence. *Psychol Bull, 129*(5), 674-697.

23. Rooney C., Whittington C., Durso E. (2018). *Protecting basiv living standards for LGBTQ people*. Center for American Progress. https://www.americanprogress.org/issues/lgbtq-rights/reports/2018/08/13/454592/protecting-basic-living-standards-lgbtq-people/.

24. Synder B., Burack G., Petrova A. (2017). LGBTQ youth's perceptions of primary care. *Clinical Pediatrics, 56*(6), 443-450.

25. Turner H., Shattuck A., Finkelhor D., Hamby S. (2015). Effects of poly-victimization on adolescent social support, selfconcept, and psychological distress. *Journal of Interpersonal Violence, 32*(5), 755-780.

26. World Health Organization [WHO]. (2014). *Strengthening of palliative care as a component of comprehensive care throughout the life course.* Geneva: World Health Organization.

Health Disparities Related to Stroke in the LGBTQIA Population

Roesch, Zachary

Introduction

The term LGBTQIA is an umbrella term used to describe the sexual minority population previously referred to as "the gay community". This acronym specifically stands for Lesbian, Gay, Bisexual, Transgender, Queer, Intersex, or Asexual (Gold, 2018). However, in society the terms LGBT, LGBTQ, or LGBTQIA+ are also used. Approximately 9 million people in the United States identify as lesbian, gay, or bisexual, and over 700,000 identify as transgender ("Best practices in LGBT care," 2016). As the gender and sexuality spectrum is become more understood, this acronym is becoming more fluid. On top of this, since this is becoming more understood, it is also becoming more accepted in mainstream American culture.

Unfortunately, just because it is becoming more accepted, that does not mean that people understand or respect these concepts the ways that they should. This is very prevalent in medicine when we treat patients who are part of the LGBTQIA population. Although there is not much literature on medical treatment of the LGBTQIA population, there is evidence of health disparities between this population and the heterosexual population (Baptiste-Roberts, Oranuba, Werts, & Edwards, 2017). This paper will focus on determining if there is a health disparity between the LGBTQIA and heterosexual population in regard to stroke specifically.

Background

A stroke occurs when, for one reason or another, there is a lack of blood supply to a certain area of the brain. When this happens, that part of the brain does not receive the amount of oxygen that it needs to survive, and this causes damage to that area of the brain. This can occur due to bleeding in the brain, low blood pressure, or a blockage preventing blood from reaching the brain. Sometimes, this damage can be irreversible and causes permanent effects ("Stroke | cdc.gov," 2019).

Stroke is currently the fifth leading cause of death in the United States. The rate of death from stroke has decreased over the last decade, likely due to the use of medications like statins and antihypertensives. Although there has been an improvement in stroke incidence and mortality, many strokes can be prevented. The most important risk factors for stroke occurrence are hypertension, diabetes mellitus, hyperlipidemia, obesity, poor lifestyle/nutrition, lack of physical activity, and cigarette smoking (Guzik & Bushnell, 2017).

In regard to health care for the LGBTQIA population, there is a clear disparity between them and the heterosexual population. This disparity exists, most likely, for many different reasons. One is the victimization and harassment that this population has experienced in society in general. The Human Rights Campaign conducted a survey of over 10,000 children aged 13-17 to discuss their lives and some of the troubles that they face in it. 51% of LGBT youths have stated that they were verbally harassed at school, compared to 25% of youths in the heterosexual population. On top of this, 29% of LGBT youths did not feel they had an adult they could talk to, compared to 13% of heterosexual youths. The most alarming statistic is that 42% of the survey respondents stated they live in a community where it is not accepting of LGBT people (Human Rights Campaign, 2019). These are important statistics to note because if people do not feel comfortable in their own communities, they will be much less likely to reach out to others for help. This could make traveling to doctors a lengthier endeavor, as some may need to see a physician in a different town to feel comfortable expressing themselves. On top of this, all the extra stress that this harassment causes would negatively impact anybody's health.

In addition to being harassed and persecuted by society, many people in the LGBTQIA population do not feel that they are treated the same by the health care system as their heterosexual counterparts. 13% of older LGBT adults reported the denial of health care, or being given poor care, due to their gender or sexual identities. In the transgender population specifically, this number increased to 40% ("Aging LGBT seniors a 'major public health issue,'" 2018). This is incredibly unfortunate, especially as a future physician, since we are supposed to be the people to put all of our personal bias's aside to provide our patients with the best, most comprehensive care that we can. However, I believe that this statistic exists because of personal bias that some physicians have in their personal lives, as well as a lack of understanding of the health care team in treating the LGBTQIA population. In the past 15 years, there have been a huge increase in the amount of research to understand the disparities and needs that this population has. However, there is still a large disparity between what medical professionals are learning in school and the cultural competency that is necessary to adequately treat the LGBTQIA population (Bonvicini, 2017).

In regards specifically to stroke in the LGBTQIA population, there is not much data on the rates of stroke compared to the heterosexual population. The small fraction of data that is mostly present is based on transgender individuals. Transgender females have a higher rate of stroke then transgender males, which is most likely due to exogenous estrogen replacement therapy. Transgender female have a 5x increased risk for venous thromboembolism. Testosterone therapy in transgender males has been shown to increase systolic blood pressure and may also increase diastolic blood pressure. Hormone therapy may increase triglyceride levels in transgender males and transgender females, and testosterone therapy increases LDL cholesterol in transgender males (Irwig, 2018).

Besides this paper, I could not find many articles on this topic specifically. However, the LGBTQIA population has higher rates of some of the risk factors associated with stroke. This will be discussed in the Public Health section, as I believe these risk factors are general public health concerns.

Public Health

Stroke in the LGBTQIA population is a public health concern because of the risk factors associated with stroke. Many of these risk factors are much more prevalent in this population when compared to the rest of the American population.

Tobacco smoking is an important public health concern. On top of this, it is also a significant risk factor for the development of stroke. It not only increases the risk for first time ischemic stroke, but also increases the risk of recurrent strokes in older smokers. Second hand smoke is also thought to contribute to the risk of stroke development (Oza, Rundell, & Garcellano, 2017). In the LGBTQIA population, there is a higher use of tobacco when compared to the general heterosexual population. The National Adult Tobacco Survey reported that 38.5% of LGBT respondents reported current tobacco use, while 25.3% of heterosexual adults reported current tobacco use (King, Dube, & Tynan, 2012).

Obesity is another critical public health issue in the United States. The CDC reports that 39.8%, or approximately 93.3 million adults in the United States suffer from obesity ("Adult Obesity Facts | Overweight & Obesity | CDC," 2019). Unfortunately, obesity seems to be more prevalent in parts of the LGBTQIA population. One study reported that transgender women and transgender men were both found to be more likely overweight when compared to cisgender women. (Caceres, Jackman, Edmondson, & Bockting, 2019). The prevalence of obesity was also found to be higher in lesbian African American women when compared to heterosexual African American women (Hafeez, Zeshan, Tahir, Jahan, & Naveed, 2017).

The role of obesity in stroke occurrence is a more debated topic. Many studies have shown that there is no direct relationship between stroke development and obesity. However, obesity can be seen as a risk factor for stroke when it causes other risk factors like hypertension, hyperlipidemia, or impaired glucose tolerance. At the same time, other papers state that abdominal obesity is a risk factor for cerebral infarction (Isozumi, 2004). A meta-analysis from 2016 showed that being overweight or obese in young adulthood is associated with increased risk of stroke, most likely independent of other cardiovascular risk factors (Guo et al., 2016). Although we do not know for certain if obesity is a direct risk factor for stroke, we do know it is more prevalent in the LGBTQIA population, and that it is at the least linked to other risk factors for stroke development.

Hypertension is also a known public health issue that is a major risk factor for the development of stroke. The CDC reports that 1 in 3, or about 75 million, American adults suffer from hypertension ("High Blood Pressure | cdc.gov," 2019). Interestingly, there have been no found differences in hypertension between the LGBTQIA population and the heterosexual population. One online survey for men who have sex with men, or MSM, reported numbers of hypertension similar to that of the general population (Hirshfield, Downing, Horvath, Swartz, & Chiasson, 2018). Another study of lesbian and bisexual women also reported hypertension rates similar to that of the general population (Simoni, Smith, Oost, Lehavot, & Fredriksen-Goldsen, 2017).

Global Perspective

The issues that the LGBTQIA population deals with socially, and in healthcare, do not exist solely in the United States. These health disparities exist globally and are often due to the segregation that this population endures from the rest of society. Successful medical care involves building trust in a doctor-patient relationship, but if the patient does not feel safe or wanted in their physician's office, then they cannot build the relationship required to adequately treat them.

In Turkey, LGBT+ individuals explained they feel they are exposed to segregating and stigmatizing attitudes by the healthcare team (Keleş, Kavas, & Yalım, 2018). They stated, as we already know, that the physician's approach in working with and treating a patient is one of the most important factors for providing adequate health care in the LGBT+ population.

In Nepal and other South Asian countries, having a different sexual identity than the societal norm is associated with "shame", mostly due to family expectations of having children in a heterosexual setting. However, there is more research being done into the disadvantages that the LGBTQIA population endures. They, like in the United States, report higher rates of alcohol, drug, and tobacco use when compared to the rest of the population. The thought is that these actions are being used as coping strategies for anxiety, stress, harassment, and discrimination that may come from society (Regmi & van Teijlingen, 2015).

Stroke is also an issue that is prevalent globally, not just in the United States. The World Health Organization, or WHO, says that noncommunicable diseases kill 41 million people each year, which accounts for 71% of deaths globally. Noncommunicable diseases are diseases that cannot be transmitted from person to person, and include cardiovascular disease, cancer, respiratory diseases, and diabetes, to name a few. 17.1 million people die directly from cardiovascular disease each year, and a portion of this is due to stroke ("Non communicable diseases," 2018).

Worldwide, stroke caused 6.5 million deaths and caused irreversible neurologic damage in 25.7 million patients (Feigin et al., 2015). The data of stroke occurrence for the international population differs from that of stroke occurrence in the United States. Globally, ischemic strokes occur 68% of the time, while 32% of strokes are due to either ICH or SAH (Krishnamurthi et al., 2013). In the United States, 87% of strokes are ischemic strokes, while only 13% of strokes are hemorrhagic in nature (Benjamin et al., 2017).

Although there is not much data specifically on stroke risk in the international LGBTQIA population, this group is exposed to risk factors for stroke at a higher rate than the general population, like smoking and drug use.

This is the same trend that is unfortunately seen in the United States, which could potentially lead to increased stroke rates in this disadvantaged population.

Research

I spoke with Dr. Gr and Dr. T about this topic. They both echoed the same concept, which is that in this population there is no genetic link to increased stroke risk. However, the psychosocial stressors and societal pressure that this population would increase cortisol and raise stress levels significantly. Some of the outlets for relaxation that this population uses at a higher rate than in the rest of the population, like cigarette smoking, unfortunately increase stroke risk. It would be interesting to find, or conduct, a study that specifically looks at stroke rates in this population to determine if these increased risk factors truly do cause an increased rate of stroke.

Recommendations

I think the most important thing that we can do as healthcare providers is to look at ourselves. A common theme throughout this paper, when dealing with the LGBTQIA population, is that they often times do not feel comfortable talking to healthcare professionals about their health concerns. This is for two reasons. One is that some healthcare professionals are not accepting of the LGBTQIA population. However, the more common reason is that most healthcare providers are simply unaware of the special considerations that need to be given to this population.

The amount of cultural competency training that we need to treat this population versus what we actually receive throughout training is not adequate. Medical training has been making an effort to include considerations in treating the LGBTQIA population, but some schools emphasize this more than others. We need to, uniformly, emphasize the correct language to use when working with this population.

I also think societally, there is so much work to be done on creating an environment where people of the LGBTQIA population can express themselves freely and without fear of criticism or rejection. The psychosocial stressors that this population encounters on a daily basis undoubtedly lead to bad habits in order to relax and decrease stress levels. Unfortunately, many of these habits also increase their risk of stroke. If the environment that we live in becomes more accepting, than this will give them a health environment to live in and also make this population more comfortable in discussing their health needs.

Conclusions

In conclusion, there is not much data on stroke in the LGBTQIA population. However, there is significant data on risk factors for stroke associated with this population. Risk factors for stroke are increased in this population when compared to the heterosexual population, and they experience societal pressures that the rest of the population doesn't encounter. Therefore, I do believe, from the research that I have conducted, that this population is certainly at a higher risk for stroke development than in the heterosexual population.

This is an area of research that requires more investigation in the future. I plan on looking into this during my Neurology residency to determine if a definitive link does, or does not, exist between stroke rates and the LGBTQIA population.

References

1. Adult Obesity Facts | Overweight & Obesity | CDC. (2019, January 31). Retrieved December 10, 2019, from https://www.cdc.gov/obesity/data/adult.html

2. Aging LGBT seniors a "major public health issue." (n.d.). Retrieved December 10, 2019, from Www.heart.org website: https://www.heart.org/en/news/2018/07/13/aging-lgbt-seniors-a-major-public-health-issue

3. Baptiste-Roberts, K., Oranuba, E., Werts, N., & Edwards, L. V. (2017). Addressing Healthcare Disparities among Sexual Minorities. *Obstetrics*

and Gynecology Clinics of North America, 44(1), 71–80. https://doi.org/10.1016/j.ogc.2016.11.003

4. Benjamin, E. J., Blaha, M. J., Chiuve, S. E., Cushman, M., Das, S. R., Deo, R., ... American Heart Association Statistics Committee and Stroke Statistics Subcommittee. (2017). Heart Disease and Stroke Statistics-2017 Update: A Report From the American Heart Association. *Circulation, 135*(10), e146–e603. https://doi.org/10.1161/CIR.0000000000000485

5. Best practices in LGBT care: A guide for primary care physicians. (n.d.). Retrieved December 10, 2019, from https://www.mdedge.com/ccjm/article/109822/adolescent-medicine/best-practices-lgbt-care-guide-primary-care-physicians

6. Bonvicini, K. A. (2017). LGBT healthcare disparities: What progress have we made? *Patient Education and Counseling, 100*(12), 2357–2361. https://doi.org/10.1016/j.pec.2017.06.003

7. Caceres, B. A., Jackman, K. B., Edmondson, D., & Bockting, W. O. (2019). Assessing gender identity differences in cardiovascular disease in US adults: An analysis of data from the 2014-2017 BRFSS. *Journal of Behavioral Medicine.* https://doi.org/10.1007/s10865-019-00102-8

8. Campaign, H. R. (n.d.). Growing Up LGBT in America: View and Share Statistics. Retrieved December 10, 2019, from Human Rights Campaign website: https://www.hrc.org/youth-report/view-and-share-statistics/

9. Feigin, V. L., Krishnamurthi, R. V., Parmar, P., Norrving, B., Mensah, G. A., Bennett, D. A., ... GBD 2013 Stroke Panel Experts Group. (2015). Update on the Global Burden of Ischemic and Hemorrhagic Stroke in 1990-2013: The GBD 2013 Study. *Neuroepidemiology, 45*(3), 161–176. https://doi.org/10.1159/000441085

10. Gold, M. (2018, June 21). The ABCs of L.G.B.T.Q.I.A.+. *The New York Times.* Retrieved from https://www.nytimes.com/2018/06/21/style/lgbtq-gender-language.html

11. Guo, Y., Yue, X.-J., Li, H.-H., Song, Z.-X., Yan, H.-Q., Zhang, P., ... Li, T. (2016). Overweight and Obesity in Young Adulthood and the Risk of

Stroke: A Meta-analysis. *Journal of Stroke and Cerebrovascular Diseases: The Official Journal of National Stroke Association, 25*(12), 2995–3004. https://doi.org/10.1016/j.jstrokecerebrovasdis.2016.08.018

12. Guzik, A., & Bushnell, C. (2017). Stroke Epidemiology and Risk Factor Management. *Continuum (Minneapolis, Minn.), 23*(1, Cerebrovascular Disease), 15–39. https://doi.org/10.1212/CON.0000000000000416

13. Hafeez, H., Zeshan, M., Tahir, M. A., Jahan, N., & Naveed, S. (n.d.). Health Care Disparities Among Lesbian, Gay, Bisexual, and Transgender Youth: A Literature Review. *Cureus, 9*(4). https://doi.org/10.7759/cureus.1184

14. High Blood Pressure | cdc.gov. (2019, November 18). Retrieved December 10, 2019, from https://www.cdc.gov/bloodpressure/index.htm

15. Hirshfield, S., Downing, M. J., Horvath, K. J., Swartz, J. A., & Chiasson, M. A. (2018). Adapting Andersen's Behavioral Model of Health Service Use to Examine Risk Factors for Hypertension Among U.S. MSM. *American Journal of Men's Health, 12*(4), 788–797. https://doi.org/10.1177/1557988316644402

16. Irwig, M. S. (2018). Cardiovascular health in transgender people. *Reviews in Endocrine & Metabolic Disorders, 19*(3), 243–251. https://doi.org/10.1007/s11154-018-9454-3

17. Isozumi, K. (2004). Obesity as a risk factor for cerebrovascular disease. *The Keio Journal of Medicine, 53*(1), 7–11. https://doi.org/10.2302/kjm.53.7

18. Keleş, Ş., Kavas, M. V., & Yalım, N. Y. (2018). LGBT+ Individuals' Perceptions of Healthcare Services in Turkey: A Cross-sectional Qualitative Study. *Journal of Bioethical Inquiry, 15*(4), 497–509. https://doi.org/10.1007/s11673-018-9874-5

19. King, B. A., Dube, S. R., & Tynan, M. A. (2012). Current Tobacco Use Among Adults in the United States: Findings From the National Adult Tobacco Survey. *American Journal of Public Health, 102*(11), e93–e100. https://doi.org/10.2105/AJPH.2012.301002

20. Krishnamurthi, R. V., Feigin, V. L., Forouzanfar, M. H., Mensah, G. A., Connor, M., Bennett, D. A., … GBD Stroke Experts Group. (2013). Global and regional burden of first-ever ischaemic and haemorrhagic stroke during 1990-2010: Findings from the Global Burden of Disease Study 2010. *The Lancet. Global Health*, *1*(5), e259-281. https://doi.org/10.1016/S2214-109X(13)70089-5

21. Non communicable diseases. (n.d.). Retrieved December 2, 2019, from https://www.who.int/news-room/fact-sheets/detail/noncommunicable-diseases

22. Oza, R., Rundell, K., & Garcellano, M. (2017). Recurrent Ischemic Stroke: Strategies for Prevention. *American Family Physician*, *96*(7), 436–440.

23. Regmi, P. R., & van Teijlingen, E. (2015). Importance of Health and Social Care Research into Gender and Sexual Minority Populations in Nepal. *Asia-Pacific Journal of Public Health*, *27*(8), 806–808. https://doi.org/10.1177/1010539515613413

24. Simoni, J. M., Smith, L., Oost, K. M., Lehavot, K., & Fredriksen-Goldsen, K. (2017). Disparities in Physical Health Conditions Among Lesbian and Bisexual Women: A Systematic Review of Population-Based Studies. *Journal of Homosexuality*, *64*(1), 32–44. https://doi.org/10.1080/00918369.2016.1174021

25. Stroke | cdc.gov. (n.d.). Retrieved November 24, 2019, from https://www.cdc.gov/stroke/

Disparities in the Prescription of PrEP in the LGBTQ+ Community

Pfeifer, Bradley

Introduction:

From a public health perspective, the advent of modern pharmaceutical advancements has rendered HIV a largely preventable disease. This has been accomplished because of patient use of pre-exposure prophylaxis, also known as PrEP. The majority of PrEP usage is in LGBTQIA+ individuals and IV drug users at high risk of contracting HIV.[2] There are significant barriers to patients using PrEP including getting healthcare appointments, receiving a prescription, finance and insurance deterrents, as well as cultural and psychosocial stigma that contribute to HIV being more transmissible than it should be.[1,2,11,12] Due to the multiple healthcare disparities impacting PrEP's usage nationally and globally, much progress must be made to ensure individuals are aware of and comfortable using PrEP. This must be addressed particularly amongst marginalized and impoverished individuals, transgender patients, as well as both developed and underdeveloped nations where HIV remains a prime public health interest.[7,14,18]

Background:

The US Food & Drug Association approved the first prescription drug, emtricitabine and tenofovir disoproxil (commercially known as Truvada), for use as PrEP against HIV in 2012.[1] In order to use PrEP, a patient must schedule care with a prescribing provider, be screened for their HIV status, be tested for multiple sexually transmitted diseases, and have their kidney and liver function assessed. The CDC already recommends annual screening for HIV in all men who have sex with men, not limited to men identifying as gay and bisexual, as well as users of illicit injection drugs. This is due to higher rates of HIV exposure and acquisition compared to heterosexual individuals and non-members of the LGBTQIA+ communities and IV drug users.[2,3] Barriers to healthcare access for LGBTQIA+ individuals, as well as the poor and marginalized including IV drug users, decreases how many PrEP-eligible patients actually seek preventative healthcare services and are prescribed PrEP.[16] Additionally, the usage of PrEP in terms of daily compliance varies from user to user: taking PrEP daily is the only way to achieve the highest risk reduction of acquiring HIV, but another method of taking PrEP, including the "2-1-1 method", or "on-demand PrEP" where patients only take PrEP before/after sex instead of daily dosing, alters the effectiveness of PrEP.[6]

Public Health:

In the United States, there are approximately 1.2 million people living with HIV, and only 14% of them are aware of their HIV-positive status.[2] On a year to year average, 13.3 of every 100,000 individuals are diagnosed with HIV.[2] African American LGBTQ men have the highest rates of diagnosis, followed up Latino LGBTQ men and then Caucasian LGBTQ men. Men who have sex with men account for about 69% of new HIV diagnoses every year.[2] Globally, there are approximately 38 million people living with HIV, of which 36.2 million are adults and 1.8 million are children.[22] Fortunately, 25.4 million are receiving antiretroviral therapy, but unfortunately, this means only 82% of HIV-positive individuals are accessing treatment. Since the peak of AIDS in 2004, deaths from AIDS (the immunosuppressed state following HIV infection without treatment) has declined by 60%.[22] Regionally, 79% of all diagnosed HIV infections are in African countries, 15% are in Asia and Pacific countries, and 6% are in Europe and North America.[22]

PrEP is prescribed to individuals at high-risk of being exposed to and acquiring HIV infection. High-risk groups are men who have sex with men and injection drug users, especially younger patients who are commonly less familiar with PrEP as a whole.[2,3] High-risk groups often exclude transgender individuals, female sex workers, and women exposed to HIV through high-risk male sex partners.[4,13] Of women exposed and diagnosed with new HIV infections, it is disproportionally in black and Latina.[13] For college-aged young adults (age 18-24), it is more commonplace in clinical settings to have sexual health screenings quarterly thanks to widespread access to low-cost/free HIV and STD testing.[1,3] Prescription of PrEP does not, however, mirror the increased screening protocols for young adults aged 18-24, as this age group has been underinformed about PrEP and its indications, usages, and benefits in recent years compared to adult males aged 34-41 and 52-59, but young adults have heard of PrEP more commonly.[3] Insurance coverage knowledge also varies, as each insurance provides different coverage and co-payment prices for prescriptions. For someone on Medicare, the annual price varies from \$1,354 to \$2,277, or \$3.70/pill to \$6.23/pill.[12] The manufacturer of PrEP, Gilead Sciences, does offer a discount coupon program that covers up to a certain threshold annually as secondary insurance. However, Medicare Part D users cannot use prescription discount programs unfortunately. Public health measures are needed to cover more of the prescription cost for PrEP, but much progress is yet to be made.[3,12]

A notable lapse in data surrounds PrEP usage for patients who are unfamiliar with their partner's status. Not knowing one's own status, as well as the status of other sexual partners, puts all involved parties at risk for contracting HIV, including females whose partners are men who have sex with other men, sex workers, as well as transgender individuals.[4] Transgender individuals and sex workers are less likely to have adequate health insurance, access to HIV testing, and experience less perceived comfort seeking preventative healthcare services due to common misunderstandings and judgment from healthcare providers not trained, accepting, and/or knowledgeable about transgender healthcare.[4,5]

The overall lack of knowledge about HIV, PrEP, and transgender healthcare collectively highlight the lack of PrEP usage adequate to stop the spread of HIV altogether. Healthcare educational systems do not routinely teach these topics but increased clinical exposure for healthcare professional students has helped educate future healthcare professionals to help responsibly reduce the spread of HIV in their future practices.[1] For individuals within the LGBTQIA+ community, the knowledge that PrEP helps to prevent the transmission of HIV has led to multiple positive and negative sociocultural changes. One such positive is that harsh conversations and negative stigmas surrounding PrEP and HIV are continuing to decline amongst users, and patients are more comfortable asking their healthcare providers for PrEP prescriptions.[1,3] Unfortunately, though PrEP is more asked for by patients, providers are not as knowledge, and the majority of primary care physicians prefer to refer to a colleague who is trained in HIV care.[15] One unexpected consequence of patients using PrEP is the belief that one does not need to use barrier protection during sex, including condoms, diaphragms, etc., because of the decreased risk of HIV spread.[2] This has led to a potentially increased transmission of curable sexually transmitted diseases (STDs) by not using protection during sex.[2] In addition many young males still believe the myth of not being at risk for HIV transmission despite actually being in a high-risk category which has also led to alternate dosing regimens for PrEP like the on-demand method.[1,2,3,6,9]

On-demand PrEP follows a dosing schedule of two pills the day before having anal sex, one pill the day of sex, and one pill the day after sex.[18] On demand PrEP usage has a lower rate of effective coverage in HIV transmission through rectal tissues and not vaginal tissues but remains an effective alternative in high-risk individuals unlikely to adhere to daily PrEP usage.[6,9] Vaginal tissues require PrEP dosing 6 of 7 days of the week to maintain statistically adequate risk reduction of HIV transmission.[6] The 2-1-1 method presents a reasonably safe alternative to daily PrEP usage (which can cause undesirable side effects and long-term health consequences to patient's renal, gastrointestinal and hepatic systems).[6,9] This method is also safer for patients who simply do not have sex frequently due to the decreased side effect profile compared to PrEP.[1,9,18]

Systemically speaking, the most significant reduction of HIV transmission achieved by PrEP is through daily patient compliance, and on-demand PrEP poses a small threat to that, but still adequately assures patients disinterested in daily PrEP do not discontinue their use altogether.[6,9] Nonetheless, the single most important factor affecting HIV transmission is still that patients know their HIV status and the risks of contracting HIV.[6] Lastly, public health efforts are making the public increasingly aware of access and compliance issues affecting adolescents, heterosexual women, male sex workers, and female sex workers who desire to use PrEP, but more research is needed to know what dosing regimens are most protective for these patients.[10,13,14]

Global Perspective:

The most vicious cycle of HIV infection and transmission is less problematic in most developed healthcare systems where PrEP is becoming more accepted and used but is more problematic in some African countries which lack robust preventative healthcare systems. However, certain moderately-developed nations like the Czech Republic and Russia are seeing increased rates of HIV as well, and well-funded public health programs remain the last guarding barrier to an HIV epidemic in these countries.[18,19] The Czech Republic has largely had HIV prevalence of under 0.025%, but that has recently been increasing because of decreased public health funding and no longer sponsoring PrEP as part of the funding decrease.[19] In Russia, there were over 1.16 million HIV diagnoses by 2017 (and undoubtedly many more because of lack of testing) largely due to use of injection drugs.[18] For LGBTQ individuals in Russia, it is unfortunately illegal to discuss use of PrEP for men who have sex with men because of the largely negative political perspectives about the LGBTQ community in Russian culture.[18]

In Kenya, researchers followed female sex workers, men who have sex with men, and young women taking PrEP. It is illegal to be gay in Kenya, thus men who have sex with men face significant fear of seeking healthcare services for PrEP and other preventative sexual healthcare.[20] Many Kenyan LGBTQ patients have also cited discrimination from their healthcare providers if they report sexual acts with the same sex, and cannot receive PrEP, thus contributing to continued unprotected sexual acts.[20] LGBTQ Kenyans lack access to Prep, but conversely, it is important to note that the largest annual incidence of newly diagnosed HIV infections in Africa is in married women. This is because many do not believe in the need to take PrEP because of perceived safety from being married despite apparent non-monogamous sexual acts by partners due to continued increases in HIV diagnoses.[7,14] Of patients who started PrEP but stopped use the most common reasons for discontinuation were low self-perception of risk of contracting HIV, having a sexual partner who is on antiretroviral therapy, community myths, misconceptions, and negative stigmas, as well as unwelcoming attitudes from health care workers.[7] In contrast to Kenya, Mali has seen decreased transmission of HIV from pregnant women to fetus because of increased screening and treatment.[21] For Mali men who have sex with men, receptiveness to PrEP is increasing but is still at an overall lower rate than desired, especially since 90.1% of surveyed men did not know they were HIV-positive, thus uninterested in using protection during sex and/or using PrEP to decrease transmission.[21]

Patients were more likely to continue taking PrEP as prescribed if their partner or peers showed support, if there was greater access to sexual health preventative services, and if there were increased feelings of shared social responsibility to decrease HIV transmission.[7,13] Unfortunately females are often discouraged from PrEP by peers due to negative social stigma that the patients are sexually promiscuous or they are already ill.[7,13] Daily PrEP usage remains the gold standard in Kenya. In other countries like France, research concludes no significant difference in risk of HIV transmission between daily usage of PrEP and on-demand PrEP, but acknowledges the need for greater patient education in on-demand PrEP usage because of a more laissez faire culture surrounding sex.[8,18] Overall, education about HIV paired with increased preventative healthcare services including PrEP access are the most powerful means for global health efforts to reduce HIV transmission.[2,7,8]

Personal Research Interviews:

I had the opportunity to witness first-hand the prescription and follow-up care of individuals using PrEP during my third-year family medicine clerkship with Dr. MG. There I learned the intricacies of the patient-physician relationship necessary to make patients feel safe coming to the office to seek PrEP prescription and proactive preventative sexual health care. Additionally, in conversations with Dr. Michael Greene, I learned about more specific barriers to PrEP access including language barriers, mistrust in the medical community and the inconsistent use of prescription drugs. Simply feeling welcome in the clinical office setting is not a typical day for these patients. Perhaps one of the greatest recent advances his offices have achieved is making their clinic building more representative of diverse patients through having healthcare team members who speak the native languages of patients, diversifying the décor and photography in the clinic and having open and proactive communication with patients about all services offered.

These successes his clinic has experienced affirm the unique lifestyle and health history of patients who seek preventative sexual health care and are likely to encourage other patients to seek similar healthcare through community referral.[1,4] He also noted that the patients who come in most frequently are at the polar ends of the financial spectrum including wealthy individuals and impoverished individuals, but not working-class individuals who do not often see him because of time constraints and lack of transportation.[12] Insured individuals remain four times as likely to come to the office for visits compared to uninsured patients, but there is a growing patient population of impoverished individuals who seek care because of little concern over their lack of finances to manage.[11] Nonetheless, another challenge Dr. Greene faces is patients beliefs that their risk of HIV exposure is low, resulting in PrEP noncompliance despite good insurance coverage; the main tool to combat this is more patient education.[6,11,12]

Further, I had the opportunity to speak to a case management employee of Advocate Aurora Health in Wisconsin, Denise. Denise is a quality care manager overseeing clinics where HIV care and routine preventative healthcare services are offered. She noted routine preventative health care services are used more frequently each year per total reasons for office visits.[2] She also noted minority populations comprise the largest increases in usage of these services. For PrEP specifically, she did not have specific statistics on prescribing by physicians but knows her organization is increasingly advertising and offering it to patients. Denise continued by stating that the largest disparity in access to PrEP is insurance, not just for pharmacy benefits and co-pays, but the cost of office visits and the delay between scheduling and the actual appointment without including patient time-constraints and rescheduling needs.[11,12]

Recommendations:

PrEP and HIV healthcare are becoming less stigmatized and more widely accessible and used by high-risk individuals. Much more work is needed to provide equal access to PrEP to non-high-risk individuals. This includes female sex workers, transgender individuals, and adolescent patients.[5,10,14] I believe one of the most urgent tasks for healthcare professionals is to educate more healthcare workers and patients about the young adults who are at high-risk of HIV exposure but deny they are high-risk, with the goal of increasing usage of PrEP in these populations appropriately. Many medical schools have done a partially good job including HIV education into their curriculums, but it is commonly limited to a few hours of instruction maximum, thus medical students need more clinical exposure to both LGBTQ and HIV healthcare. Increased use of public health marketing is needed to reinforce use of barrier protection during sex to decrease STD spread while on PrEP.[15,16] Lastly, global access and education regarding PrEP remains a top priority in endemic areas, especially among individuals to simply understand their risks of HIV exposure.

Conclusion:

PrEP remains a highly effective public health tool to decrease HIV transmission in all countries where HIV is present and is indicated for all high-risk individuals. Greater preventative sexual healthcare services are needed, as many countries are still not prescribing PrEP as much as they could be.[20,21] Financial and insurance barriers to PrEP are on the decline, but more cost-savings measures are needed surrounding preventative healthcare office visits. The on-demand PrEP approach helps to ensure partial compliance but is not a catch-all for HIV exposure prophylaxis, so patient education is needed.[6,8,10,18] Overall, the disparities which LGBTQ individuals most commonly face are fear of rejection and discrimination from healthcare workers, as well as financial and insurance barriers to access preventative healthcare resources like PrEP.

References:

1. Sun, C.J., et. al. (2019). "Little Tablets of Gold: An Examination of the Psychosocial and Social Dimensions of PrEP Among LGBTQ Individuals". *AIDS Education and Prevention*, 31(1), 51–62.

2. CDC. (2017). "Preexposure Prophylaxis for the Prevention of HIV Infection in the United States – 2017 Updates". DHHS/CDC, March 2018. Online.

3. Hammack, P.L. et. al. (2018). "HIV testing and pre-exposure prophylaxis (PrEP) use, familiarity, and attitudes among gay and bisexual men in the United States: A national probability sample of three birth cohorts." *PLOS ONE*. https://doi.org/10.1371/journal.pone.0202806

4. Connolly, M.D., et. al. (2020). "Outcomes of a PrEP Demonstration Project with LGBTQ Youth in a Community-Based Clinic Setting with Integrated Gender-Affirming Care." *Transgender Health*, 5, 2. 10.1089/trgh.2019.0069

5. Reiser, S.L., et, al. (2019). "High risk and low uptake of pre-exposure prophylaxis to prevent HIV acquisition in a national online sample of transgender men who have sex with men in the United States." *Journal of the International AIDS Society*. https://doi.org/10.1002/jia2.25391

6. Haberer, J. (2017). "Pro and Cons of On Demand PrEP." Presentation at IAPAC Adherence Conference. Online.

7. Kyongo, J.K, et. al. (2016). "How long will they take it? Oral pre-exposure prophylaxis (PrEP) retention for female sex workers, men who have sex with men and young women in a demonstration project in Kenya."

8. Molina, J.E. (2018). "Incidence of HIV-infection in the ANRS Prevenir study in Paris region with daily or on-demand PrEP with TDF/FTC"

9. Hojilla, J.C. et, al. (2020). "Early Adopters of Event-driven Human Immunodeficiency Virus Pre-exposure Prophylaxis in a Large Healthcare System in San Francisco." *Clinical Infectious Diseases: Brief Report.*"

10. Yusuf, H. et, al. (2020). "HIV Preexposure Prophylaxis Among Adolescents in the US: A Review." *JAMA Pediatrics.*

11. Patel, R.R., et. al. (2017). "Impact of insurance coverage on utilization of pre-exposure prophylaxis for HIV prevention." *PLOS ONE.* https://doi.org/10.1371/journal.pone.017873

12. Kay, E.S. and Pinto, R.M. (2020). "Is Insurance a Barrier to HIV Preexposure Prophylaxis? Clarifying the Issue." *American Journal of Public Health*, 110, 1.

13. Goparaju, L. (2015). "Women want Pre-Exposure Prophylaxis but are Advised Against it by Their HIV-positive Counterparts." *Journal of AIDS Clinical Research*, 6(11): 1-10. doi:10.4172/2155-6113.1000522.

14. Sheth, A.N, Rolle, C.P., and Gandhi, M. (2016). "HIV pre-exposure prophylaxis for women." *Journal of Virus Eradication,* 2.: 149-155.

15. Petroll, A.E., et, al. (2017). "PrEP Awareness, Familiarity, Comfort, and Prescribing Experience among US Primary Care Providers and HIV Specialists." *AIDS Behavior*, 21(5): 1256-1267. doi:10.1007/s10461-016-1625-1.

16. Mayer, K.H., Agwu, A., and Malebranche, D. (2020). "Barriers to the Wider Use of Pre exposure Prophylaxis in the United States: A Narrative Review." *Adis* https://doi.org/10.1007/s12325-020-01295-0

17. Molina, J.E., et. al. (2015). "On-Demand Preexposure Prophylaxis in Men at High Risk for HIV-1 Infection." *New England Journal of Medicine*, 373: 2237-2246. DOI:10.1056/NEJMoa1506273

18. Beyrer, C., et. al. (2017). "The expanding epidemic of HIV-1 in the Russian Federation." *PLOS Medicine.* https://doi.org/10.1371/journal.pmed.1002462

19. Mravcik, V., et. al. (2017). "HIV epidemic among men who have sex with men in the Czech Republic, 2016: high time for targeted action." *Euro Surveillance.* https://doi.org/10.2807/1560-7917.ES.2017.22.48.17-00079

20. Okall, D.O., et. al. (2016). "Men Who Have Sex With Men in Kisumu, Kenya: Comfort in Accessing Health Services and Willingness to Participate in HIV Prevention Studies." *Journal of Homosexuality.* doi:1 0.1080/00918369.2014.951261.

21. Lahuerta, M., et. al. (2018). "HIV Prevalence and Related Risk Factors in Men Who Have Sex with Men in Bamako, Mali: Findings from a Bio-behavioral Survey Using Respondent Driven Sampling." *AIDS and Behavior.* doi:10.1007/s10461-017-1793-7

22. HIV.gov. (2020) "Global Statistics." *HIV.gov.* Retrieved from https://www.hiv.gov/hiv-basics/overview/data-and-trends/global-statistics on 08/02/2020.

Sexual Coercion Among Homosexual Men in Prison and Mental Health Repercussions: A Case Study in Pollsmoor Prison, Khayelitsha, Cape Town, South Africa.

Tahseen, Ahmed

Introduction

Sexual minorities suffer from an increased rate of mental health problems including suicide attempts and completions (Ploderl & Trembly 2015). In addition, there is an even higher risk of mental health disorders among homosexual men who have been sexually victimized (Ratner et al 2003). Sexual victimization is also an especially major risk factor for men within the prison system displaying higher rates of suicide (Salive et al 1989). Taken together, the vulnerability of homosexual men who have been forced into sexual activity in prison is of notable concern. With the known increased risk of mental health problems among homosexual men who have been sexually victimized, homosexual prisoners deserve special consideration and protections to prevent future suicide. A particularly salient case study is Khayelitsha township in South Africa, which serves as host to prisons that are notoriously dangerous for inmates in an environment where homosexual men face extreme homosexual prejudice.

Background

Identifying the rate of sexual coercion among prison populations is difficult, though attempts to quantify the matter repeatedly reflect a higher prevalence of unwanted sexual contact and assault among prisoners (Malacova et al 2012). Vulnerable populations remain at an elevated risk of sexual victimization including gay, bisexual, and transgender inmates (Beck et al 2013). The most recent National Inmate Survey revealed that 12.2% of non-heterosexual prison inmates report sexual abuse by inmates and 5.4% report sexual abuse by staff just within the past 12 months versus 1.2% by inmates and 2.1% by staff reported by heterosexual prisoners (Ratkalkar & Atkin-Plunk 2017). Figures like these are worrisome and still there are many regions where the facts on sexual victimization are unknown and prisoners may be even more susceptible. Such an environment is seen in Pollsmoor Prison in Khayelitsha township. Notorious as one of the most dangerous maximum-security prisons, over half of the prison population belongs to the Numbers Gang. It is an extreme example of prison overcrowding, with 20-24 prisoners jammed into a cell meant to house 11 at most (Kemp 2006) (Schurink 1989).

This is the environment in which the Numbers Gang resides and thrives, with many prisoners and guards alike admitting that guards tend to look away and allow the rampant inmate violence and drug use to continue—dangerous prisoners vastly outnumber guards who often sustain stab injuries from inmates. For every 100 prisoners, there is one warden. Stabbings, beatings, rituals, and rape are all used to showcase loyalty and acceptance into the Numbers Gang. Non-gang members are immediately robbed and raped upon admission into Pollsmoor Prison. Newcomers must eventually comply to sexual demands by the head Numbers Gang figure of their prison cell. Ultimately, newcomers are left with the option of becoming a member of the Numbers gang or a sex slave of sorts if they don't join (Kemp 2006) (Hayson 1981).

Public Health

A large body of evidence indicates higher incidence of depression and suicide in sexual minorities. Studies assessing risk factors for suicide using Denmark's extensive registries and sociodemographic data found that same sex registered domestic partners were three to four times more likely than heterosexual partners to die by suicide (Qin 03) (Haas et al 2011). In fact, men who had ever participated in same sex relationships were eight times more likely to die by suicide than men in heterosexual partnerships (Mathy 2011). A recent meta-analysis of 25 international population-based studies measuring suicidal behavior in LGB adolescents and adults concluded that lifetime prevalence of suicide attempts in gay/bisexual men was four times that of comparable heterosexual men (King et al 2008).

Sexual minorities exhibit increased susceptibility to mental health disorders at baseline and exposure to sexual abuse is dangerous among this group. Just the fear of rape for victims, especially for homosexual men, critically influences inmate mental wellbeing. Studies in the US have found of those prisoners targeted for sexual coercion, 38% made suicide gestures reflecting a 17-fold increase in suicide attempts compared to non-targeted prisoners (Lockwood 1980). A qualitative review on the prevalence of mental health disorders among survivors of sexual abuse revealed 17-65% develop PTSD, 13%-51% meet major depressive disorder criteria, 13-49% develop alcohol use disorder, 23-44% develop suicidal ideation, and 2-19% actually attempt suicide (Campbell et al., 2009). When controlling for other risk factors for PTSD, sexual abuse has consistently been associated with the highest increase in risk for suicidality in epidemiological studies (Ullman & Brecklin, 2002) (Stein et al., 2010).

In addition to mental health repercussions, a history of sexual abuse among males predisposes to revictimization and increased difficulty in forming healthy relationships (Maitland & Slunder 1998) (Desai et al., 2002). One third of inmates experience severe anxiety and over 55% of targeted men in prison relay their extreme fear of future assaults (Lockwood 1982). These fears are unfortunately justified as a victim of rape in prison will experience on average nine sexual assaults (Struckman-Johnson 1999). Sexual abuse begets sexual abuse as it may lead to the very same victims engaging in future sexually predatory behavior (Warren et al 2009).

Global Health Perspective

Homosexual men have a tough time in Khayelitsha township as it is. To this day, young adults are shot, stabbed, stoned to death because of their sexual orientation and religious figures in the community denounce homosexual behavior as a curse to the community (Sefali 2013) (Sefali 2014). Homosexual men already face many pressures, which are exponentially increased in the face of such cultural prejudice. Researchers agree that this type of social stigma, prejudice and discrimination associated with minority sexual orientation is a part of the observed elevation in rates of suicide attempts and mental disorders found in LGB people. One especially powerful stressor for LGB youth is rejection by parents and other family members (Ryan et al 2009). Those who experience frequent rejection by their parents or caregivers during adolescence are over eight times more likely to make a suicide attempt than those with accepting parents (Ryan et al 2009). Cultures fostering such environments contribute to the epidemic.

Surely, men around the globe who are homosexual and find themselves in institutions like Pollsmoor Prison or born in townships like Khayelitsha are at increased risk of suicide. Already facing extreme cultural stigma from an early age, these young homosexual men are put into a prison where virtually everyone is raped, and homosexuals are indicted by their peers for their sexual orientation. Both guards and prisoners admit as much (Kemp 2006). Rape in prison profoundly affects an individual's ability to cope with imprisonment, and the devastating and debilitating psychological consequences have been well documented (Lockwood 1982). Cross-national epidemiological studies indicate that sexual abuse is more strongly associated with suicidality than any other form of trauma, and this may be due to the high degree of stigma and shame associated with sexual abuse victimization (Stein et al., 2010) (Rudd 2006).

Internationally, marginalized youth of lower socioeconomic status make up a significant portion of prisoners, and multiple studies confirm not only an increased frequency of suicide attempts in gay and bisexual youth, but specifically the highest frequency seen in gay/bisexual men of low socioeconomic status (Garofalo 1999) (Kulkin 2000) (Grossman 2007) (Paul et al 2002). Limited health care resources compound institutional barriers to care for homosexual prisoners (Brinkley-Rubinstein 2013).

Research/Interactions

The township of Khayelitsha is ruled by gang and mob violence and Khayelitsha Emergency Department treats several victims of stabbings on a daily basis (Yates 2014). An inmate who presented to the emergency department at Khayelitsha District Hospital after having been stabbed revealed a central tenet of the Numbers Gang; one must either stab someone or let a head gang member rape him to be accepted into the gang. He described this as an almost ubiquitous occurrence. But he added to his account: 'Who wouldn't want to be a part of the Numbers Gangs?' Joining the Numbers Gang meant being afforded protection from other prisoners and guards, amenities, and a sense of belonging to the largest family in the prison system. Truly disturbing was the matter-of-fact attitude the patient had towards the rampant sexual coercion employed by the Numbers Gang. Forcing and being forced into sexual acts is a daily exercise in gang dynamics and survival in the prison. In the midst of his nonchalant account of the man-on-man rapes, the patient expressed his vehemence towards homosexualism. In fact, he described disdainfully an atrocity in his eyes which occurred a recently when a recent prisoner came out as homosexual. The gang members were so offended that they brutally stabbed the homosexual man to death. Men rape men on a daily basis, yet there is a paradoxical zero-tolerance policy for homosexuals in the gang and Pollsmoor Prison at large.

Recommendations

In Pollsmoor Prison, there are two clinical psychologists for the ~7,000 prisoners, and they focus on 2,000 or so prisoners who are convicted rapists (Kemp 2006). They treat the fraction they view as most in need of their help, but they might focus on the sexual minorities if they knew of the increased risk of suicide. Shifting to focus on these at-risk prisoners may save lives, and they represent a small enough proportion of the prison population that this would not drastically divert healthcare resources from others. Prison mental healthcare workers might be able to address predisposing conditions and risk factors leading to suicidal ideation. An objective assessment at intake could help identify homosexual prisoners and ascribing to a non-heterosexual orientation either on paper or via questioning may lead to early intervention. In Pollsmoor Prison, Numbers Gang members within a cell initiate the sexual assaults. If new inmates are screened and identified as homosexual at intake, placing them within a separate cell discretely but intentionally may prevent future violence, as these inmates specifically spend 96% of their time within their cells. These measures are best summarized as: recognition of an increased risk of suicide especially after assault, identification and mental healthcare worker assessment of homosexual intakes, and allocation to protected jail cells free of potential rape perpetrators (Kemp 2006).

Conclusion

Homosexual men are an extremely vulnerable population in prison with a disproportionate death by suicide representation. A strategy based on these measures may help us take steps in the right direction to prevent suicide in an at-risk population at Pollsmoor Prison, and possibly other prisons with similarly threatened populations of homosexual men. If the purpose of prison is to rehabilitate and eventually return prisoners as contributing members of society, then preventing further harm and psychiatric illness to befall homosexual men in prison is crucial—the benefit is multifold. Preventing sexual assaults in sexual minorities will help to prevent future suicides and we may also halt downstream mental health illness thereby decreasing sexual minority suffering and better allocating public healthcare resources. We may need to acknowledge the required special care for homosexual men in prison and we should begin recognizing the vulnerability of this population.

References

1. Salive, M.E., Smith, G.S., & Brewer, T.F. 1989. Suicide mortality in the Maryland state prison system, 1979 through 1987. *JAMA. 262*(3):365-369

2. Ratner, P.A., Johnson, J.L., Shoveller, J.A., Chan, K., Martindale, S.L., Schilder, A.J., Botnick, M.R., & Hogg, R.S. 2003. Non-consensual sex experienced by men who have sex with men: prevalence and association with mental health. *Patient Education and Counseling. 49*(1):67-74.

3. Ploderl, M., & Tremblay, P. 2015. Mental health of sexual minorities. A systematic review. *International Review of Psychiatry 27*(5):367-385.

4. Kemp, R., & Bennett, M. 2006. Ross Kemp on Gangs: Cape Town. *Tiger Aspect Productions.*Cape Town, South Africa.

5. Malacova, E., Butler, T., Yap, L., Grant, L., Richards, A., Smith, A.M., & Donovan, B. 2012. Sexual Coercion prior to imprisonment: prevalence, demographic and behavioral correlates. *International Journal of STD and AIDS. 23*(8):533-539.

6. Beck, A., Berzofsky, D., Caspar, R., & Krebs, C. 2013. Sexual victimization in jails and prisons reported by inmates, 2011-12 update. *Bureau of Justice Statistics.*

7. Ratkalkar, M., & Atkin-Plunk, C.A. 2017. Can I ask for help? The relationship among incarcerated males' sexual orientation, sexual abuse history, and perception of rape in prison. *Journal of Interpersonal Violence.*

8. Yates, R., & Abiola, K. 2014. Reggie Yates: Extreme South Africa. *BBC.* Cape Town, South Africa.

9. Hayson, N. 1981. Towards an Understanding of Prison Gangs. *National Criminal Justice Reference Service. NCJ* 144249, 50.

10. Schurink, W.J. 1989. The World of Westlaners: an analysis of some organizational features in South African prisons. *Southern African Journal of Criminology.* 2(2), 60-70.

11. Haas, A.P, Eliason, M., Mays, V.M., Mathy, R.M., Cochran, S.D., D'Augelli, A.R., Silverman M.M., Fisher, P.W., Hughes, T., Rosario, M., Russell, S.T., Malley, E., Reed, J., Litts, D.A., Haller, E., Sell, R.L., Remafedi, G., Bradford, J., Beautrais, A.L., Brown, G.K., Diamond, G.M., Friedman, M.S., Garofalo, R., Turner, M.S., Hollibaugh, A., & Clayton, P.J. 2011. Suicide and suicide risk in lesbian, gay, bisexual, and transgender populations: review and recommendations. *Journal of Homosexuality.* 58(1), 10-51.

12. Qin, P, Agerbo, E., & Mortensen, P.B. 2003. Suicide risk in relation to socioeconomic, demographic, psychiatric, and familial factors: a national register-based study of all suicides in Denmark, 1981-1997. *American Journal of Psychiatry.* 160(4), 765-772.

13. Sefali, P. 2014. Too few gay men get involved, says Khayelitsha Activist. *GroundUp.*

14. Sefali, P. 2013. What's it like to be gay or lesbian in Khayelitsha? *GroundUp.*

15. Mathy, R.M. 2011. The association between relationship markers of sexual orientation and suicide: Denmark, 1990-2001. *Social Psychiatry and Psychiatric Epidemiology.* 46(2), 111-117.

16. Garofalo, R. 1999. Sexual orientation and risk of suicide attempts among a representative sample of youth. *Archives Pediatric Adolescent Medicine.* 153(5), 487-493.

17. Kulkin, H.S. 2000. Suicide among gay and lesbian adolescents and young adults: a review of the literature. 2000. *Journal of Homosexuality.* 40(1), 1-29.

18. Grossman, A.H. 2007. Transgender youth and life-threatening behaviors. *Suicide and Life-Threatening Behavior.* 37(5), 527-537.

19. King, M., Semlyen, J., Tai, S.S., Killaspy H., Osborn, D., Popelyuk, D., & Nazareth, I. 2008. A systematic review of mental disorder, suicide, and deliberate self harm in lesbian, gay and bisexual people. *BioMedCentral Psychiatry.* 18(8), 70.

20. Struckman-Johnson, C.J. 1996. Sexual Coercion reported by men and women in prison. *The Journal of Sexual Research. 33,* 67-76.Lockwood, D. 1982. The contribution of sexual harassment to stress and coping in confinement. *Sage Publications. 45-64.*

21. Ullman, S.E., & Brecklin, L.R. 2002. Sexual assault history and suicidal behavior in a national sample of women. *Suicide and Life-Threatening Behavior. (32):*117-130.

22. Stein, D.J., Chiu, W.T., Hwang, I., Kessler, R.C., Sampson, N., Alonso, J., & Nock, M.K. 2010. Cross-national analysis of the associations between traumatic events and suicidal behavior: findings from the WHO World Mental Health Surveys. *PloS ONE. 5(5):*e10574

23. Maitland, A., & Sluder, R. 1998. Victimization and youthful prison inmates: an empirical analysis. *The Prison Journal, (78):*55-73.

24. Desai, S., Arias, I., Thompson, M., & Basile, K. 2002. Childhood victimization and subsequent adult revictimization assessed in a nationally representative sample of women and men. *Violence and Victims. (17):*639-653

25. Warren, J., Jackson, S., Booker, A., & Burnette, I. 2009. Risk markers for sexual predation and victimization in prison. *National Institute of Justice.*

26. Dworkin, E.R., Menon, S.V., Bystrynski, J., & Allen, N.E. Sexual assault victimization and psychopathology: A review and meta-analysis. *Clinical Psychology Review.*

27. Lockwood, D. 1980. Prison Sexual Violence. *Elsevier.*

28. Fergusson, D.M. 2005. Sexual orientation and mental health in a birth cohort of young adults. *Psychological Medicine. 35(7),* 971-981.

29. Paul, J.P., Catania, J., Pollack, L., Maskowitza, J., Canchola, J., Mills, T., Binson, D., & Stall, R. 2002. Suicide attempts among gay and bisexual men: Lifetime prevalence and antecedents. *American Journal of Public Health*. *92*(8), 1338-1345.

30. Brinkley-Rubinstein, L. 2013. Incarceration as a catalyst for worsening health. *Health & Justice, (1)*:1-17.

31. Bontempo, D.E., et al. 2002. Effects of at-school victimization and sexual orientation on lesbian, gay or bisexual youths' health risk behavior. *Journal of Adolescent Health. 30*, 364-374.

32. Friedman, M.S., Koeske, G.F., Silvestre, A.J., Korr, W.S, & Sites, E.W. 2006. The impact of gender-role nonconforming behavior, bullying, and social support on suicidality among gay male youth. *Journal of Adolescent Health. 38*, 621-623.

33. Ryan, C., Huebner, D., Diaz, R.M., & Sanchez, J. 2009. Family rejection as a predictor of negative health outcomes in White and Latino LGB young adults. *Pediatrics. 123*, 346-352.

Depression and Suicidality Among Gay, Lesbian, and Bisexual Youth Populations

Morelli, John

Introduction

Depression and suicidality among American youth continue to be one of the primary sources of morbidity and mortality in the United States. An estimated 3.2% of children between the ages of three through seventeen have an active diagnosis of major depressive disorder (Ghandour et al., 2019). Incidences of major depressive episodes among adolescents between the ages of twelve to seventeen have more than doubled between 2005-2017. The rates of non-suicidal self-injury and hospitalizations for suicidal ideations and suicide attempts have also significantly increased during this period. The increase in the rate of suicidality among this population are multifaceted. Experts have speculated on a range of theories, including increased self-reporting, increasing rates of opioid abuse, decreasing hours of sleep, and the influence of social media among the adolescent population (Twenge et al., 2019). "Intentional self-harm (suicide)" remains the second leading cause of death among US males and females between the ages of 10-14 as well as the ages of 15-19 (Heron, 2019). Adolescent youth who identify as gay, lesbian, or bisexual (GLB) are at a significant disparity in rates of depression and suicidality when compared to their heterosexual peers (Marshal et al., 2011). This paper aims to explore the disparity of depression and suicidality among GLB adolescent youth, with particular emphasis on the role that supportive parents and caregivers have in the mitigation of depression, suicidality, and other mental health disparities. Of note, while the subject of this paper aims to specifically address GLB youths, researchers, datasets, and interviewers may make reference to GLB persons and also include persons who identify as transgendered; when this occurs, the term lesbian, gay, bisexual, and transgendered (LGBT) will be used.

Background

In a recent government survey of 9,175 Americans between the ages of 18-44, 1.9% of men and 1.3% of women identified as "homosexual, gay, or lesbian," with an additional 5.5% of women and 2.0% of men identifying as bisexual (Copen et al., 2016). As sexual preference or orientation may not be precisely reported, known, or identified by individual within the adolescent age rage, rates of gay, lesbian, and bisexual youth in US are imprecisely estimated. Adolescent individuals identifying as gay, lesbian, or bisexual appear to be a growing subset of the American populous. A 1991 survey among 34,706 adolescents (grades 7-12) reported rates of bisexual or homosexual identity at 1.1%, with 88.2% identifying as heterosexual, and 10.7% as "unsure" (Remafedl et al., 1991). Among more recent surveys investigating self-reported attraction among 93,817 youth between 12.5-18 years of age in northern California, 1.7% reported exclusive same-sex attraction, while 3.2% reported attraction to both sexes and 3.9% reporting "unsure" or "neither" (Parmar et al., 2020).

The rate of pediatric depression increases with age, with prevalence estimates at 0.5% for children ages 3 to 5, 1.4% for children ages 6 to 11, and 3.5% for children ages 12 to 17 (Perou et al., 2013). Risk factors of pediatric depression among children and adolescents include a variety of biological, environmental, and psychological elements, including family history of depression, obesity, low birth weight, lack of peer support, and poor self-esteem (Clark et al., 2012). Adolescents identifying as gay, lesbian, or bisexual are at a significantly increased risk of depression due to a number of secondary factors such as lack of parental support and bullying from peers (Luk et al., 2018).

The seminal 1989 *Report of the Secretary's Task Force on Youth Suicide* was the first US health agency to highlight the disparity of gay and lesbian youth suicidality, which estimated adolescent gay and lesbian suicidality at 2 to 3 times more than the general adolescent population (Feinleib, 1989). A 2018 report from the *Youth Risk Behavior Surveillance System* revealed that a staggering 7.4% of students in grades 9 through 12 had attempted suicide at least once in the 12 months preceding the survey questionnaire. When stratified by sexual orientation, 5.4% of heterosexual students had attempted suicide in the year previous to the study, while 23.0% of students who identified as gay, lesbian or bisexual had attempted suicide during the same period – a 430% increase in relative risk. This suicide risk remained elevated when only comparing students who have experienced sexual contact with partners of an opposite (8.1%) vs. same/both sex(es) (23.8%). 1.7% of students who identify as heterosexual vs 7.5% of student identifying as gay, lesbian, or bisexual had made a suicide attempt in the previous calendar year which resulted in "injury, poising, or overdose" necessitating intervention by a medical professional (Kann et al., 2018).

Adolescents who experience depression have also been shown to have augmented neurocircuitry in the emotional regulation centers of the brain. When compared to controls, adolescents with depression experience hyperactivity of the amygdala, the brain's emotional response processing center. The amygdala also experiences dense connections with the subgenual anterior cingulate cortex (sgACC), involved in cognitive organization and emotional affect to stimuli. The resting-state functional connectivity (RSFC) is used as a metric for quantifying brain activity under MRI; when observing the sgACC and amygdala of depressed adolescents, the RSFC between the amygdala and sgACC shows heightened activity compared to controls, indicating that adolescents who are depressed likely experience heightened emotional activity to outside stimuli than their controlled peers (Henje Blom et al., 2016).

Public Health

Pediatric depression affects both short- and long-term health outcomes. A number of prospective studies have independently linked adolescent depression to a multitude of physical comorbidities into adulthood, including obesity, smoking, alcohol and substance abuse, migraine headaches, generalized self-rated health, and higher utilization of health care resources (Goodman & Whitaker, 2002; Naicker et al., 2013; Keenan-Miller et al., 2007). In 2018, Johnson, et al, produced one of the largest meta-analysis on the role depression in adolescents and the risk of adult mental health disorders, which found a significant association between adolescent depression and a number of adult depressive and anxiety disorders (Johnson et al., 2018). There is also a significant association between adolescent depression and several long-term social outcomes, including decreased odds of finishing high school. (Clayborne et al., 2019).

As outlined above, depression and suicidality of gay, lesbian, and bisexual adolescents remain a grave public health concern. It is well understood that GLB adolescents have poorer physical, mental, and substance use health trajectories into adulthood when compared to their heterosexual peers (Needham, 2011). When compared to heterosexual adolescents, depressive symptoms and suicidal ideation among GLB adolescents are significantly more likely to persist into adulthood; these persistent depressive symptoms and suicidal ideations are most likely to occur in persons identifying as lesbian or bisexual (Marshal et al., 2013).

The cultural stigma surrounding mental health care is well understood to be a barrier to receiving treatment (Parcesepe & Cabassa, 2012). This phenomenon has been shown to be more pronounced among gay and lesbian adolescents when compared to their heterosexual peers. Gay and lesbian adolescent youth are more likely than their contemporaries to be ashamed about accessing of mental health care and are more likely to have an unaddressed mental health condition (Williams & Chapman, 2011).

Familial support of gay, lesbian, and bisexual youth and the development of adolescent depression and suicidality haven been found to be intrinsically linked. In 2009, Pediatrics published one of the largest and most robust studies surrounding GLB adolescent health outcomes. Among the most startling statistics from this study: GLB-identifying youth were 8.4 times more likely to attempt suicide if they reported high levels of familial rejection secondary to their sexual orientation when compared to families with low or no reported levels of familial rejection. Similar findings were associated with rates of depression (5.9 times), use of illegal drugs (3.2 times), and rates of unprotested sexual intercourse (3.2 times) (Ryan et al., 2009).

Other studies have demonstrated similar assortations. When assessing prevention of suicidality among GLB youth, family connectedness was the most important social protective factor and was found to be more important than caring teachers, other caring adults, and school safety (Eisenberg & Resnick, 2006). Gay and lesbian adolescents are also more likely to report having an unaddressed mental or physical health condition secondary to fear of their parents discovering their sexual orientation (Williams & Chapman, 2011).

Among the most difficult situations plaguing American youth is the rising rate of homelessness; this is pertinent problem among sexual minority youth and is directly associated with familial support in light of their sexual identity. A 2004 study projected that 25-40% of LGBT youth are, at some point, displaced from their home as a direct result of familial conflicts secondary to their sexual and/or gender identity (Whitbeck et al., 2004). Another study analyzing LGBT youth in foster care found that 42% of these individuals were placed into the system as a direct result of familial rejection or conflict relating to their gender and/or sexual identity (Wilber et al., 2006, p. 4). LGBT youth are 120% more likely than their peers to report experiencing at least one episode of homelessness (Morton et al., 2017).

Global Perspective

As of 2019, six countries impose the death penalty upon individuals caught having sexual relations with someone of the same sex. Twenty-six countries punish gay or lesbian relationships with a prison sentence ranging from 10 years to life in prison. In total, seventy countries continue to criminalize consensual same-sex relations (Ramón Mendos, 2019). As a result of the various number of countries that legally and/or socially discriminate against persons identifying as gay, lesbian, or bisexual, it remains extraordinarily difficult to gather statistics on the identities, practices, and medical disparities of these communities throughout the world. In a report from Kenya's Men Against AIDS Youth Group, surveyed Kenyan male youths who identified as gay universally reported at least once incidence of victimization; the perpetrators were most commonly identified as friends and family members of the victim (Keifer & Arshad, 2016). In a 2013 survey out of Vietnam, 77% of LGBT youth stated they had personally faced verbal abuse by a classmate, 44% had been physically assaulted by a peer at school, 54% stated that their school was unsafe for LGBT students, and 19% reported at least once incident of sexual assault and/or rape (Hahn & Tung, 2014).

According to estimates from the World Health Organization (WHO), suicide remains the second leading cause of death worldwide for children and young adults between the ages of ten and twenty-four. The WHO also cites certain groups at risk of discrimination, including those identifying as gay, lesbian, or bisexual, as those who remain at high risk of suicide (World Health Organization, 2014). In a birth to age twenty-one cohort study out of New Zealand, individuals identifying as GLB were at a six-fold greater risk of attempting suicide when compared to their heterosexual peers (Hawton et al, 2012). From the Philippians, female youth (ages 15-24) who reported identifying as lesbian or bisexual were more than two times more likely to attempt suicide than their heterosexual equivalents. A survey profiling Estonian men who have sex with men found a lifetime prevalence of suicidal ideation at 45%, with 11% reporting at least one lifetime suicide attempt (Rüütel et al, 2016). Outside the United States, the available data suggests the link between GLB youth depression and familial support trends similarly to the research conducted within the United States: In a large (n = 1,738) cohort study out of the Netherlands, the rate of depression among GLB youth were directly associated with the youths' perceived parental support of the youth's identity (la Roi et al., 2016). A study out of Thailand of LGBT secondary school students also found that rates of depression, suicidality, and happiness were associated with parental acceptance of the youths' identity (Ojanen et al, 2016).

Public Health Perspective – Interview with Omaha Youth Emergency Services, Street Outreach Coordinator Conner Garges

The Youth Emergency Services (YES) Omaha was founded "to serve youth experiencing homelessness and near-homelessness by providing critically-needed resources which empower them to become self-sufficient." Connor Garges is the Street Outreach Coordinator for YES Omaha, where he is responsible for finding and housing homeless youth as well as overseeing their transition towards finding permanent housing options. Conner reports that gay and lesbian youth are among the most common minority population to find themselves in the position of homelessness at YES. "Many LGBT youth who we serve become homeless as a result of their identity, and more often than not, [these youth are] running away from an unsupportive environment, are kicked out of their home because of their identity, or feeling like they desire a safe space to express their identity." Mr. Garges states that many of these homeless LGBT youth are especially susceptible to resorting to sexual exploitation to maintain food and shelter: "Studies have demonstrated that LGBT youth who are homeless are more likely to engage in prostitution, human trafficking, or survival sex than heterosexual homeless youth and we do see a considerable number of cases at YES that fall into this category." Mr. Garges has seen how unsupportive home environments of gay and lesbian youth result not only in homelessness, but also deleterious mental health issues, as well as physical health and substance abuse issues. "At our outreach center, we have a partnership with Lutheran Family Services therapists who staff our mental health clinic and provide free mental health counseling for all our displaced LGBT youth. Nearly all of our youth have some sort of unaddressed mental health concern which the therapists can at least begin to address." The average length of stay at YES's emergency shelter is 26 days (2019 YES Impact Report, 2020). During this time, if YES determines the GLB youth's home situation to be unreconcilable, YES will then use a rapid rehousing program attempts to place the youth in independent stable housing. "We have a rapid rehousing case manager and job coordinator to get the youth a permanent place to live. Our goal is to provide them with a job and an apartment of their own." Displaced LGBT youth who resort to prostitution, survival sex, or are forced into sex trafficking are at an increased risk of acquiring sexually transmitted infections. "We also have a Nurse Practitioner on staff three days per week who is able to screen for and treat any [STIs] our youth may have. In addition, our LBGT youth are at a higher risk of acquiring HIV infections, so YES partners with the Nebraska AIDS Project to also help educate all our youth on safe sex practices and provides condoms free of charge." Finally, Mr. Garges states that many youths are reluctant to be checked for STIs. "As a result, we have found the best tactic to be incentivizing them to be checked with $25 gift cards to restaurants, which has been a very effective motivating factor." (C. Garges, personal communication, May 1, 2020).

Recommendations

Among the most impactful public policies which has helped mitigate gay, lesbian, and bisexual youth suicides has been the acceptance of state-recognized gay marriage. Utilizing the CDC's Youth Risk Behavior Surveillance System, researchers led by Dr. Julia Raifman, ScD, were able to track youth suicide rates state-by-state as individual states implemented same-sex marriage. They found that, on average, that states which had adopted same-sex marriage observed a 0.6% drop in suicide attempts among all high school students and resulted in a 7% relative reduction in overall suicides in this demographic; among GLB students, the rate of suicide attempts dropped by 4% (> 95% CI) (Raifman et al., 2017). Other researchers have demonstrated that, prior to the Supreme Court's landmark decision in Obergefell v. Hodges, state-wide bans against same sex marriage were associated with increased rates of mood disorders (30%), anxiety disorders (48%) among GLB individuals with compared to states without state-wide bans (Hatzenbuehler et al., 2010). As Dr. Raifman has speculated, the passage and acceptance of same-sex marriages in these states likely signaled a wider cultural shift of acceptance of the sexual identity of these adolescents: "[P]ermitting same-sex marriage reduces structural stigma associated with sexual orientation... [making] students feel less stigmatized and more hopeful for the future" ("Same-Sex Marriage Legalization Linked to Reduction in Suicide Attempts Among High School Students," 2017). While generalization of this phenomenon may not be directly attributable to other countries and cultures, wider cultural acceptance and passage of same-sex marriage laws may result in similar findings of reduced rates of suicides among adolescents identifying as gay, lesbian, or bisexual. Wider cultural acceptance may also be among the best influencers to increase the rates of parental acceptance and family connectedness of GLB youth.

Along with family connectedness, other investigations have demonstrated the importance of school connectedness in mitigating GLB youth suicidality. Multivariable models indicate that US counties with higher proportion of school-hosted gay-straight alliances and firm school antibullying and antidiscrimination policies (measurable variables of school connectedness) observe significantly lower county-wide rates of gay, lesbian, and bisexual youth suicides (Hatzenbuehler, 2011). Binding of state public school funding with firm school district-wide antibullying and antidiscrimination policies would likely decrease the rates of GLB youth suicides. In addition, increasing the accessibility and funding of grants for schools to adopt gay-straight alliance organizations may encourage schools to adopt their own chapters and may also be an effective tool to curb the prevalence of suicidality among sexual minority adolescents.

As issues surrounding gay, lesbian, and bisexual youth homelessness secondary to family connectedness will likely never be fully resolved, changes to better support these youth, as well as their families, may help mitigate this disparity. In 2013, The Center for American Progress released a report on LGBT youth homelessness and made several recommendations to help protect this vulnerable population. Among their suggestions included a recommendation to extend the Runaway and Homeless Youth Act with specific language to better support homeless LGBT youth. The Runaway and Homeless Youth Act, which is reauthorized every five years, provides grants for organizations to provide essential services, including housing and job placement programs, for homeless youth (Cray et al., 2013). However, as of 2017, the Runaway and Homeless Youth Act has yet to require organizations to have antidiscrimination standards towards gender identity or sexual orientation (Page, 2017). By requiring antidiscrimination language of organizations receiving grant funding, homeless LBGT youth would be better served by their communities. In addition to protecting LGBT youth, extra efforts towards restoring family relationships among homeless LGBT youth and their families may help decrease the prevalence of homelessness among this population. As many as 40% of organizations or agencies which provide services to homeless LGBT youth do not offer specific programs to confront conflict and restore family relationships (Cray et al., 2013). Extending grants directly for the funding of family therapy could help reduce the overall burden of homelessness faced by this population.

For GLB youths facing depression and/or suicidal ideations, practitioners must be attuned to the various and unique needs of young GLB persons. As outlined above, GLB persons are more likely have an unmet healthcare need when compared to their peers out of fear on condemnation. Screening for depression and suicidality has become common practice among pediatric and family medicine practitioners, however, more can be done by primary care physicians in ameliorating this disparity among GLB youth. In 2013, the American Academy of Pediatrics issued their first policy guidelines on the proper clinical care for LGBT youth, which help outline best practices for physicians treating this population: To create a positive and welcoming environment of adolescent patients, physicians and staff should offer an inclusive environment and never presume the sexuality of their patients. Practitioners who wish to treat sexual minority patients should also be familiar with local organizations who can also provide resources to these patients and their families. In addition, while still respecting the confidentially and autonomy of the patient, pediatricians and family medicine physicians have the opportunity to be a source of support for families who may be resistant or uncomfortable by the identity of the patient. This may be accomplished by acknowledging family members' feelings, having the practitioner express support for the patient, and by providing information and additional resources to the families, including individual therapy referrals and support groups such as Parents, Families, Friends of Lesbians and Gays (Levine, 2013).

Physicians should make efforts to encourage and refer their GLB patients who are suffering from depression and/or suicidal ideations to participate in cognitive behavioral therapy (CBT), as CBT has been shown to be an effective tool in reducing symptoms of depression in pediatric patients (Spirito et al., 2011). Finally, "restorative" or "conversion therapy" is an inappropriate and ineffective option for GLB patients and may cause undue harm to the patient by way of shame, stigmatization, and an increase in depressive symptoms (Graham 2011).

Conclusion

Gay and lesbian adolescents are at an increased risk of depression and suicidality – nearly one in four GLB high schoolers attempt suicide each year in the United States; yearly, one in every thirteen GLB youth undergo a suicide attempt resulting in stabilization by medical intervention. The increased risks of depression and suicidality among this population appears to be related to social/peer support, school support, and, most importantly, familial support. Gay and lesbian youth lacking familial support increases the disruptions in physical and mental health and also increases the risk of homelessness among this population, exacerbating underlying physical and mental health disparities. Incentivizing schools and peers to provide better support for this population will likely lead to decreased rates of depression and suicidality. Broadening government-recognized same-sex marriage has also proven to be an effective tool in limiting suicides among GBT youth. Finally, more can be done on the federal level to support homeless LGBT youth to broaden their resource availability as well as to support the reunification of families

References:

1. 2019 YES Impact Report (pp. 1–18). (2020). Youth Emergency Services Omaha. https://issuu.com/miwatkins/docs/yes_2019_annual_report_-_with_indiv_79b84c01f1c590

2. Clark, M., Jansen, K., & Cloy, J. (2012). Treatment of Childhood and Adolescent Depression. *American Family Physician, 86.*

3. Clayborne, Z. M., Varin, M., & Colman, I. (2019). Systematic Review and Meta-Analysis: Adolescent Depression and Long-Term Psychosocial Outcomes. *Journal of the American Academy of Child & Adolescent Psychiatry, 58*(1), 72–79. https://doi.org/10.1016/j.jaac.2018.07.896

4. Copen, C., Chandra, A., & Febo-Vazquez, I. (2016). *Sexual Behavior, Sexual Attraction, and Sexual Orientation Among Adults Aged 18–44 in the United States: Data From the 2011–2013 National Survey of Family Growth.* US Department of Health and Human Services. https://www.cdc.gov/nchs//data/nhsr/nhsr088.pdf

5. Cray, A., Miller, K., & Durso, L. (2013). *Seeking Shelter: The Experiences and Unmet Needs of LGBT Homeless Youth.* Center for American Progress. https://www.americanprogress.org/wp-content/uploads/2013/09/LGBTHomelessYouth.pdf

6. D'Augelli, A. R., Hershberger, S. L., & Pilkington, N. W. (2001). Suicidality Patterns and Sexual Orientation-Related Factors Among Lesbian, Gay, and Bisexual Youths. *Suicide and Life-Threatening Behavior, 31*(3), 250–264. https://doi.org/10.1521/suli.31.3.250.24246

7. Eisenberg, M. E., & Resnick, M. D. (2006). Suicidality among Gay, Lesbian and Bisexual Youth: The Role of Protective Factors. *Journal of Adolescent Health, 39*(5), 662–668. https://doi.org/10.1016/j.jadohealth.2006.04.024

8. Feinleib, M. (Ed.). (1989). *Report of the Secretary's Task Force on Youth Suicide.* U.S. Department of Health and Human Services. https://files.eric.ed.gov/fulltext/ED334503.pdf

9. Garges, C. (2020, May 1). *Youth Emergency Services and LGBT Youth* [Personal communication].

10. Ghandour, R. M., Sherman, L. J., Vladutiu, C. J., Ali, M. M., Lynch, S. E., Bitsko, R. H., & Blumberg, S. J. (2019). Prevalence and Treatment of Depression, Anxiety, and Conduct Problems in US Children. *The Journal of Pediatrics, 206*, 256-267.e3. https://doi.org/10.1016/j.jpeds.2018.09.021

11. Goodman, E., & Whitaker, R. C. (2002). A prospective study of the role of depression in the development and persistence of adolescent obesity. *Pediatrics, 110*(3), 497–504. https://doi.org/10.1542/peds.110.3.497

12. Graham, R., Berkowitz, B., Blum, R., Bockting, W., Bradford, J., de Vries, B., & Makadon, H. (2011). The health of lesbian, gay, bisexual, and transgender people: Building a foundation for better understanding. *Washington, DC: Institute of Medicine, 10*, 13128.

13. Hahn, D. H., & Tung, T. K. (2014). *Being LGBT in Asia: Viet Nam Country Report* (p. 20). USAID. https://www.usaid.gov/sites/default/files/documents/1861/Being_LGBT_in_Asia_Viet_Nam_report_ENG.pdf

14. Hatzenbuehler, M. (2011). The Social Environment and Suicide Attempts in Lesbian, Gay, and Bisexual Youth. *Pediatrics, 127*(5), 896–903. https://doi.org/10.1542/peds.2010-3020

15. Hatzenbuehler, M., McLaughlin, K., Keyes, K., & Hasin, D. (2010). The Impact of Institutional Discrimination on Psychiatric Disorders in Lesbian, Gay, and Bisexual Populations: A Prospective Study. *American Journal of Public Health, 100*(3), 452–459. https://doi.org/10.2105/ajph.2009.168815

16. Hawton, K., Saunders, K. E., & O'Connor, R. C. (2012). Self-harm and suicide in adolescents. *The Lancet, 379*(9834), 2373–2382. https://doi.org/10.1016/s0140-6736(12)60322-5

17. Henje Blom, E., Ho, T. C., Connolly, C. G., LeWinn, K. Z., Sacchet, M. D., Tymofiyeva, O., Weng, H. Y., & Yang, T. T. (2016). The neuroscience and context of adolescent depression. *Acta Paediatrica, 105*(4), 358–365. https://doi.org/10.1111/apa.13299

18. Heron, M. (2019). *Deaths: Leading Causes for 2017.* National Vital Statistics. https://www.cdc.gov/nchs/data/nvsr/nvsr68/nvsr68_06-508.pdf

19. Johnson, D., Dupuis, G., Piche, J., Clayborne, Z., & Colman, I. (2018). Adult mental health outcomes of adolescent depression: A systematic review. *Depression and Anxiety, 35*(8), 700–716. https://doi.org/10.1002/da.22777

20. Kann, L., McManus, T., Harris, W. A., Shanklin, S. L., Flint, K. H., Queen, B., Lowry, R., Chyen, D., Whittle, L., Thornton, J., Lim, C., Bradford, D., Yamakawa, Y., Leon, M., Brener, N., & Ethier, K. A. (2018). Youth Risk Behavior Surveillance — United States, 2017. *MMWR. Surveillance Summaries, 67*(8), 1–114. https://doi.org/10.15585/mmwr.ss6708a1

21. Keenan-Miller, D., Hammen, C. L., & Brennan, P. A. (2007). Health Outcomes Related to Early Adolescent Depression. *Journal of Adolescent Health, 41*(3), 256–262. https://doi.org/10.1016/j.jadohealth.2007.03.015

22. Keifer, M., & Arshad, U. (2016). *Lesbian, Gay, Bisexual, and Transgender (LGBT) Youth in the Global South.* Advocates for Youth. https://www.advocatesforyouth.org/wp-content/uploads/storage//advfy/documents/Factsheets/lesbian-gay-bisexual-and-transgender-youth-in-the-global-south.pdf

23. la Roi, C., Kretschmer, T., Dijkstra, J. K., Veenstra, R., & Oldehinkel, A. J. (2016). Disparities in Depressive Symptoms Between Heterosexual and Lesbian, Gay, and Bisexual Youth in a Dutch Cohort: The TRAILS Study. *Journal of Youth and Adolescence, 45*(3), 440–456. https://doi.org/10.1007/s10964-015-0403-0

24. Levine, D. (2013). Office-Based Care for Lesbian, Gay, Bisexual, Transgender, and Questioning Youth. *Pediatrics, 132*(1), e297–e313. https://doi.org/10.1542/peds.2013-1283

25. Luk, J. W., Gilman, S. E., Haynie, D. L., & Simons-Morton, B. G. (2017). Sexual Orientation Differences in Adolescent Health Care Access and Health-Promoting Physician Advice. *Journal of Adolescent Health, 61*(5), 555–561. https://doi.org/10.1016/j.jadohealth.2017.05.032

26. Luk, J. W., Gilman, S. E., Haynie, D. L., & Simons-Morton, B. G. (2018). Sexual Orientation and Depressive Symptoms in Adolescents. *Pediatrics*, *141*(5), e20173309. https://doi.org/10.1542/peds.2017-3309

27. Marshal, M. P., Dermody, S. S., Cheong, J., Burton, C. M., Friedman, M. S., Aranda, F., & Hughes, T. L. (2013). Trajectories of Depressive Symptoms and Suicidality Among Heterosexual and Sexual Minority Youth. *Journal of Youth and Adolescence*, *42*(8), 1243–1256. https://doi.org/10.1007/s10964-013-9970-0

28. Marshal, M. P., Dietz, L. J., Friedman, M. S., Stall, R., Smith, H. A., McGinley, J., Thoma, B. C., Murray, P. J., D'Augelli, A. R., & Brent, D. A. (2011). Suicidality and Depression Disparities Between Sexual Minority and Heterosexual Youth: A Meta-Analytic Review. *Journal of Adolescent Health*, *49*(2), 115–123. https://doi.org/10.1016/j.jadohealth.2011.02.005

29. Morton, M., Dworsky, A., & Samuels, G. (2017). *Missed Opportunities: Youth Homelessness in America. National Estimates*. University of Chicago.

30. Naicker, K., Galambos, N. L., Zeng, Y., Senthilselvan, A., & Colman, I. (2013). Social, Demographic, and Health Outcomes in the 10 Years Following Adolescent Depression. *Journal of Adolescent Health*, *52*(5), 533–538. https://doi.org/10.1016/j.jadohealth.2012.12.016

31. Needham, B. L. (2011). Sexual Attraction and Trajectories of Mental Health and Substance Use During the Transition from Adolescence to Adulthood. *Journal of Youth and Adolescence*, *41*(2), 179–190. https://doi.org/10.1007/s10964-011-9729-4

32. Ojanen, T., Ratanashevorn, R., & Boonkerd, S. (2016). *Gaps in responses to LGBT issues in Thailand: Mental health research, services, and policies* (pp. 41–59). Psychology of Sexualities Review. https://www.researchgate.net/publication/318528375_Gaps_in_responses_to_LGBT_issues_in_Thailand_Mental_health_research_services_and_policies

33. Page, M. (2017). Forgotten Youth: Homeless LGBT Youth of Color and the Runaway and Homeless Youth Act. *Northwestern Journal of Law &*

Social Policy, 2(2). https://scholarlycommons.law.northwestern.edu/cgi/
viewcontent.cgi?article=1150&context=njlsp

34. Parcesepe, A. M., & Cabassa, L. J. (2012). Public Stigma of Mental Illness
in the United States: A Systematic Literature Review. *Administration
and Policy in Mental Health and Mental Health Services Research, 40*(5),
384–399. https://doi.org/10.1007/s10488-012-0430-z

35. Parmar, D. D., Alabaster, A., Vance, S., Ritterman Weintraub, M. L., &
Lau, J. S. (2020). Identification of Sexual Minority Youth in Pediatric
Primary Care Settings Within a Large Integrated Healthcare System
Using Electronic Health Records. *Journal of Adolescent Health, 66*(2),
255–257. https://doi.org/10.1016/j.jadohealth.2019.10.003

36. Patel, V. (2013). Why Adolescent Depression Is a Global Health Priority
and What We Should Do About It. *Journal of Adolescent Health, 52*(5),
511–512. https://doi.org/10.1016/j.jadohealth.2013.03.003

37. Perou, R., Bitsko, R., Blumburg, S., Pastor, P., Ghandour, R., & Gfroerer,
J. (2013). *Mental Health Surveillance Among Children — United States,
2005–2011.* Centers for Disease Control and Prevention. https://www.cdc.
gov/mmwr/preview/mmwrhtml/su6202a1.htm

38. Raifman, J., Moscoe, E., Austin, S. B., & McConnell, M. (2017). Difference-
in-Differences Analysis of the Association Between State Same-Sex
Marriage Policies and Adolescent Suicide Attempts. *JAMA Pediatrics,
171*(4), 350. https://doi.org/10.1001/jamapediatrics.2016.4529

39. Ramón Mendos, L. (2019). *State Sponsored Homophobia: Global
Legislation Overview Update.* IGLA World. https://ilga.org/downloads/
ILGA_World_State_Sponsored_Homophobia_report_global_
legislation_overview_update_December_2019.pdf

40. Remafedl, G., Resnick, M., Blum, R., & Harris, L. (1991). The demography
of sexual orientation in adolescents: A population-based study.
Journal of Adolescent Health, 12(2), 165. https://doi.org/10.1016/0197-
0070(91)90473-y

41. Rüütel, K., Valk, A., & Lõhmus, L. (2016). Suicidality and Associated Factors Among Men Who Have Sex With Men in Estonia. *Journal of Homosexuality, 64*(6), 770–785. https://doi.org/10.1080/00918369.2016.1236578

42. Ryan, C., Huebner, D., Diaz, R. M., & Sanchez, J. (2009). Family Rejection as a Predictor of Negative Health Outcomes in White and Latino Lesbian, Gay, and Bisexual Young Adults. *Pediatrics, 123*(1), 346–352. https://doi.org/10.1542/peds.2007-3524

43. Same-Sex Marriage Legalization Linked to Reduction in Suicide Attempts Among High School Students. (2017, February 20). *Johns Hopkins Bloomberg School of Public Health.* https://www.jhsph.edu/news/news-releases/2017/same-sex-marriage-legalization-linked-to-reduction-in-suicide-attempts-among-high-school-students.html

44. Spirito, A., Esposito-Smythers, C., Wolff, J., & Uhl, K. (2011). Cognitive-Behavioral Therapy for Adolescent Depression and Suicidality. *Child and Adolescent Psychiatric Clinics of North America, 20*(2), 191–204. https://doi.org/10.1016/j.chc.2011.01.012

45. Twenge, J. M., Cooper, A. B., Joiner, T. E., Duffy, M. E., & Binau, S. G. (2019). Age, period, and cohort trends in mood disorder indicators and suicide-related outcomes in a nationally representative dataset, 2005-2017. *Journal of Abnormal Psychology, 128*(3), 185–199. https://doi.org/10.1037/abn0000410

46. Uma, R., & Chen, L. (2009). Characteristics, correlates, and outcomes of childhood and adolescent depressive disorders. *Dialogues in Clinical Neuroscience, 11*(1). https://www.ncbi.nlm.nih.gov/pmc/articles/PMC2766280/

47. Whitbeck, L. B., Chen, X., Hoyt, D. R., Tyler, K. A., & Johnson, K. D. (2004). Mental disorder, subsistence strategies, and victimization among gay, lesbian, and bisexual homeless and runaway adolescents. *Journal of Sex Research, 41*(4), 329–342. https://doi.org/10.1080/00224490409552240

48. Wilber, S., Ryan, C., & Marksamer, J. (2006). *CWLA Best Best Practice Practice Guidelines: Serving LGBT Youth in Out-of-Home Care* (p. 4). Child Welfare League of America. http://www.nclrights.org/wp-content/uploads/2013/07/bestpracticeslgbtyouth.pdf

49. Williams, K. A., & Chapman, M. V. (2011). Comparing Health and Mental Health Needs, Service Use, and Barriers to Services among Sexual Minority Youths and Their Peers. *Health & Social Work, 36*(3), 197–206. https://doi.org/10.1093/hsw/36.3.197

50. World Health Organization. (2014). Preventing suicide: a global imperative. *Who.Int.* https://doi.org/9789241564779

The Impact of Discrimination on Transgender Health

Simon, Brittany

Introduction

Every day, transgender patients experience social and economic marginalization due to their gender identity. In comparison to gay/lesbian adults, transgender adults experience more family estrangement and conflict. Transgender adults are two times more likely than gay/lesbian adults to experience discrimination and victimization, which can lead to shame and emotional distress. The purpose of this writing assignment is to reveal the impact of social stigma and discrimination on transgender patient health and examine methods of how transgender health disparities can be effectively reduced.

Studies have shown that transgender people report high rates of discrimination across many areas, including healthcare, housing and employment (Clements-Nolle, 2001). A needs assessment of 182 transgender people in Philadelpha, Pennsylvaina found that 26% had been denied medical care because they were transgender and 52% had difficulty accessing one or more health services in the past year (Kenagy, 2005). The San Francisco Transgender Community Project revealed that 39% of female-to-male (FTM) transgender patients reported being denied health care or having difficulties obtaining health care compared with 13% of male-to-female (MTF) patients (Clements, 1999). A Chicago, Illinois study sampled 111 transgender people and found that 12% were refused routine health care, 3% were refused mental health care, and 14% reported difficulty getting emergency health care because they were transgender (Kenagy & Bostwick, 2005).

Advocates who work with transgender patients continue to work with clients to obtain health benefits, find housing, or to save jobs terminated due to discrimination. Many times, policy makers, the media, and society dismiss the unique needs of transgender people in their communities. Insufficient data on the scope of anti-transgender discrimination within healthcare settings has hindered the fight for basic fairness within this population. In 2008, the National Center for Transgender Equality and the National Gay and Lesbian Task Force formed a research partnership to address this problem by launching the first comprehensive national transgender discrimination study. Over 70,000 people responded to the survey, which provided great insight into transgender health and health care discrimination and disparities. Survey participants reported very high levels of postponing medical care when sick or injured due to discrimination or inability to afford the care. Respondents faced hurdles to accessing health care including refusal of care, harassment and violence in medical settings and lack of provider knowledge. 19% of patients reported being refused care due to their transgender or gender non-conforming status, with even higher numbers among people of color (Grant, 2010). 28% were subjected to harassment in medical settings and 2% were victims of violence in doctor's offices (Grant, 2010). 50% of the sample reported having to teach their medical providers about transgender care (Grant, 2010).

Real or perceived stigma and discrimination within our healthcare system may impact transgender patients' desire and ability to access appropriate health care. Transgender patients have reported avoiding medical care because of negative and/or discriminatory experiences or fear of negative experiences. These experiences occur in both the outpatient and inpatient settings. The Trans PULSE Project conducted an emergency department experience survey of transgender patients in Ontario, Candada in 2009 to 2010. 24% of the 408 respondents reported ever avoiding emergency department care because of a perception that their transgender status would negatively affect that encounter.

This was consistent with non-peer-reviewed United States reports showing high frequencies of avoidance or postponement of care across healthcare settings.

As a result of less access to care, transgender patients are at risk for suffering significant health disparities in multiple areas. MTF are recognized world-wide as a group that carries a disproportionate burden of HIV infection, with a worldwide HIV prevalence of 20% in 2011 (Baral, 2013). A United States sample of 1093 transgender patients demonstrated a high prevalence of clinical depression (44.1%), anxiety (33.2%), and somatization (27.5%) (Lombardi, 2011). The National Center for Transgender Equality and the National Gay and Lesbian Task Force's 2008 study found that 30% of the respondents reported current smoking, which is nearly double the rate of the general population. 26% reported current or former alcohol or drug use to cope with mistreatment and 41% report having attempted suicide, which is 26 times higher than the general population (Grant, 2010). Respondents also reported over four times the national average of HIV infection; 2.64% in the study sample versus 0.6% in the general population (Grant, 2010). Over a quarter of the respondents misused drugs or alcohol specifically to cope with discrimination (Grant, 2010). While some of these health care barriers are faced by other minority groups, many are unique and many are significantly magnified for transgender persons.

In order to improve transgender patient access to care, several actions can be taken by healthcare providers and the medical education community to combat discrimination and reestablish trust with our transgender community. The first step is to educate current and future health care providers in transgender medicine and how to appropriately care for the transgender patient.

More competent and knowledgeable providers are needed in the transgender healthcare community. According to Dr. Michael White, the Chief Medical Officer of CHI Health Creighton University Medical Center in Nebraska and university's Associate Dean for Educational Innovation, one way to improve rapport with FTM patients and decrease distrust is through undergraduate and graduate medical education and continuing medical education. Through early education of medical students and new physicians, future negative provider encounters can be prevented. Most medical schools provide a curriculum designed to introduce and address the health care disparities faced by lesbian and gay patients. However, transgender medicine is underrepresented in medical schools. A 2011 JAMA article found that out of 132 allopathic and osteopathic medical schools in Canada and the United States, 70% reported zero coverage of gender transitioning (Obedin-Maliver, 2011).

Conversely, lesbian and gay topic areas of HIV, sexual orientation, gender identity and sexually transmitted infections had zero-coverage rates of less than 30%. Therefore, while lesbian and gay curriculum coverage in medical schools is overall positive, transgender medicine is represented in numbers that are disproportionately low. Students taking a transgender curriculum within the organ system-based course Endocrine-Reproduction reported feeling more prepared to care for transgender patients (Marshall 2017). This additional needed curriculum may yield providers who are more comfortable treating transgender patients and/or offering gender-affirming care. Medical schools can further educate students about transgender patient disparities by incorporating transgender standardized patient (SP) cases within advanced clerkship curriculum. Underman et al developed a transgender SP encounter which took place as part of a half-day workshop on communication challenges with patients. 179 United States fourth-year medical students participated in the through undergraduate and graduate medical education and continuing medical education. Through early education of medical students and new physicians, future negative provider encounters can be prevented. Most medical schools provide a curriculum designed to introduce and address the health care disparities faced by lesbian and gay patients. However, transgender medicine is underrepresented in medical schools. A 2011 JAMA article found that out of 132 allopathic and osteopathic medical schools in Canada and the United States, 70% reported zero coverage of gender transitioning (Obedin-Maliver, 2011).

Conversely, lesbian and gay topic areas of HIV, sexual orientation, gender identity and sexually transmitted infections had zero-coverage rates of less than 30%. Therefore, while lesbian and gay curriculum coverage in medical schools is overall positive, transgender medicine is represented in numbers that are disproportionately low. Students taking a transgender curriculum within the organ system-based course Endocrine-Reproduction reported feeling more prepared to care for transgender patients (Marshall 2017). This additional needed curriculum may yield providers who are more comfortable treating transgender patients and/or offering gender-affirming care. Medical schools can further educate students about transgender patient disparities by incorporating transgender standardized patient (SP) cases within advanced clerkship curriculum. Underman et al developed a transgender SP encounter which took place as part of a half-day workshop on communication challenges with patients. 179 United States fourth-year medical students participated in the workshop. In preliminary uses of the case, 80% of students agreed or strongly agreed that it increased their skills for working with transgender patients. Observational data from debrief discussions following the case revealed that students identified gaps in their medical training regarding LGBT health and expressed interest in their program incorporating more information on transgender health.

In addition to being knowledgeable about transgender health concerns and hormone therapies, providers must provide a safe, non-judgmental space for their patients. Dr. Mark Goodman, a Professor of Family Medicine at Creighton University School of Medicine establishes rapport and trust with his patients before discussing health issues and recommendations. He tells patients that he is their advocate, reassures them that they are in a safe space and confirms that he is benevolent and competent in transgender medicine. This is a very important step because when providers are judgmental or express disapproval, patients may be less honest with medical history which may cause missed opportunities for needed health screenings and prevention.

References

1.   Baral S. D., Poteat T., Stromdahl S., Wirtz A. L., Guadamuz T. E., Beyrer C. (2013) Worldwide burden of HIV in transgender women: a systematic review and meta-analysis. *Lancet Infect Dis.*;13:214–22

2. Bradford, J., Reisner, S. L., Honnold, J. A., Xavier, J. (2013). Experiences of Transgender-Related Discrimination and Implications for Health: Results from the Virginia Transgender Health Initiative Study. *Am J Public Health*. 103(10): 1820-1829.

3. Braveman P., Gruskin S. (2003). Poverty, equity, human rights and health. *Bull World Health Organization*. 81 (7): 539-545

4. Clements-Nolle K, Marx R, Guzman R, Katz M. (2001). HIV prevalence, risk behaviors, health care use, and mental health status of transgender persons: implications for public health intervention. *Am J Public Health* ;91(6):915–921

5. Clements K, Katz M, Marx R. (1999) The Transgender Community Health Project: Descriptive Results. San Francisco, CA: San Francisco Department of Public Health

6. Grant JM, Mottet LA, Tanis J. National Transgender Discrimination Survey report on health and health care: findings of a study by the National Center for Transgender Equality and the National Gay and Lesbian Task Force. National Gay and Lesbian Task Force Web site. http://www.thetaskforce.org/static_html/downloads/resources_and_tools/ntds_report_on_health. pdf. Published October 2010.

7. Kenagy G. P. (2005) Transgender health: findings from two needs assessment studies in Philadelphia. *Health Soc Work*. 30(1):19–26

8. Kenagy G. P., Bostwick W.B. (2005). Health and social service needs of transgender people in Chicago. In: Bockting WO, Avery E, editors. Transgender Health and HIV Prevention: Needs Assessment Studies From Transgender Communities Across the United States. Binghamton, NY: Haworth Medical Press; pp. 57–66.

9. Lombardi E. (2011) Transgender Health: A Review and Guidance for Future Research—Proceedings from the Summer Institute at the Center for Research on Health and Sexual Orientation, University of Pittsburgh. *International Journal of Transgenderism*; 12:211–29

10. Marshall A, Pickle S, Lawlis S (2017). Transgender medicine curriculum: integration into an organ system–based preclinical program. *MedEdPORTAL*; 13:10536.Newfield, E., Hart, S., Dibble, S., & Kohler, L., (2006). Female-to-male transgender quality of life. *Quality of Life Research*. 15: 1447-1457.

11. Obedin-Maliver J, Goldsmith ES, Stewart L, et al (2011). Lesbian, gay, bisexual, and transgender–related content in undergraduate medical education. *JAMA*; 306(9):971-977.

12. Safer, J.D., Coleman E., Feldman, J., Garofalo, R., Hembree, W., Radix, A., & Sevelius, J. (2016). Barriers to Health Care for Transgender Individuals. *Curr Opin Endocrinol Diabetes Obes*; 23(2): 168-171.

13. Underman K, Giffort D, Hyderi A, Hirshfield LE. (2016)Transgender health: a standardized patient case for advanced clerkship students. *MedEdPORTAL*;12:10518

Barriers to Cervical Cancer Screenings in Transgender Men

Williams, Christopher

Background

As healthcare in the United States continues to focus ever increasingly on preventative care, greater attention has been given to populations that do not receive adequate preventative screenings due to minority statuses including gender identity. Gender identity refers to the inherent feelings of being male, female, both, or neither that is common among all humans (Streed, 2017). In contrast, a person's sex is determined by the physical reproductive organs that they possess at birth. Commonly, an individual's gender identity is congruent with the cultural norms that surround their assigned sex at birth. Such persons whose gender identity matches their physical sex are called cis-gender or are alternatively referred to as cis-men or cis-women (Streed, 2017). An individual who identifies as both a man and a woman, neither man nor woman, or possess any other identity outside typical binary gender identities can be referred to as genderqueer, non-binary, or gender non-conforming (Streed, 2017). If the sex assigned to an individual at birth does not match their internal gender identity and the individual makes efforts to correct this discordance, they are referred to as transgender or alternatively as a trans-man or trans-woman. A transgender man specifically refers to someone who was assigned female at birth, but identifies as a male (Streed, 2017).

A common routine health screening performed in the United States is the Papanicolaou or Pap smear, which is used to screen for cervical cancer.

A Pap smear requires insertion of a sterile speculum into the vaginal canal to allow a physician to visualize and collect epithelial cells from the transitional zone of the uterine cervix to be sent for visual inspection and analysis for cellular abnormalities. The transitional zone refers to the zone between the squamous epithelium of the ectocervix and the columnar epithelium of the endocervix. The squamous epithelial cells of the ectocervix are the cells most at risk for malignant transformation. Screening guidelines for cervical cancer include cervical cytology every 3 years for women aged 21 – 65. Alternatively, women aged 30 – 65 or women at high risk for HPV infection can have concurrent cervical cytology and HPV testing administered every 5 years (The American College of Obstetricians and Gynecologists, 2017).

Because transgender men possess a uterine cervix, unless they have undergone a total hysterectomy, this population is still at risk for developing cervical dysplasia or cancer. While case reports of transgender men with cervical cancer exist in the literature, little is known about the epidemiology of chronic conditions like cervical cancer in this population (Braun, et al., 2017). Hence, transgender men should receive Pap smears using the same schedule that is used for cis women as outlined above. Despite these recommendations, transgender men are less likely to receive Pap smears than their cis-women counterparts (Peitzmeier, Khullar, Reisner, & Potter, 2014). Transgender men are also more likely to have inadequate or abnormal Pap smears compared to cis women (Gatos, 2018). This paper will serve to identify barriers to proper cervical cancer screening in the transgender men population and suggest changes that can be implemented to improve patient care.

Cervical Cancer

Cervical cancer is a disease process that exists on a spectrum of severity. The earliest, premalignant form of cervical cancer is referred to as cervical intraepithelial neoplasia, although the term cervical dysplasia is still sometimes encountered. Cervical intraepithelial neoplasia or CIN is defined as disordered growth, development, or morphology of cervical epithelial cells that is graded by the thickness of epithelium involved. CIN can be graded as

CIN I, CIN II, or CIN III. Once dysplasia involves the entire thickness of the cervical epithelium without invasion of the basement membrane, the abnormal changes are referred to as CIN III or carcinoma in situ. Once the abnormal cells invade through the basement membrane layer of the uterine cervix, the disease is termed invasive cervical cancer or, more commonly, cervical cancer (Callahan and Caughey, 2013).

The primary causative agent of cervical epithelial abnormalities resulting in CIN and cervical cancer is human papilloma virus or HPV. Certain HPV types including types 16, 18, 31, and 45 are especially carcinogenic. Because of advances in routine cervical cancer screening and HPV prevention, the rates of cervical cancer have dropped dramatically in the United States. Pap smears became widely accepted and performed screening examinations in the 1950s and 1960s. Testing for HPV through genetic testing has further reduced cervical cancer deaths. The combination of regular Pap smears and HPV testing reduces the risk of death from cervical cancer by 90%. Furthermore, immunizations against the risk strains of HPV have decreased the risk of developing cervical cancer by 70% (Callahan and Caughey, 2013).

Besides HPV infections, other risk factors for CIN and cervical cancer are cigarette smoking, immunodeficiency such as HIV or iatrogenic immunosuppression. Each of these risk factors inhibit the ability of the body's natural defenses against HPV from clearing the virus resulting in a more rapid progression of CIN to cervical cancer (Callahan and Caughey, 2013). These risk factors are particularly important as transgender persons are more likely to smoke than cis-gender persons (Bernstein, Peitzmeier, Potter, and Reisner, n.d.)

Barriers to Care

Transgender men face many different barriers to accessing comprehensive healthcare and screenings. Of these barriers, some of the most well documented are lack of access to care, negative experiences within the healthcare industry, feelings of self-conflict over gender identity due to the invasiveness of the exam, and complications due to transition-related surgical and hormonal treatments.

Access to care is a significant barrier to transgender patients receiving proper medical screenings and treatment. As in many populations, cost is a deterrent from transgender patients from seeking medical care. Nearly one-third of transgender patients reported not seeing a physician in the past year due to cost. Cost is a major concern in transgender patients in particular because of problems with health insurance coverage (James et al., 2016). Insurance coverage rates are potentially lower in transgender patients because of higher rates of poverty and less access to employment-based insurance because of job loss due to bias (Stroumsa, 2014). While not all private insurance will cover hormone replacement therapies or gender confirmation surgeries, private health insurance companies are required to cover preventative services regardless of sex assigned at birth or current gender identity if recommended by a physician or advanced care practitioners under the Affordable Care Act (U.S. Centers for Medicare & Medicaid Services, n.d.). It should be noted, however, that many medical professional organizations including the American Medical Association and American Psychological Association have advocated for increased coverage of hormone replacement therapy and gender confirmation surgeries as these treatments have been shown to be beneficial to the overall health of transgender patients resulting in a more cost-effective insurance coverage for private insurance companies (Stroumsa, 2014). As healthcare policies, such as the Affordable Care Act are strongly influenced by the political leanings and opinions of administrations within the United States government, the potential for these protections to be repealed and replaced by less inclusive regulations is a real threat to the health of transgender patients.

Cost is not the only deterrent that transgender men face. In a study conducted by the National Center for Transgender Equality (2016), 42% of transgender men respondents reported that they had had at least one negative experience in a healthcare setting because of identifying as transgender. Negative experiences were more likely to be reported by transgender individuals who are part of racial or ethnic minorities and were more common in transgender men compared to transgender women and non-binary persons (James et al., 2016). Negative screenings can be the result of discrimination or the creation of an unwelcoming environment for transgender men. As a respondent to a study conducted by Potter, et al. stated "It being an OB/GYN office, I was pretty much the only male sitting there…People think, why is he here? I don't want to be outed. I don't want to be sitting there looked at like, "Who is this person?"" (Potter et al., 2015). Such feelings of unease can negatively impact the patient's experience and cause the individual to not seek care when they are due for another Pap smear. Other negative experiences by transgender men included blatant discrimination or harassment in healthcare settings, lack of knowledge about transgender care by physicians, and refusal of care by physicians (James et al., 2016). Even the most positive of experiences with competent staff and physicians can become negative if incorrect names or gendered language is used during the visit (Potter et al., 2015).

Gynecological exams such as Pap smears are invasive tests that require penetration, inspection, and manipulation of genitalia. Such invasive screening forces transgender patients to acknowledge the discord between their gender identity and their physical sex. Despite the emotional difficulties and potential for discrimination that transgender patients face during gynecological examinations, they typically place the priority on their physical health. A transgender male patient was quoted as saying, "That's my biology … I just say to myself before I go in, 'You know what they are going to call you, she, and they are going to call you, [name], and that is okay because that is my body and that is my biology and I need to make sure I'm healthy so that is my priority in that moment." (Dutton, Koenig, & Fennie, 2008). Hormone replacement therapy, HRT, used in transgender men for masculinization of features includes the administration of testosterone. Testosterone or androgen hormone replacement therapy induce atrophy of the vaginal mucosa and uterine cervix, which are normally sustained by the female hormone estrogen. Such atrophic changes can make speculum insertion more painful in transgender men, making the pelvic examination and Pap smear more difficult for both the provider and the patient to complete (Peitzmeier et al, 2014). If a transgender male patient has difficulty with pelvic exams and Pap smears due to vaginal atrophy, it may be appropriate to offer co-testing with both cytology and HPV testing to ensure accurate results (Gorton, 2016).

A final potential barrier to proper cervical cancer screening in transgender men is the effect that transition-related surgeries and treatments have on Pap smear frequency and quality. The most commonly performed transition-related surgeries in transgender men are chest reconstructions and hysterectomies (James et al, 2016). According to the National Center for Transgender Equality, only 8% of transgender men receive gender-affirming hysterectomies (James et al., 2016). Hysterectomies can be performed as total hysterectomies where the uterine corpus and uterine cervix are removed or as supracervical hysterectomies where the uterine cervix is maintained. Patients may not always be aware of which surgery was performed (Potter et al., 2015). Because the uterine cervix is removed in a total hysterectomy, there is no indication for routine cervical cancer screenings to be carried out. If patients are unaware of the type of hysterectomy that they receive, patients may believe that they no longer require Pap smears when, in fact, they do. Another transition-related barrier that transgender men face regarding cervical cancer screening is a high rate of unsatisfactory or inadequate Pap smears in transgender men. Unsatisfactory Pap smears refer to samples that cannot be evaluated by a pathologist due to a lack of sufficient cells or an obscuring factor. In cis-gender women, unsatisfactory Pap smears are associated with an increased risk of developing cervical cancer and a need for re-screening to rule out any abnormal cervical changes. While the exact significance of unsatisfactory Pap smears in transgender men is unknown, it is known that the longer the duration that a transgender man is on testosterone for transition-related therapy the higher the risk of unsatisfactory Pap smears. It is thought that these atrophic changes mimic the abnormal morphology seen in CIN leading to an unsatisfactory pathological specimen on Pap smear (Peitzmeier et al., 2014). As such, healthcare providers should be aware of the effects that hormone replacement therapy may have on cytological samples and inform both laboratory specialists and the patient about the potential for an abnormal result.

Healthcare providers themselves can serve as barriers to transgender patients from receiving proper gynecological care. Many transgender patients report that they had to teach healthcare providers about how-to best care for transgender persons and others report that healthcare providers asked unnecessary or invasive questions that were unrelated to the chief complaint of the visit (James et al., 2016). These complaints by transgender patients bring to light the knowledge deficits present in many U.S. healthcare providers. United States and Canadian medical schools across the board offer a median of 5 hours of devoted lecture time about the lesbian, bisexual, gay, and transgender (LGBT) community (Obedin-Maliver et al., 2011). The impact of such limited education was apparent in a study published in the Journal of Women's Health in which a survey of 352 OBGYNs revealed that only 29% felt comfortable caring for transgender men and 88.7% were willing to perform a Pap smear on transgender men (Unger, 2015). Lack of education about caring for LGBT patients may also result in physicians being unclear about stereotypes and myths that surround transgender individuals. Common misconceptions that the lay public and physicians may have about transgender individuals may include that transgender people have few sexual partners, never engage in penetrative vaginal sex, or that transgender men who do not have penis-in-vagina sex do not require Pap smears. However, transgender individuals may have multiple sexual partners, engage in a variety of sexual behaviors, and should receive routine Pap smears regardless of types of sexual activities that the patient is involved in (Potter, et al., 2015).

Healthcare providers also can intentionally or unintentionally discriminate against transgender patients by not creating a safe and welcoming environment. Other times, complacency and lack of awareness of transgender patients can lead to what is likely largely unintentional discrimination of this patient group. This author has witnessed attending physicians call transgender patients by the name or pronouns that they were assigned at birth rather than by their preferred name and pronouns. Most of the times that this has been witnessed, there is no attempt by the physician to elicit the preferred name or pronouns of the patient. Such behavior by healthcare providers is a huge indignity to patients who come in a state of vulnerability, seeking medical care like all humans are entitled to. Physicians, like all healthcare providers, can lose the sensitivity and empathy that should be employed when dealing with transgender patients or any other minority group under the mounting pressures of efficiency and outcome standards, but no healthcare providers should lose fact of the sight that they entered the medical field to help people.

Recommendations to Healthcare Providers

As previously stated, the invasive nature of Pap smears can make these screenings awkward and potentially emotional for transgender men to endure. Potter, et al (2015) provide many recommendations for medical providers who provide gynecological exams and Pap smears to transgender men. Providers should first determine what type of anatomical terms the patient feels comfortable with. For instance, some transgender men may prefer that providers use the terms "internal parts" or "internal organs" when referring to the uterus or use the term "genital opening" rather than vagina. Similarly, the highly female-associated Pap smear could be referred to simply as a "cancer screening". Some transgender men may also find the phrases that physicians use when performing pelvic exams and Pap smears to have violent or even sexual connotations. For this reason, Potter et al. (2015) suggest that providers avoid terms like "stirrups" or phrases like "open your legs" when performing these sensitive exams. More inclusive language could include "footrests" rather than stirrups and instructing patients to "let your legs drop to either side" (Potter, et al 2015). This author also would suggest encouraging family medicine and general internal medicine physicians to perform more Pap smears to reduce the stigma that transgender men and non-binary individuals face when being forced to go to a gynecological specialist's office for these screenings.

Healthcare providers should always strive to provide a welcoming environment for all patients to promote high quality care. There are many ways in which healthcare providers, especially physicians, can create a welcoming environment for transgender patients. One of the simplest methods that physicians can employ is ensuring that physicians are aware of the preferred gender, pronouns, and name of all patients that they care for. Dr. Mark

Goodman, a family medicine physician at Creighton University, stated that to improve the inclusive environment of the CHI Health – Creighton University partnership hospitals, CHI Health will be upgrading medical record systems to reflect a patient's sex at birth, preferred gender, preferred name, and status of transition. Having this personal information will allow physicians to ensure that they call patients by their preferred name and pronouns to ensure that all patients feel welcome. Creating welcoming and safe environments for transgender men will make these patients more likely to return to the clinic and establish longstanding relationships with their provider, which has been shown to increase adherence to the recommended Pap smear screening schedule (Peitzmeier et al., 2014).

Ashley Kuykendall, CHES, is a public health professional who provides education and recommendations to medical providers to improve their knowledge of treating LGBT patients. She recommends that providers implement changes to their clinical practices and the clinical environment to ensure full inclusion of LGBT individuals, particularly transgender patients. She states that one of the most important clinical practices that physicians can provide is a non-judgmental and non-intimidating method of collecting identifying patient information, including the patient's sex at birth, gender identity, sexual orientation, preferred name, etc. She cites self-reported surveys filled out by patients as the most effective way of procuring this information, as patients are most likely to feel comfortable filling out a survey rather than verbally answering questions. Ms. Kuykendall also recommends setting up clinical spaces in a way that provides a private and inclusive environment for all patients. Examples include setting up waiting areas with barriers such as large chairs that can provide privacy for all patients or allowing transgender patients to wait in a private waiting area if they would prefer. Welcoming and inclusive visual clues such as posters and signs can also help to make LGBT patients feel safe in healthcare settings. Taking these recommendations into account is extremely important in creating the most inclusive setting possible for all LGBT individuals.

Similar sentiments were echoed by Anonymous, who was assigned female at birth and now identifies as genderqueer. They state that in their experiences, physicians often make assumptions about patient gender identities and typically do not ask about preferred gender, pronouns, and other identifiers. They state that they would like to see surveys about gender identity employed in healthcare settings, but also expressed that physicians should acknowledge these preferences verbally and should clarify information like preferred names, gender identities, or preferred pronouns if there are any uncertainties.

While the overwhelming majority of young healthcare students and providers undoubtedly go into medicine with altruistic intentions, there is clearly a lack of training in how to best care for patients who identify as transgender. As these young professionals are trained, there should be a continued push to include teaching on transgender healthcare and disparities in medical school curriculum. Teaching about transgenderism in a psychiatry or public health course alone is not sufficient in training the next generation of physicians. These providers need to know not only about the mental aspects of care, but also the physical and biosocial challenges faced by transgender patients. A certain cultural competence should be taught and promoted in young medical providers to encourage proper interactions with transgender patients to ensure no transgender patients feel that their doctors are incompetent in dealing with their medical care. Changes such as those proposed to medical curriculum are often slow to be implemented. While waiting for such changes to be enacted, all medical students, residents, and attending physicians should be encouraged to research ways to address their own biases and knowledge deficits on an individual basis to ensure that all people receive high quality care.

References

1. Bernstein, I., Peitzmeier, S., Potter, J., & Reisner, S. (n.d.). If You Have It, Check It: Overcoming Barriers to Cervical Cancer Screening with Patients on the Female-to- Male Transgender Spectrum. Retrieved from https://www.lgbthealtheducation.org/wp-content/uploads/Overcoming-Barriers-to-Cervical-Cancer-Screening.pdf

2. Braun, H., Nash, R., Tangpricha, V., Brockman, J., Ward, K., & Goodman, M. (2017). Cancer in Transgender People: Evidence and Methodological Considerations. *Epidemiologic Reviews,39*(1), 93-107. doi:10.1093/epirev/mxw003

3. Callahan, T. L., & Caughey, A. B. (2013). *Blueprints: Obstetrics and Gynecology* (6th ed.). Baltimore, MD: Lippincott, Willams, &Wilkins.

4. Dutton, L., Koenig, K., & Fennie, K. (2008). Gynecologic Care of the Female-to-Male Transgender Man. *Journal of Midwifery & Womens Health,53*(4), 331-337. doi:10.1016/j.jmwh.2008.02.003

5. Gatos, K. C. (2018). A Literature Review of Cervical Cancer Screening in Transgender Men. *Nursing for Womens Health,22*(1), 52-62. doi:10.1016/j.nwh.2017.12.008

6. James, S. E., Herman, J. L., Rankin, S., Keisling, M., Mottet, L., & Anafi, M. (2016). *The Report of the 2015 U.S. Transgender Survey.* Washington, DC: National Center for Transgender Equality.

7. Obedient-Maliver, J., Goldsmith, E. S., Stewart, L., White, W., Tran, E., Branman, S., . . . Lunn, M. R. (2011). Lesbian, Gay, Bisexual, and Transgender–Related Content in Undergraduate Medical Education. *JAMA,306*(9), 971-977.

8. Peitzmeier, S. M., Khullar, K., Reisner, S. L., & Potter, J. (2014). Pap Test Use Is Lower Among Female-to-Male Patients Than Non-Transgender Women. *American Journal of Preventive Medicine,47*(6), 808-812. doi:10.1016/j.amepre.2014.07.031

9. Potter, J., Peitzmeier, S., Bernstein, I., Reisner, S. L., Alizaga, N. M., Agenor, M., & Pardee, D. J. (2015). Cervical Cancer Screening for Patients on the Female-to-Male Spectrum: A Narrative Review and Guide for Clinicians. *Journal of General Internal Medicine,* 30(12), 1857-1864. doi:0.1007/s11606-015-3462-8

10. Streed, C. G., Jr. (2017, March 22). Terminology Related to Sexual Orientation, Gender Identity, and More. Retrieved from https://mfdp.

med.harvard.edu/sites/default/files/files/HMS SOGI terminology 3.22.17. pdf

11. Stroumsa, D. (2014, March). The State of Transgender Health Care: Policy, Law, and Medical Frameworks. *American Journal of Public Health*, *104*(3), e31-e38.

12. The American College of Obstetricians and Gynecologists. (2017). Practice Advisory: Cervical Cancer Screening. Retrieved from https:// www.acog.org/Clinical-Guidance-and-Publications/Practice-Advisories/ Practice-Advisory-Cervical-Cancer-Screening

13. U.S. Centers for Medicare & Medicaid Services (n.d.). Transgender health care. HealthCare.gov. https://www.healthcare.gov/transgender

14. Unger, C. A. (2015). Care of the Transgender Patient: A Survey of Gynecologists Current Knowledge and Practice. *Journal of Womens Health,24*(2), 114-118. doi:10.1089/jwh.2014.4918

Unintended Pregnancies in LGBTQIA Adolescents

Mulder, Hanna

Introduction

Various populations of children and adolescents are currently underserved in the United States health care system. Recent medical and psychosocial information alludes to astonishing health disparities facing sexual minority youth (Calzo *et al.*, 2017). Pediatricians play an essential role in promoting the health and well-being of all children for which they care, especially sexual minority patients whom they must continue to learn how to best serve and support their unique health needs (Granado-Villar *et al.*, 2013).

Lesbian, gay, bisexual, transgender, queer or questioning, intersex and asexual (LGBTQIA) adolescents endure substantial adversity as they face continual identity related stigma. These individuals are at an unreasonable risk to experience a surplus of negative social and health outcomes (Calzo *et al.*, 2017). According to the World Health Organization (WHO), sexual and reproductive health are critical parts of an individual's overall health, affecting their physical, mental, and social wellbeing (Leonardi *et al.*, 2019). Despite continuous efforts by WHO to improve and promote the sexual health of all individuals, much work is needed in these areas. People who identify as lesbian, gay, bisexual or are unsure of their sexual identity continue to be at increased reproductive health risk (Leonardi *et al.*, 2019). Reproductive health becomes especially important in adolescence as youth begin developing their sexual and gender identity.

Non-heterosexual adolescent women have a higher rate of unintended pregnancy than their heterosexual peers, a finding that may seem counterintuitive without further investigation (Ela and Budnick, 2017). There has been a historical lack of demographic attention to individuals not defined as heterosexual, reflecting a common assumption that these individuals are not at risk of pregnancy (Ela and Budnick, 2017). In a 2007 study of 12,000 youth grades 7-12, 28% of participants who identified as a sexual minority had been pregnant or were involved in conceiving a pregnancy compared to 7% of heterosexual respondents (Leonardi *et al.*, 2019). It is crucial that pediatricians are aware that some youth in their care may be questioning their sexual orientation and provide factual, current, and nonjudgmental information in a confidential manner to all patients (Levine, 2013).

Background

Adolescence

The World Health Organization defines adolescence as a transitional phase of growth and development between childhood and adulthood occurring between ages 10 and 19 years (World Health Organization, 2019). However, the exact ages of adolescence are frequently changing with decreasing age of puberty and rising age of reaching social maturity. The adolescence time in an individual's life is one of rapid physical, emotional and sexual change and often one of sexual discovery, exploration and experimentation (Levine, 2013). Adolescence is a critical life phase when opportunities for health are huge and habits for future health in adulthood are ingrained (Cole *et al.*, 2007).

LGBTQIA

Gender identity is an internal, self- conception of one's gender (Levine, 2013). It is impossible to predict what gender a child will ultimately identify with certainty. Between the ages 1 and 2 years, children are aware of physical differences between the two sexes, by 3 years most children can identify themselves as a boy or girl, and by 4 years of age gender identity generally stabilizes (Levine, 2013). Gender identification is solidified throughout childhood upon observation of the gender roles of parents, adults, siblings and peers (Levine, 2013). Children may undergo a period of gender-role confusion, most often in preschool, in which they identify with traits of the opposite sex, feel opposed about their gender or distaste a part of themselves that is a boy or girl (Levine, 2013). Most children will resolve their dysphoria by the completion of adolescence, but a few will seek treatment to transition to the opposite gender (Levine, 2013).

Transgender individuals are those whose gender or identity does not match their anatomic and chromosomal sex. Gender nonconforming refers to individuals who do not follow other's ideas of how they should act according to gender roles and such people may or may not be distressed about the nonconformity (Levine, 2013). Gender minority further includes people whose gender expression is different from the sex they were assigned at birth (Calzo et al., 2017).

Sexual orientation is defined as the direction of one's sexual attractions, identity and behavior; and it most often emerges between 12 to 14 years of age (Calzo et al., 2017). The term sexual minority encompasses all individuals with same-gender attractions, romantic, or sexual experiences and/or identify as gay, lesbian or bisexual. Asexual individuals describe no sexual attractions to men or women. LGBTQIA is used a shorthand referring to the community of sexual and gender minority individuals (Levine, 2013).

A precise estimate of the number of United States adolescents who identify as a sexual minority is currently lacking. Two important data collections, the U.S. Census Bureau and American Community Survey, do not collect information on sexual identity (Stoffel et al., 2018). According to a Youth Risk Behavior Surveillance taken in 2011, 4.5% of 9-12th graders identified as LGBTQIA with a further 4.5% reportedly questioning their sexual or gender identity (Desai and Romano, 2018). Data from The National Longitudinal Study of Adolescent to Adult Health found that 15% of U.S. female adolescents in grades 7 to 12 identified as a sexual minority (Stoffel et al., 2018). It often takes some time for a young adult to reach an understanding of their sexual identity before they can label it or discuss it with others (Levine, 2013). Interestingly, new data suggests that the proportion of young individuals identifying as LGBTQIA is increasing compared to previous generations (Stoffel *et al.*, 2018)

Sexual Activity

Approximately 45% of 15 to 19-year-old youth in the U.S. report having vaginal intercourse with an opposite-sex partner, 2.5% of 15 to 19-year-old males report having had oral or anal sex with another male and 11% of 15 to 19-year-old females report having a sexual experience with another female (Marcell and Burstein, 2017). Sexual minority youth are more likely than heterosexual youth to self-report having ever had intercourse, having intercourse before 13 years of age and to have had intercourse with more than four people in their lifetime (Levine, 2013).

In a National Survey of Family Growth taken from 2006-2008 reportedly 13.4% of females and 4.0% of males ages 15 to 24 years reported having sex with someone of the same gender. This was a larger percentage than those who self-described themselves as LGBTQIA (Levine, 2013). In addition, many adolescents who self-report as lesbian will occasionally have sex with males and many males who self-report as gay will have sex with females. Therefore, sexual behaviors do not always equal identity and many adolescents will struggle with their sexual attractions and identity formation at some point (Levine, 2013).

Pregnancy

Unintended pregnancy rates among young females in the U.S. have fallen in recent years but remain high compared to other developed countries (Ela and Budnick, 2017). Data indicates that pregnancy is a relatively common experience for sexual minority women with approximately 37% reporting having a child in their lifetime (Stoffel *et al.*, 2018). In the 1999 Minnesota Adolescent Health Survey, women who identified as lesbian or bisexual were about as likely to have had vaginal intercourse as heterosexual youth (33% vs. 29%) but had nearly twice the rate of pregnancy (12% vs 6%) with many having more than two pregnancies (Levine, 2013). Unintended pregnancies are often associated with negative health and social results for both the mother and child (Ela and Budnick, 2017).

Further investigation separating lesbian and bisexual adolescents found that those who identified as bisexual had a higher rate of pregnancy and pregnancy termination than heterosexual peers; whereas those who identified as lesbian had no difference in teen pregnancy rate (Everett *et al.*, 2019). More recent data from the 2013 Youth Risk Behavior Survey supports this trend that young sexual minority women, classified as women who have sex with women or women who have sex with men and women, were significantly more likely to have been pregnant in the last 12 months than female peers who have sex with men only (Stoffel *et al.*, 2018). Data compiled from 2006 to 2010 found that 8.4% of bisexual women age 14 to 21 years had been pregnant and were three times as likely as their heterosexual peers to have terminated a pregnancy, suggesting pregnancy was not desired (Stoffel *et al.*, 2018).

It is important to note that female youth who identified as a sexual minority or had partners of both genders were more likely to have been physical forced to have sexual intercourse than heterosexual individuals of comparable age (Leonardi *et al.*, 2019). This trend was paralleled in the 2013 Youth Risk Surveillance Survey in which almost 25% of LGBTQIA surveyed individuals reported a history of forced sex (Leonardi *et al.*, 2019).

Public Health

LGBTQIA adolescents face a multitude of disparities that make this vulnerable population often daunting for pediatricians and other health care providers assisting in their care. These disparities include but are not limited to a higher rate of attempted and completed suicide, higher rates of homelessness and disheartening levels of tobacco, alcohol and illicit substance use compared to heterosexual peers (Desai and Romano, 2018).

While significant health disparities exist in several sexual health outcomes with respect to HIV and sexually transmitted infections (STIs), this paper will focus on the higher rate of unintended pregnancy in LGBTQIA adolescents compared to heterosexual individuals of the same age. Given higher rates of earlier sexual initiation, greater number of partners and less contraceptive use, adolescents in the LGBTQIA population are at a greater risk of teen pregnancy than youth who only have sex with the opposite gender (Desai and Romano, 2018). However, disparities are likely not only due to differences in sexual behavior but other factors including variances in the care provided to these patients by the provider. (Stoffel *et al.*, 2018).

Adolescent Pregnancy

Adolescent pregnancy represents a significant developmental harm as the individual is working to grow physically and emotionally while also adjusting to the physical and emotional demands that accompany their pregnancy (Grady and Bloom, 2004). The adolescent is faced with building a relationship with their child while also understanding their new identity as a mother. Further, many adolescents enter pregnancy with poor health habits and do not make the needed changes for a healthy pregnancy (Grady and Bloom, 2004). Social support for the parenting adolescent is often lacking with common social isolation from friends and alienation from family (Grady and Bloom, 2004). Only 30% of adolescent mothers will complete high school and those that do are unlikely to go to college (Grady and Bloom, 2004). The consequences of adolescent motherhood are great for the mother and child.

Infant Outcomes

Compared to heterosexual women, bisexual and lesbian women are more likely to experience miscarriage (30% vs. 19%), a pregnancy ending in stillbirth (4.1% vs. 0.8%), preterm birth (34% vs. 12%) or low birth weight infant (22% vs. 8%) (Everett *et al.*, 2019). Smoking during pregnancy was nearly twice the level in heterosexual women inand sexual minority groups (Everett *et al.*, 2019). These risks are added to the well-established factors of adolescent pregnancies in general including increased gestational morbidity, greater cesarean-section rates, eclampsia and complications at birth (Grady and Bloom, 2004).

Contraception

It has been shown that most adolescents prefer identifying as "mostly heterosexual" or "mostly homosexual" when asked of their sexual attraction (Levine, 2013) This range of sexuality is further reflected in startling rates of teen pregnancies in women who report having sex with women. Women who report having sex with women have lower rates of contraceptive use then do women having sex with men (Everett *et al.*, 2019). Gay or lesbian youth were about half as likely as heterosexual youth (35.8% vs. 65.5%) to report use of hormonal or barrier contraceptives during their last sexual encounter with the opposite gender (Levine, 2013). Adolescents females who reported having male and female's sexual partners had higher alcohol and drug use during sex than females with only male sexual partners (Everett *et al.*, 2019).

LGBTQIA women have more relationships and spend less weeks without a partner compared to heterosexual individuals (Ela and Budnick, 2017). They are also more likely than exclusively heterosexual women to have sexual intercourse in a higher proportion of weeks (16% vs. 7%) (Ela and Budnick, 2017). While studies indicate that contraception use is not uncommon among sexual minority youth, their rates of lifetime contraception are much lower than the general population. It is estimated that 99% of women ages 15 to 44 who have ever had sexual intercourse with a male have used any form of contraception (Ela and Budnick, 2017). In the Women's Health Initiative, it was found that only 19% of women who had sex with both men and women had used contraception in the past year (Stoffel *et al.*, 2018). In addition to reporting less frequent contraceptive use, sexual minority youth use less effective contraceptive methods compared to heterosexual peers. Sexual minority adolescents have markedly less use of a more effective dual method such as condoms plus hormonal pills (Ela and Budnick, 2017).

It is well studied that infrequent intercourse is a risk factor for nonuse of contraception in heterosexual women and has recently been shown to predict sexual minority adolescent's contraceptive behavior as well. In these circumstances when intercourse may not be planned, the women may not be using hormonal contraception or partners may not have condoms available

(Ela and Budnick, 2017). It has been suggested that the increased risk of pregnancy among sexual minority youth may be related to attempts to avoid stigmatization by engaging in intimate relationships with males (Everett *et al.*, 2019). Further, if sexual minority women are experiencing intellectual discord regarding their sexual orientation, they are even less likely to use a hormonal contraception method or purchase condoms (Ela and Budnick, 2017). Intended

Pregnancy

While rates of unintended pregnancy are higher among sexual minority women than their heterosexual peers, not all wish to avoid pregnancy. Successful conception requires special considerations of challenges social minority women face (Stoffel *et al.*, 2018). It is important for pediatricians to provide referrals to experienced Obstetrics and Gynecological (Ob/Gyn) providers who can assist in fertility options, surrogacy, and adoption as the patient wishes. In a study completed at a pediatric gender clinic from 2013 to 2016, 18 of 105 adolescents seen underwent formal consultation for fertility preservation, sperm or oocyte preservation (Leonardi *et al.*, 2019). This suggest that even at a young age many LGBTQIA youth are considering future plans for children.

LGBTQIA-Competent Physicians

Many LGBTQ adolescents self-reported that a lack of LGBTQIA-competent physicians was a significant barrier to them seeking and accessing health care (Stoffel *et al.*, 2018). LGBTQIA youth who are open about their sexuality with friends and family may not feel comfortable disclosing their sexuality to their health care provider. In a study of 131 sexual minority youth attending an empowerment conference, it was reported that only 35% had shared their sexual orientation with their pediatrician despite 70% "being out" to their family and friends (Meckler *et al.*, 2006).

Global Perspective

Sexual identity is multidimensional and continuously changing making it extremely difficult to estimate the stigma faced. It is estimated that globally, 5-10% of the population is made of LGBTQIA individuals who each have unique health needs (Adam, 2016). The stigma of sexuality can begin early in life for adolescents who do not have adequate societal, family and health care support. Approximately sixteen million girls aged 15-19 give birth each year, and 95% of these births occur in low – and middle-income countries (Morris and Rushwan, 2015). Limited research has been done on unintended pregnancies in LGBTQIA individuals in international countries and the sparse information that is available has occurred primarily in developed countries. Pregnancy in transgender Canadian youth was found to be nearly one in twenty, which is comparable to the general population (Veale *et al.*, 2016). Disregarding the health of LGBTQIA adolescents will lead to life-long health disparities and increased pressure on health care systems as they pay the cost of caring for things such as HIV and mental health issues.

In recent years the U.S. has led the way for the rights of the LGBTQIA population and begun addressing their health care needs also. Progress has been made in countries like Greece which legalized same-sex marriage in 2016 and the Malawi government which prohibited prosecution of homosexual activity the same year (Adam, 2016). Despite positive momentum with the granting of legal rights, for many people in various countries LGBTQIA civil rights and access to basic health care are vastly inferior. For example, in Japan following the 2004 Gender Identity Disorder Special Act, a transgender person is only recognized after meeting several criteria including having a diagnosed identity disorder, being over the age of 20 years, being unmarried, having no children younger than 20 years of age, and having absent or non-functioning gonads (The Lancet, 2019). This legal restriction of transgender people prevent adolescents who might benefit greatly from early gender-affirmation assistance from seeking the health care they may desire and should receive.

Research

In my study of this issue, I was able to talk with Dr. MG, family medicine physician at Catholic Health Initiative (CHI) in Omaha, Nebraska. He provided great insight into a complicating factor for LGBTQIA unintended pregnancies that I did not encounter in my research. Dr. MG informed me of the higher rate of homelessness and run-away LGBTQIA youth compared to their heterosexual peers. In the U.S., these youth often leave home for fear or not fitting in. Run-away adolescents in general also have a much higher rate of sexual abuse; individuals of female gender who are more likely to be picked up as sex workers. Dr. G. shared that a "sex worker" implies some level of consent but this is questionable in the adolescent population.

In regard to overall adolescent sexual health, Dr. MG recommends inquiring about the patient's current understanding of sexuality and sexual health. In his own experience, Dr. MG has observed a great variety in health literacy of his patients. For example, he recently saw a patient for follow up whom he had placed an intrauterine contraceptive device (IUD) for about six months prior. The patient was concerned that she may be pregnant and asking for a pregnancy test. After further questioning, the patient shared that she was worried her doctor hadn't placed anything in her throat or stomach to prevent her from getting pregnant. Her lack of knowledge of the anatomy and physiology of conception and pregnancy was causing her great distress. This patient is an excellent example that just because an individual is born in the U.S. and educated in the public-school system as she was, does not assure a good health literacy understanding. Dr. MG further shared that health literacy is lower now amongst adolescents than it was twenty years ago. He believes this is in part to youth in the 1970-1990s growing up with great concern of contacting the HIV which has now become a chronic, manageable disease that is less talked about among young populations. Lastly, he touched on the importance of using the language the adolescent uses to talk about sexuality and what they understand as "sexually active." It is important to be as descriptive as possible while also recognizing that most medical descriptions are not well understood by many in the U.S.. Thankfully, there are many more resources available today than in past decades to support LGBTQIA adolescents. Overall, Dr. MG believes that working to have less run-aways will lead to less sex workers and in turn fewer unintended pregnancies.

I further had the opportunity to talk with Dr. KN, an Obstetrician and Gynecologist at CHI in Omaha. She shared that in her experience working with transgender individuals, she has not seen as many adolescents who are sexually active since they are trying to figure out where they fall in the gender spectrum. In her practice she works with trans-males (assigned female sex at birth, perceives gender identity as male) who have been on continuous birth control pills or an IUD to completely stop periods and are mostly sexually active with females. She also shares stories of trans-males that she works with who have intercourse with cis-males (assigned male sex at birth, perceives gender identity as male) and spends a great deal of time discussing with these individuals the chance of pregnancy even if they are not having regular menstrual periods on testosterone therapy. For these patients she often recommends an IUD as it would not interfere with their testosterone. For the trans-female (assigned male sex at birth, perceives gender identity as female) patients she treats she is thorough on discussing pregnancy risks in their partners depending on who they are sexually active with and in all circumstances gives thorough birth control options when appropriate.

Dr. KN discussed what she sees as the biggest challenge the LGBTQIA adolescent population faces in regard to their reproductive health. She believes they are lacking in their access to knowledgeable healthcare providers that have received training and education about issues specific to sexual minority health care. Many individuals she has worked with who identify as LGBTQIA are afraid to seek healthcare for fear of being discriminated against or having to educate their physician about being LGBTQIA. She shares that an important resource in the Omaha community for LGBTQIA adolescents is Planned Parenthood organizations. Many of the patients she sees learn of her practice by word of mouth and the knowledge within the community that she is a "LGBTQIA friendly" physician.

Recommendations

After speaking with Dr. MG and Dr. KN and watching the LGBT healthcare training video "To Treat Me, You Have to Know Who I Am," it is clear to me that we must work to remove barriers to care for LGBTQIA youth and create a welcoming environment for all adolescents. Providing early support to sexual and gender minority youth is essential to prevent the emergence of health disparities later in life (Calzo *et al.*, 2017). Avoiding unintended pregnancies and sexually transmitted infections as well as promoting healthy relationships should be a central concern for OBGyn and for pediatricians caring for LGBTQIA adolescents.

Clinic Environment

It is important that all staff members are trained about LGBTQIA health and are dedicated to creating a safe clinical environment. Any unrecognized internalized homophobia or heterosexism in the clinic staff may inadvertently interfere with quality care. For example, a nurse asking a teenage girl who is in a relationship with another woman about her boyfriend may be perceived as non-accepting of her choice and hinder the provider's ability to form a trusting relationship with the patient (Levine, 2013). The use of gender-neutral terms throughout the clinic and on intake forms and questionnaires can encourage teenagers to openly discuss questions they may have about their sexual behavior or orientation (Levine, 2013). The clinic should also display posters in waiting areas highlighting both same and opposite gender couples as well as having readily available brochures on a spectrum of adolescent topics, including sexual orientation, in the waiting room and restrooms for adolescents to pick up (Levine, 2013).

Patients should be given the opportunity to reveal sensitive information before their face-to-face encounter with the pediatrician. Adolescents have reported they are most comfortable sharing information such as their sexual behavior or identity on a computer or paper questionnaire compared to in conversation (Levine, 2013). It is then the pediatrician's responsibility to initiate a discussion during the visit about what they reported, without the patient's parents in the room. In a questionnaire sent to lesbian and gay youth, 75% shared they had not disclosed their identity with their pediatrician because their parents were in the room (Meckler *et al.*, 2006). Confidentiality is of utmost importance in all levels of health care, especially in facilities providing care for LGBTQIA youth. These policies should be shared proactively with patients and their families (Desai and Romano, 2018).

<u>Physician Role</u>

Many health care providers have limited experience with individuals of sexual or gender minority status and lack the cultural competency to adequately support these youth, encourage open dialogue, and screen for risk behaviors (Calzo *et al.*, 2017). Young people need the assistance of their pediatricians as they develop their identities to avoid the consequences of unwanted pregnancy, regardless of sexual orientation. LGBTQIA adolescents, like all adolescent patients, should be assessed individually for challenges, vulnerabilities and strengths. Health care providers must take caution not to make assumptions based on an individual's sexual identity and forgo assessing sexual behaviors and offering contraception (Stoffel *et al.*, 2018). Pediatricians should reinforce patients' positive behaviors and work to address behavioral interventions to reduce existing risk behaviors (Levine, 2013).

It is important that pediatricians assess for unintended pregnancy risk by asking about the gender of all partners. Young women who report having sex with other women should not stop pediatricians from providing contraception counseling. Condoms should be strongly encouraged for all sexual activities involving insertive or receptive intercourse. Providers should also discuss contraceptive methods that are easy to hide, such as long-acting reversible contraception, for patients who fear their use of contraceptive will share their sexual behaviors with unwanted parties (Stoffel *et al.*, 2018). Every individual is likely at a different place in terms of their own "coming out" process in addition to the acceptance of their family and friends. It is important that providers realize that their social situation greatly affects their health outcomes.

LGBTQIA Evidence Based Programs

Various explanations have been proposed for disparities in contraception use by sexual minority youth. Importantly, some sexual minority individuals may not perceive themselves at risk of pregnancy. Sexual education curriculum often equates health risks with penetrative sex and excludes information on safe sex practices relevant to sexual minorities (Stoffel *et al.,* 2017). Despite growing attention to gay and lesbian concerns, current school sex education curriculum in the U.S. remains heterosexually focused (Estes, 2017).

Evidence-based programs (EBPs) have been impactful in changing sexual behavior in adolescents and improving sexual health outcomes. They are the standard for sexual health education in all federally or state funded programs but often fail to include LGBTQIA identities and inclusive health information (Boyce *et al.,* 2018). The role-play scenarios included in EBPs curriculum highlight only heterosexual couples and rarely mention LGBTQIA sexual health risks. Serious efforts are needed to adapt these programs to be more LGBTQIA inclusive. In a survey of students who completed a piloted program with a LGBTQIA supplementation, 70% reported they had excellent sex education compared to 57% of peers who did not have the supplement (Boyce *et al.,* 2018). It is important that any sexual and reproductive health program offered include LGBTQIA information.

There remains a longstanding argument whether the school environment is the appropriate place to discuss sexual topics. Further, many parents do not feel comfortable discussing sexual topics and assume their child is heterosexual and will receive information at school (Estes, 2017). Because parental conversations and school-based sex education often exclude LGLBTQIA individuals' needs, an adolescent's pediatrician can make sure they learn the information needed until changes are made at large to school sex education curriculum.

Conclusion

Sexual minority adolescents have increased sexual and reproductive health risks compared to their heterosexual peers. The population faces provider barriers to safe and inclusive health care in addition to a multitude of sociocultural stigma. LGBTQIA teens are an underserved population composed of many young adults who struggle with acceptance of their sexuality and managing the many rigors of adolescence (Levine, 2013). Pediatricians have an important obligation to ensure that sexual minority youth have full access to all appropriate health care services and to provide them with honest and compassionate answers as they deal with issues around sexual orientation, identity, and sexual behavior. It is crucial that pediatricians are addressing their patient's sexual and reproductive health needs to prevent health outcomes with serious permanent sequelae.

References

1. Adam, R. (2016). Meeting the unique health-care needs of LGBTQ people. *The Lancet, 387(95)*.

2. Boyce, K. S., Travers, M., Rothbart, B., Santiago, V., & Bedell, J. (2018). Adapting evidence based teen pregnancy programs to be LGBT-inclusive: Lessons learned. *Health promotion practice, 19*(3), 445-454.

3. Calzo, J. P., Melchiono, M., Richmond, T. K., Leibowitz, S. F., Argenal, R. L., Goncalves, A., ... & Burke, P. (2017). Lesbian, gay, bisexual, and transgender adolescent health: an interprofessional case discussion. *MedEdPORTAL: the journal of teaching and learning resources, 13*

4. Cole, T. J., Flegal, K. M., Nicholls, D., & Jackson, A. A. (2007). Body mass index cut offs to define thinness in children and adolescents: international survey. *Bmj, 335*(7612), 194.

5. Desai, N., & Romano, M. E. (2018). Pediatric and adolescent issues in underserved populations. *Primary Care of the Medically Underserved, An Issue of Physician Assistant Clinics, Ebook, 4*(1), 47.

6. Ela, E. J., & Budnick, J. (2017). Non-heterosexuality, relationships, and young women's contraceptive behavior. *Demography, 54*(3), 887-909.

7. Estes, M. L. (2017). "If there's one benefit, you're not going to get pregnant": The sexual miseducation of gay, lesbian, and bisexual individuals. *Sex Roles, 77*(9-10), 615-627Everett, B. G.,

8. Kominiarek, M. A., Mollborn, S., Adkins, D. E., & Hughes, T. L. (2019). Sexual orientation disparities in pregnancy and infant outcomes. *Maternal and child health journal, 23*(1), 72-81.

9. Everett, B. G., Turner, B., Hughes, T. L., Veldhuis, C. B., Paschen-Wolff, M., & Phillips, G. (2019). Sexual Orientation Disparities in Pregnancy Risk Behaviors and Pregnancy Among Sexually Active Teenage Girls: Updates from the Youth Risk Behavior Survey. *LGBT health, 6*(7), 342-349.

10. Grady, M. A., & Bloom, K. C. (2004). Pregnancy outcomes of adolescents enrolled in a Centering Pregnancy program. *Journal of midwifery & women's health, 49*(5), 412-420.

11. Granado-Villar, D. C., Gitterman, B. A., Brown, J. M., Chilton, L. A., Cotton, W. H., Gambon, T. B., & Zind, B. (2013). Community pediatrics: navigating the intersection of medicine, public health, and social determinants of children's health. *Pediatrics, 131*(3), 623-628.

12. Leonardi, M., Frecker, H., Scheim, A. I., & Kives, S. (2019). Reproductive health considerations in sexual and/or gender minority adolescents. *Journal of pediatric and adolescent gynecology, 32*(1), 15-20.

13. Levine, D. A. (2013). Office-based care for lesbian, gay, bisexual, transgender, and questioning youth *Pediatrics, 132*(1), e297-e313.

14. Marcell, A. V., & Burstein, G. R. (2017). Sexual and reproductive health care services in the pediatric setting. *Pediatrics, 140*(5), e20172858.

15. Meckler, G. D., Elliott, M. N., Kanouse, D. E., Beals, K. P., & Schuster, M. A. (2006). Nondisclosure of sexual orientation to a physician among

a sample of gay, lesbian, and bisexual youth. *Archives of pediatrics & adolescent medicine, 160*(12), 1248-1254.

16. Morris, J. L., & Rushwan, H. (2015). Adolescent sexual and reproductive health: The global challenges. *International Journal of Gynecology & Obstetrics, 131*, S40-S42.

17. Stoffel, C., Carpenter, E., Everett, B., Higgins, J., & Haider, S. (2017, September). Family planning for sexual minority women. In *Seminars in reproductive medicine* (Vol. 35, No. 05, pp. 460-468). Thieme Medical Publishers.

18. The Lancet. (2019). Coercive sterilisation of transgender people in Japan. *Lancet (London, England), 393*(10178), 1262.

19. Veale, J., Watson, R. J., Adjei, J., & Saewyc, E. (2016). Prevalence of pregnancy involvement among Canadian transgender youth and its relation to mental health, sexual health, and gender identity. *International Journal of Transgenderism, 17*(3-4), 107-113.

20. World Health Organization (2019). *Adolescent Health and Development.* Retrieved from: http://www.searo.who.int/entity/child_adolescent

The Gender Nonconforming and/ or Transgender Pediatric Patient

Van Galder, Hannah

Introduction

A child is assigned a gender very quickly after birth based on external genitalia or chromosomes. When the gender that the child experiences does not align with what gender was assigned, the child can experience gender nonconformity. Sometimes the child grows up to be cisgender, identifying as the gender assigned at birth, but sometimes the child grows up to be transgender, identifying as a gender different from what was assigned at birth. Pediatricians must understand the issues facing gender nonconforming and transgender patients and put into practice the recommendations for pediatricians with gender nonconforming and transgender patients.

The epidemiology of the transgender youth population is not well studied, but it is well documented that the number of children and adolescents presenting with gender identity concerns is increasing ([1]). Gender nonconformity affects children assigned both male and female genders at birth. Prepubertal clinical referrals for gender dysphoric children were 3:1 to 6:1 male to female; after 12 years old, clinical referrals for gender dysphoria were 1:1 male to female ([2]-[4]). The presentation of a gender nonconforming patient varies and can manifest in preferences in clothes, hairstyles, toys, etc. It is important to acknowledge that how the patient appears or acts is not necessarily a choice but an inherent desire.

Prepubertal presentations of gender nonconformity may not display gender dysphoria because, for younger children, societal consistency between gender identity and genitalia can be less apparent. As gender identity and primary and secondary sex characteristics become more synonymous, especially with the physical changes of puberty, gender dysphoria can develop ([1]). The dysphoria can cause an emotional toll, causing anxiety, depression, suicidality, and risky behaviors ([1]). In a study of over 900 transgender youth in Canada, nearly two-thirds reported seriously considering suicide in the past year, remarkably high compared to the 13% found in a Canadian general adolescent survey ([8]). The transgender youth also reported nearly six times higher attempt rate compared to the general adolescent population ([8]). In a smaller study of 180 transgender youth in Boston, the suicide attempt and suicidal ideation rates were three times higher in transgender youth than cisgender youth ([9]). There are several psychosocial concerns for children with gender dysphoria. Family understanding of gender dysphoria and transgenderism may vary and can be negative causing conflicts in families and potentially endangering the child. This obviously can occur in social situations, such as in school and friend groups, as well, and can create isolation of the transgender child.

Access to healthcare is a large disparity for gender nonconforming and transgender youth. A study of 15 transgender youth and 50 caregivers of transgender youth found several barriers specific to transgender youth to gender-affirming healthcare, including few pediatric providers trained in gender-affirming healthcare and inconsistent use of patient's chosen name/pronouns ([7]). Primary care providers, including pediatricians, are often the first stop for families with gender nonconformity questions. The way the provider responds can set the tone of the physician-patient-family relationship and influence how the family and patient move forward.

Approaching the Gender Nonconforming and/or Transgender Pediatric Patient

Safe Space

Just as one would hope for any child, the pediatrician office should be a safe and comforting place for a transgender child. A negative experience at the clinic can negatively affect the patient's long-term health. In a survey of over 900 Canadian transgender adolescents, over 50% of transgender adolescents stated that they forewent medical and mental health care because they were afraid of their physician's reaction ([12]). Over a quarter forewent medical care and over two-thirds forewent mental healthcare because of a past negative experience ([12]). Awareness of staff members to transgender issues and educating staff members of the patient's current gender expression will help the patient build trust in the care providers. Maintaining an environment that is safe to play with gender nonconforming toys or read gender nonconforming material helps welcome the patient. Making sure that there is comfort for transgender patients in a pediatric office is essential in making sure that patients return for both medical and mental health care. As will be described below, bathroom use is a great source of concern for transgender youth. Providing access to gender neutral bathrooms and/or having gender neutral signage at clinic can provide a source of comfort for the patient.

There are several communicative ways that can help build trust with transgender patients. Specifying preferred name and pronouns with consistent usage is of paramount importance to transgender patients. In a structured interview of 15 transgender patients, preferred name and pronoun usage was often described as a barrier to healthcare access for transgender patients. One patient stated it made his/her day when his/her physician used the preferred pronouns for the patient ([7]). As for all patients, it is important to place a great emphasis on physician-patient confidentiality, especially for patients that have yet to disclose that they are transgender. As gender can be nonbinary, it is also important for pediatricians to understand gender fluidity. This requires distinguishing what the patient finds necessary in gender expression and supporting the patient ([6]).

Addressing Concerns

All pediatricians must be prepared for the concerns of patients and families. In a survey of 118 transgender patients and 103 caregivers of transgender children, both patients and caregivers had concerns in both social work and medical domains, emphasizing the importance of having a strong social work presence in the pediatric office ([11]). The top three concerns endorsed by the patient were medically related, with concerns about gender-affirming hormones, gender-affirming surgery, and steps in transitioning ([11]). The caregiver top concerns contained a mix of social and medical issues ([11]). The pediatrician should be prepared to be able to provide information about transitioning as well as provide resources for social issues such as bathroom use, legal assistance, and child's safety in public.

It is important to acknowledge that the concerns in regard to transgender patients vary depending on the age of the patient and stage of transition. The concerns are best broken down in relationship to pubertal status.

Prepubertal Patient

Often, parents will come with concerns of their child's gender nonconformity in prepubertal children. In discussing gender with the prepubertal patient, it is recommended to make the child feel comfortable by keeping the questions open. One suggestion is to ask, "Most children have a feeling of being a boy or a girl. How do you feel? Do you feel like a boy, girl, in between or different?" Asking about the patient's gender in this manner keeps the question open but provides options. Providing options gives the appearance of an understanding physician to young patients. The patient does not have to feel uncomfortable trying to articulate that they feel different than the gender assigned to them at birth.

It is also important to note that the concerns of the patient may differ from those of the caregivers. The top concerns for children 6-10 years old were related to bathroom use and safety in public along with puberty blockers ([11]). Caregiver concerns are generally social, especially for children 6-10 years old. Issues of family acceptance, bathroom use, and discussing transgender issues with nonfamily members were the most common concerns for caregivers along with a desire for general resources on transgender ([11]). The pediatrician should be ready to address these concerns with patients and caregivers. It is important to stay educated on bathroom use laws specific to the region and state of practice. For parents and caregivers, pediatricians should suggest parents encourage a wide range of activities and interests for their child. If gender dysphoria develops in the prepubertal transgender patient, the pediatrician can suggest a social transition. A social transition between the ages of 6 and 14 years old was found to be associated with decreased anxiety and depression ([5]). The pediatrician should encourage the parents to follow the child's lead regarding gender expression; however, safety and protection of the child should be of utmost importance. For instance, for a transgender boy that may have developing breasts, it may not be safe to play in public without a shirt even though cisgender boys are. It is also important for the pediatrician to encourage caregivers to address family problems that affect the child's well-being in order to provide a cohesive, supportive unit for the child.

Older patient

The transgender patient often faces more concerns as puberty looms. Gender dysphoria that persists through the onset of puberty and increases at the onset of puberty is unlikely to subside ([3]). With puberty, the concerns of the patient become more medical. At 11-14 years old, the top concerns were bathroom use and resources to meet other transgender youth as well as gender-affirming hormones ([11]). At 15-17 years old, the top concerns became more medical with concerns of gender-affirming hormones and steps in transition, but social concerns remained high with bathroom use and legal issues ([11]). At 18-22 years old, the top concerns were all medical with gender-affirming hormones, steps in transition, and gender-affirming surgery ([11]). Social concerns remain high for caregivers of transgender patients through puberty and young adulthood, but as puberty occurs, parents become more concerned with gender-affirming hormones and acute mental health issues ([11]). The pediatrician must be prepared to discuss the gender-affirming medical options as well as discussing mental health and social issues facing the transgender patient. It is also important to understand for adolescent patients that not all patients are comfortable transitioning socially first, especially with pubertal changes (6).

Screening for the Gender Nonconforming and/or Transgender Patient

Discussions of the following are important in all children in the pediatric office, but these are problems that the transgender patient faces in disproportionate numbers. Bullying and social isolation is a common problem in childhood, but research shows that bullying seriously affects transgendered patients. In a survey of over 80,000 youth in Minnesota, transgender youth reported at least twice as more physical and cyber bullying than cisgender youth ([10]). While there are no specific screening tools for bullying, the American Academy of Pediatricians (AAP) recommends opening a conversation about bullying by stating that other children are experiencing bullying as well ([14]). The AAP also recommends acknowledging that in-person bullying is not the only stress children face but that bullying online is present as well. Keeping this in mind, it is important to ask about cyberbullying specifically. The pediatrician can counsel youth to respond to bullying by staying calm, leaving the situation when able, and confiding in a trusted adult ([13]). It is important for the pediatrician to be encouraging to the patient and to reinforce that this treatment by others is not something that patients deserves ([14]).

The pediatrician should also inquire about the patient's family/home life. Being gender nonconforming can cause strife in a family unit, especially with family members that are less understanding. Family strife has in part led to transgender and other LGBT youth to make up 20-40% of the 1.6 million homeless youth in the United States ([15]). Fortunately, in a survey of over 80,000 youth in Minnesota, there was no significant difference in the ranking of family connectedness, teacher-student relationships, and safety in the community between transgender and cisgender youth ([10]). Minnesota is known to be a more liberal state, so this level of social connectedness for transgender youth is less likely to be the case in all communities in the United States.

Again, risk taking behaviors such as substance use and unprotected sex should be discussed with all adolescent patients, but it is especially important to address in transgender youth as these behaviors are self-reported in greater levels than cisgender youth. In a survey of over 80,000 youth in Minnesota, transgender youth reported significantly more substance use (cigarettes, alcohol, and marijuana) and significantly more binge drinking than cisgender youth ([10]). It is important to counsel patients about the dangers of using the above substances, keep discussing substance use with patients that are not ready to stop using, and provide resources for patients that would like to stop substance use. In the same survey of youth in Minnesota, transgender youth were more likely to have greater than or equal to one sexual partner in the last year and were less likely to use condoms or birth control than cisgender youth ([10]). Transgender youth were also more likely to have been intoxicated during their last sexual encounter than cisgender youth ([10]). It is important to discuss the dangers of unprotected sex, such as sexually transmitted infections, and provide options of protection for patients that choose to be sexually active. It is also important to discuss ways to keep one safe and avoid sexual assault. One substance specific to transgender youth that pediatricians must screen for are unprescribed hormones such as herbal hormones. Herbal hormones are easily accessible on the internet and could be a tempting option for patients that are yet to be prescribed gender-affirming medications. However, hormone usage has side effects and risks that should be monitored and can interfere with other medication use.

Conclusion

As the number of youths with gender identity concerns grows, it is essential for pediatricians to be aware and prepared for gender nonconforming and transgender patients. There is a large disparity in the transgender population in accessing healthcare, and some of the disparity is due to patients' fear of providers or prior negative experiences. The pediatrician should provide safe and welcoming care to transgender youth to ensure that youth feel comfortable in accessing healthcare. Pediatricians can take steps to provide a welcoming environment such as educating staff members, having access to gender neutral bathrooms, and consistently using patient preferred name and pronouns. Pediatricians should also be ready to address patient and caregiver concerns, both medical and social, as well as screening for issues that disproportionately affect transgender youth such as bullying and substance use. With these steps, gender nonconforming and transgender youth can continue to pursue healthcare comfortably.

References:

1. Forcier, M., & Olson-Kennedy, J. (2017). Gender development and clinical presentation of gender nonconformity in children and adolescents. *UpToDate.*

2. Cohen-Kettenis, P., Owen, A., Kaijser, V., Bradley, S., & Zucker, K. (2003). Demographic characteristics, social competence, and behavior problems in children with gender identity disorder: a cross-national, cross-clinic comparative analysis. *J Abnorm Child Psychol. 31(1),* 41-53.

3. Spack, N., Edwards-Leeper, L., Feldman, H., Leibowitz, S., Mandel, F., Diamond, D., & Vance, S. (2012). Children and adolescents with gender identity disorder referred to a pediatric medical center. *Pediatrics. 129(3),* 418-25

4. Zucker, K. (2004). Gender identity development and issues. *Child Adolesc Psychiatr Clin N Am. 13(3),* 551-68, vii.

5. Durwood, L., McLaughlin, K., & Olson, K. (2017) Mental Health and Self-Worth in Socially Transitioned Transgender Youth. *J Am Acad Child Adolesc Psychiatry. 56(2),* 116.

6. Olson-Kennedy, J., & Forcier, M. (2017). Management of gender nonconformity in children and adolescents. *UpToDate.*

7. Gridley, S., Crouch, J., Evans, Y., Eng, W., Antoon, E., Lyapustina, M., Schimmel-Bristow, A., Woodward, J., Dundon, K., Schaff, R., McCarty, C., Ahrens, K., &Breland, D. (2016). Youth and caregiver perspectives on barriers to gender-affirming health care for transgender youth. *J Adolesc Health. 59(3)*, 254-261.

8. Veale, J., Watson R., Peter, T., & Saewyc, E. (2017) Mental health disparities among Canadian transgender youth. *J Adolesc Health. 60(1)*, 44-49.

9. Reisner, S., Vetters, R., Leclerc, M., Zaslow, S., Wolfrum, S., Shumer, D., & Mimiaga, M. (2015) Mental health of transgender youth in care at an adolescent urban community health center: A matched retrospective cohort study. *J Adolesc Health. 56(3)*, 274-279.

10. Eisenberg, M., Gower, A., McMorris, B., Rider, G., Shea, G., & Coleman, E. (2017) Risk and protective factors in the lives of transgender/gender nonconforming adolescents. *J Adolesc Health. 61(4)*, 521-526.

11. Lawlis, S., Donkin, H., Bates, J., Britto, M., & Conrad, L. (2017). Health concerns of transgender and gender nonconforming youth and their parents upon presentation to a transgender clinic. *J Adolesc Health. 61(5)*, 642-648.

12. Clark, B., Veale, J., Greyson, D., & Saewyc, E. (2017) Primary care access and foregone care: a survey of transgender adolescents and young adults. *Fam Pract.*

13. Earnshaw, V. Reisner, S., Juvonen, J., Hatzenbuehler, M., Perrotti, J., & Schuster, M. (2017) LGBTQ bullying: Translating research to action in pediatrics. *Pediatrics. 140(4)*.

14. American Academy of Pediatricians. (2017) Bullying and cyberbullying.

15. National Center for Transgender Equality. (2017). Housing and homelessness.

Access to Healthcare of POC Gay Males and Bisexual, Lesbian and Transgender People of All Races in Comparison to White Gay Males

Safa, Hussein

Introduction

The access to healthcare in the LGBTQIA community (henceforth collectively referred to as the queer community) has been extensively documented as subpar relative to the heterosexual community. Various studies have shown that queer individuals face more barriers to healthcare, mainly due to discrimination by healthcare policies and the healthcare system, and sometimes, unfortunately, discrimination by healthcare providers (who may have not received appropriate diversity education in their training.) This has left the entire queer community as a whole disenfranchised and powerless when it comes to their health (Ard and Makadon). One does not need to go far back in history to see a manifestation of this, as exemplified by the initial response of the healthcare system to the HIV epidemic, which mainly affected the queer community at first, in addition to continued micro aggressions inflicted to this day.

The queer community, however, is an incredibly diverse community, not just when referring to gender and sexual orientation, but also in terms of race, ethnicities and cultural backgrounds. Issues of sexual identity and gender are heavily intertwined with issues of race and ethnic backgrounds. So when discussing queer politics, it is imperative to also link issues of race into the discussion, so as to obtain a complete understanding of the marginalization the queer community faces. Healthcare is no exception when it comes to the intersectionality of queerness and race. While there is plenty of research and data about the gap in access to healthcare among LGBTQIA individuals relative to heterosexuals in general, very little has been done to specifically examine the gap in access to healthcare within the queer community, comparing race and gender and sexual identity among the different groups.

The purpose of this research paper is to explore the access of persons of color (POC) gay males and bisexual, lesbian and transgender individuals of all races relative to white gay males, with the intention of showing the former group has a gap in access to healthcare relative to white gay males (GLMA Health Experts, 2001). Before fully delving into this topic, however, an examination of how this hypothesis came to be is in order.

First, it has been well documented that POCs in general have less access to healthcare. Second, societal and media influences have placed white gay males (particularly affluent ones) at the forefront of the queer community (which as mentioned previously is an extremely diverse community). From the white gay male stars and characters of *Will and Grace* to *Modern Family* to HBO's *Looking* and other various reality TV stars and personalities, the affluent white gay male has been mainstreamed, whereas bisexuals continue to experience erasure[1], lesbians face stereotypical tropes (barring *The L Word*), and the adversities of transgender people are overlooked (barring *Tangerine*). Interestingly, one study has shown that in gay pride parades, the gay males are placed in the front flashy floats, and the lesbians were relegated to the back or the sidelines (Ritzer, 2013). In addition, by virtue of living in a society where

---

1   Bisexual erasure is the phenomenon of delegitimizing the identity of bisexual people through micro aggressions such as asking bisexuals, "How many girls vs. guys have you been with?" "You'll make up your mind eventually" or "You're just doing it for the attention." For more, please see the article in the New York Times Magazine "The Scientific Quest to Prove Bisexuality Exists", published on March 20th, 2014.

the patriarchy and white privilege dominate, white individuals have better access to higher education and higher paying jobs than POCs, and males get paid more than their female counterparts for doing the same job. One study showed that black gay male couples are "six times more likely to be poor" in comparison to white gay male couples (Badgett, Durso and Schneebaum, 2013).

By extension of all these factors, white gay males have higher access to wealth in comparison to other members of the queer community, and can afford living in wealthy neighborhoods now associated with gay men such as Palm Springs in California and Chelsea-Hell's Kitchen in New York. In fact, one study has shown that while lesbians initiate the beginning stages of gentrification by moving into poorer neighborhoods, it is gay males who "accelerate the gentrification" process by bringing in wealth, and then eventually "price" out their lesbian neighbors due to rising rents (Ghaziani, 2015). Lesbians, particularly couples, initially moved into these poorer areas since they have lower income compared to gay male couples, because "thanks to the gender pay gap, times two," lesbian couples do not generally earn as much income as gay male couples (Wade, 2015).

All of these income and cost of living factors point to better access to healthcare for white gay males relative to everyone else in the queer community. However, no extensive data or research has been conducted to document this with irrefutable numbers (Ard and Makadon). The research that exists is minimal, or can be extrapolated from other studies such as those done in assessing access to HIV treatment.

In reviewing the literature, one study showed that queer people of color were more likely to be underserved in healthcare environments or by organizations focused on heterosexual POC and white LGBT populations (Charles and Conron, 2002). And speaking to the compounding issues of queerness, race and sexism, Latina and black bisexual women and lesbians in low-income neighborhoods were twice as likely to be without health insurance as their heterosexual neighbors (Charles and Conron, 2002). The Urban Men's Study, a study on "random household sample of men in census tracks with high proportions of gay men in San Francisco, New York, Los Angeles, and Chicago", found that MSM were more likely to be uninsured, and more importantly, that "economic privilege seems to predict having health insurance or a health care provider" (GLMA Health Experts, 2001). Transgender people are more likely to be uninsured, with transgender POC more likely to be "disproportionately uninsured" (GLMA Health Experts, 2001). A report by the Center for American Progress' Fighting Injustice to Reach Equality (FIRE) initiative found that "combined exposure to antigay and/or anti-transgender policies, along with institutionalized racial discrimination, derails black gay and transgender Americans' financial stability, creates barriers to accessing quality health care, and erodes safeguards for gay and transgender families. Consequently, gay and transgender people of color face high rates of unemployment or underemployment, overall lower rates of pay, higher rates of poverty, and a greater likelihood of being uninsured" (Dunn and Moodie-Ellis, 2012).

Data on HIV prevalence and treatment among the queer community also follow the same trends. One study assessing the community viral loads of individuals infected with HIV by neighborhood in New York City found that the neighborhood of Chelsea-Hell's Kitchen (a white gay male gayborhood) had low to undetectable viral loads, whereas the Bronx (the third poorest county in the country with a predominantly POC population) had high and detectable viral loads (Laraque, 2013). Other studies, however, combine demographic data of heterosexual and queer people with race, but they still show that POC had higher rates of HIV infection and less access to treatment compared to their white counterparts (Terzian et al, 2008 & Kersanske et al, 2016). It can be extrapolated that since the POC and white numbers included both heterosexual and queer individuals, and the rates for POC were higher, then the rates for queer POC are higher than white queer individuals.

After presenting all this information, what is the point of highlighting this specific disparity within the queer community relative to white gay males? The goal is to establish better public health outreach by targeting groups in more specific and focused ways. As already mentioned, POCs are underserved group in healthcare, as is the queer community. As there are endeavors targets POCs of all orientations or queer people of all races, it would be prudent to then combine forces and specifically address queer POC groups regarding access to healthcare. The CDC, for example, has already started an endeavor targeting specifically gay, bisexual and MSM men of color in getting tested and seeking treatment for HIV. They have enacted programs and specific campaigns such as *Act Against AIDS* that target and represent the POC community they are trying to reach. They have also provided funding of $11 million per year for 5 years to 34 community-based organizations "to provide HIV testing to more than 90,000 young gay and bisexual men of color, with the goals of identifying more than 3,500 previously unrecognized HIV infections and linking those who have HIV to care and prevention services" (CDC, 2016).

Before beginning a public health endeavor such as this one, it is important to obtain numbers that better represent the magnitude of the issue. Further research and studies need to be conducted to solidly document the gap in access to healthcare when combining race with queer identities.

The queer community is an incredibly diverse community in terms of genders, sexual orientation, race, ethnicities and culture. While it is easy to lump the entire community under the "queer" umbrella, the label should erase or mask the incredible variety and stories present among individuals within the community. This brief literature review has pointed that way that POC gay men and bisexual, lesbian and transgender people of all races are facing increased barriers to healthcare access in comparison to white gay males. Further research with more data acquired specifically about this issue is necessary, so that public health endeavors can properly target disenfranchised individuals by integrating other social determinants of health into LGBTQIA advocacy such as race, gender and socioeconomic status.

References:

1. Ard, Kevin, & Makadon, Harvey. Improving the Healthcare of Lesbian, Gay, Bisexual and Transgender (LGBT) people: Understanding and Eliminating Health Disparities. *The National LGBT Health Education Center, The Fenway Institute*, 1, 3-4.

2. Badgett, M. V., Durso, Laura, & Schneebaum, Alyssa (2013, June). *New Patterns of Poverty in the Lesbian, Gay and Bisexual Community*. The Williams Institute at University of California Los Angeles School of Law.

3. Center for Disease Control (2016). HIV Among African American Gay and Bisexual Men. http://www.cdc.gov/hiv/group/msm/bmsm.html

4. Charles, V. and K. Conron (2002). Double Jeopardy: How Racism and Homophobia Impact the Health of Black and Latino Lesbian, Gay, Bisexual, and Transgender (LGBT) Communities. *Boston Public Health Commission, LGBT Health*, 1-5.

5. Dunn, Melissa, Moodie-Ellis, Aisha (2012, April). The State of Gay and Transgender Communities of Color in 2012. *Center for American Progress*. Web.

6. Gay and Lesbian Medical Association and LGBT Health Experts (2001). *Healthy People 2010 Companion Document for Lesbian, Gay, Bisexual, and Transgender (LGBT) Health*. San Francisco, CA: Gay and Lesbian Medical Association.

7. Ghaziani, Amin (2015, February). Lesbian Geographies. *Contexts, Winter 2015*. Web.

8. Kersanske, Laura, & al (2016, February). Demographics and HIV Care among New Yorkers Living with HIV by Diagnostic Cohort. Poster presented at The 2016 Conference on Retroviruses and Opportunistic Infections, Boston, MA.

9. Laraque, Fabienne, & al (2013). Disparities in community viral load among HIV-infected persons in New York City. *AIDS, 27 (13)*, 2129-2139. doi: 10.1097/QAD.0b013e328360f619

10. Neaigus A, Reilly KH, Jenness SM, Wendel T, Marshall DM IV, Hagan H (2015, February). Experiences of discrimination and HIV risk among men who have sex with men in New York City. Poster presented at IMN's 3rd Annual HealthIMPACT East, New York, NY.

11. Ritzer, George, & Guppy, Neil. (2014). Social Change, Social Movements and Collective Behavior, *Introduction to sociology* (590-629) [Ebook]. San Francisco: SAGE Publications.

12. Terzian, Arpi, & al (2011, July). *Factors associated with persistent high viremia in HIV-infected New Yorkers, 2006-2007.* Poster presented at HIV Surveillance Workshop, Atlanta, GA.

13. Wade, Lisa (2015, December). Why Lesbians and Gay Men Don't Share Spaces. *Sociological Images.* Web.

Medical Considerations for Transgender Patients in the United States Military

Getchell, Courtney

Introduction

In United States medical schools, the curriculum recommended by AAMC encourages comprehensive education about LGTBQ+ (abbreviation for lesbian, gay, bisexual, transgender, queer/ questioning, with the + encompassing people who identify all along the gender identity and sexual orientation spectrum) patients. However, surveys of medical students found that there is an average of 5 hours of instruction dedicated to the care, terminology, and specific medical concerns for the LGBTQ+ patient population (10). In a survey of students and faculty at the Uniformed Services University School of Medicine (USUHS), the curriculum has 7 hours of topics focused on this patient population, which students rated as "poor to adequate" for medical training purposes (14). A 2018 Gallup poll estimated 4.5% of the United States population identifies as LGBTQ+, which is approximately 14.8 million Americans (19). This demonstrates a need for medical students to develop a strong knowledge base and comfort with treating patients within this population.

Transgender people face a different set of medical concerns than other members of the LGBTQ+ community. Compared to gay, lesbian, and bisexual persons, transgender people report twice as many instances of discrimination, and tend to have poor social supports and higher levels of emotional distress which can contribute to the diagnosis of gender dysphoria (23). While some transgender people may not seek hormonal therapies and sexual reassignment surgery, those that do face additional barriers in accessing and affording healthcare service.

In the United States, an estimated 15,500 transgender people are serving in the military in active duty, guard, and reserve forces, as well as 134,000 transgender veterans as of 2014. Compared to the civilian population, transgender people are twice as likely to serve in the US military as their cisgender peers (12). For military medical personnel, this emphasizes the need for designated training for treating transgender patients, as well as clarified policies for caring for transgender soldiers, veterans, and family members.

Background and Overview

To understand the current medical concerns of transgender people in the United States Armed Forces, we must first look at the past and present federal legal status of transgender service members. In 2011, the United States military repealed its *Don't Ask, Don't Tell* Policy, which then allowed gay, lesbian, and bisexual people to serve openly. This same year, the Veteran's Health Administration policy updated to provide transgender medical services to veterans (5). In 2014, Executive Order 11478 added a provision for the Equal Opportunity Employment of Federal Employees to prohibit discrimination based on sexual orientation or gender identity (21) In 2016, the transgender ban was lifted, and the new policy in place allowed for transgender people to openly serve in the United States military if they had been stable in their preferred gender identity for 18 months prior to joining and allowed for people to transition while serving (16).

The policy for transgender service members that is currently in place as of March 2019, relies on recommendations from the Secretary of Defense written in February 2018, which advises that transgender service members and those diagnosed with gender dysphoria should not be able to serve in their preferred gender. It does allow transgender people to serve in their biological sex and has a provision for service members who joined or transitioned while under the previous policy to remain in the military. The reasoning behind the policy change is that transgender service members who are transitioning or have gender dysphoria "undermines readiness" due to the time and risk involved in transition treatments, and that transitioning is "incompatible with sex-based standards" (17). This current memorandum is due to expire September 12, 2020 as of writing this paper (20).

The most recent recommendations for transgender and gender dysphoria treatment and care follow the World Professional Association for Transgender Health guidance. This identifies several possible courses of medical treatment of transgender individuals with or without the comorbid diagnosis of gender dysphoria. Gender affirming psychotherapy is the treatment of choice for patients with gender dysphoria and is required prior to hormonal and surgical treatment (11). Due to the high incidence of mental disorders in this population, it is recommended for all transgender patients. Patients can start gender affirming care via vocal training, hair removal, genital tucking, breast binding or padding, and using a preferred name and/ or changing legal documents to reflect this change (8). Patients who wish to start hormonal and/ or surgical treatment have to undergo psychological evaluation, have stable chronic and mental conditions, and have a referral from another medical specialist. It is also highly recommended they have Real Life Experience, wherein they live as their preferred gender (2).

Endocrinologists typically coordinate the use of hormones and expect the patient to understand the risks, side effects, and reasonable expectations of hormone treatments. Some of the special medical considerations for transgender women are that taking exogenous estrogen and anti-androgen blockers can lead to increased cardiovascular risk and cancers which require close follow up. For both transgender men and women, frequent appointments are needed every 2-3 months for the first year of hormone treatment (8, 11).

If desired, patients can also pursue gender affirming surgery including breast implants or mastectomy, internal genitalia removal, and external genitalia reconstruction. Currently, no military facilities have sexual reassignment surgery capabilities, and therefore require referral to civilian facilities (13). These procedures also carry the possibility of permanent disability that may limit the transgender patient's operational capacity via their ability to deploy.

Some additional military-specific concerns for transgender service members undergo transition are that they must coordinate their transition timeline and medical appointments with their commanding officer (9). This can interfere with ability to complete job tasks, as some specialists may not be available near smaller or more rural duty stations. This may require the patient themselves to take leave time for appointments, or for their primary care provider to coordinate the care and communicate with specialists. Additionally, during the first year of hormone therapy, patients will not be able to deploy or transfer locations because of the frequency of medical appointments (11). Following the first year of hormone treatment and/ or recovery from surgery, there are no limitations on deployments if the transgender service member is medically cleared (8).

In Practice

Dr. GC is a current US Army lieutenant colonel and endocrinologist who previously established the Transgender Care Team based out of Fort Bill, Texas in 2016 in response to the change in Department of Defense policy to allow transgender people to openly serve. This task force served duty stations in Regional Health Command-Central, which encompasses 20 states and their medical treatment facilities. The first task of the Transgender Care Team was to create and conduct educational programing for commanding officers, medical providers, and soldiers in the region. Next was to develop a clear path of communication with primary care physicians, behavioral health professionals, and patients to coordinate care. Accomplishing these first two tasks enabled Dr. Chin and his team to start hormone therapy in transgender soldiers following a diagnosis from a mental health professional with minimal interruption to the soldiers' ability to deploy.

Due to the broad region of coverage for transgender soldiers, Dr. Chin communicated with primary care physicians primarily through telemedicine. He worked closely with a family medicine at Fort Carson, Colorado who acted as the main point of contact for coordinating transgender hormone therapy via telemedicine. For other military training centers, there was little capability for telemedicine as the administrative requirements for the system were not established. At these locations, communication with various physicians was conducted via email and phone, with no streamlined process.

In his role as an endocrinologist, he prescribed hormone therapies for transgender patients and made adjustments depending on lab draws demonstrating hormone levels. Prior to starting hormone therapy, patients were required to regularly see behavioral health specialists and have a full history and physical in addition to initial labs. This is coordinated through primary care physicians and helps to establish the patient as low risk for complication with the therapy. During the first 3-6 months, lab draws are required between hormone injections which occur every 2 weeks. The timing of these is important to establish a stable hormone dosage and regimen. During these first 3-6 months, soldiers were put on a profile and were not able to be deployed with their units due to the importance of attending frequent medical appointments. With this consideration, some soldiers elected to schedule the initiation of hormone therapy so as to not interfere with deployments. For the most part, Dr. GC found the soldiers' leadership very supportive of their transitions and need to attend appointments.

Public Health

The potential financial burden of gender affirming treatment, long term psychological disorders, and military readiness of transgender service members can affect the communities in which they live and the public health of the United States. From the perspective of the federal government, the priority of the Armed Forces is readiness, meaning the ability to deploy and meet the physical requirements of job duties. Some of the factors analyzed for the health and readiness of troops include BMI, cigarette use, alcohol use, sexual behaviors, and mental disorders. LGBTQ+ service members were less likely to be overweight or obese compared to their non-LGBTQ+ peers at 54.2% to 67%. This group also shared a higher percentage of cigarette smokers, binge drinkers, and personnel who had more than one sexual partner compared to their peers (18). In addition to these high-risk behaviors, LGBTQ+ military personnel had higher rates of moderate depression, self-inflicted injury, and suicide attempts. Some of the factors that may contribute to the 3-5 times higher rates of suicide amongst LGBTQ+ service members and veterans include poor access to mental healthcare, low social support, and stigmatization. In some non-military populations, gender confirming surgery reduced suicidal ideation from 20% to 0.5-1.9% in transgender people. Additionally, disclosing gender identity and sexual orientation may be protective against suicide in service members (16).

Historically, sexually transmitted infection (STI) rates within the United States military have been reported as higher than their civilian counterparts. The yearly incidence of chlamydia and gonorrhea among soldiers is 1.8% and 0.08% respectively (1). For the civilian population, the 2018 incident rate for chlamydia is 0.54% and for gonorrhea is 0.18% (33). There are not many comprehensive statistics on transgender people's STI rates. However, one study over a 3.5-year period found that 13.1% of transgender women tested positive for chlamydia and 12.6% for gonorrhea. For transgender men, the rate of chlamydia was 7.7%, while the rate for gonorrhea was 10.5% (24). The drastically higher rates of STIs in transgender populations may be due to a lack of social support system, lower socioeconomic levels leading to being uninsured, and lack of access/ comfort within the healthcare system.

STIs were associated with binge drinking, lack of condom use, multiple sex partners in one year (especially 5 or more), and illicit substance use (32). Of these factors, transgender people in the military have a higher rate of binge-drinking and multiple sex partners. While the cost of treating STIs in the armed forces is not known, the yearly cost of treated STIs in the United States is estimated to be $16 million (29). Some ideas to reduce the costs of STIs in the military include yearly screening for soldiers who are sexually active with multiple people, free condoms, Human Papillomavirus Vaccinations, and educational materials about STIs directed at people of all sexual orientations and gender identities.

As the United States military is funded by taxpayers, the financial cost of caring for transgender troops may play a factor in analyzing troop readiness. The estimated cost per year for transition care for all transgender troops is $5.6 million as of 2015 (4). This same year, the total defense budget was $495 billion. The value did take into consideration that not all people who identify as transgender will seek hormonal or surgical treatments.

Global Perspective

While the United States currently bans transgender people from joining and serving, this is not the case throughout the world. There are currently 19 countries that have specific provisions allowing transgender people to serve in their armed forces. These include Australia, Austria, Belgium, Bolivia, Canada, the Czech Republic, Denmark, Estonia, Finland, France, Germany, Ireland, Israel, Netherlands, New Zealand, Norway, Spain, Sweden, and the United Kingdom.

The Netherlands was the first country to allow transgender people to openly serve in 1974. They have found no major changes in the overall functioning of their military after the addition of openly transgender service members. Their policies focus on the concept of LGBTQ+ inclusion, meaning the valuing and recognition of the differences of transgender people and integrating these cultural differences into the military organization, such as avoiding deployments to areas hostile to LGBTQ+ people (25).

Canada officially lifted their ban on transgender service members in 1992. Transgender military personnel are able to serve in an active duty capacity without compromising operational effectiveness. However, the inclusivity of military policy does not supersede the lack of medical expertise available for transgender troops, lack of guidance for transition, and discrimination against transgender people that exists in both the Canadian civilian and military worlds (22). Greater medical training and clearer transition policies are needed to meet the needs of Canadian transgender service members.

Many countries lack legislation or policies that explicitly ban or permit transgender people to openly serve in the military, we can extrapolate this by examining the overall policies and attitudes of nations towards LGBTQ+ people. In Africa, several tribes recognize and embrace people with gender expressions outside of the European gender binary. These include the Dogon, Dagaaba, Lugbara, Ambo, Zulu, and Neur tribes (6). However, African countries recognized by the United Nations tend to be less accepting of homosexual and non-gender conforming people. Of the 54 countries in Africa, at least 34 explicitly ban homosexuality. In Somalia, Somaliland, Mauritania, and parts of Nigeria, homosexuality is punishable by death (3). In these countries, LGBTQ+ people are not allowed to openly exist, and therefore would be banned from military service. By far, the country with the most liberal LGBTQ+ rights policies in Africa is South Africa. The Defense Act of 2002 protects members of the force from discrimination on the basis that the South African Defense Force "is subservient to the Constitution of South Africa and therefore does not discriminate against people in terms of race, ethnicity, gender, cultural, language, [and] sexual orientation"(15). The broad anti-discrimination policies allow for transgender people to openly serve in the military, and they are also able to change gender on official forms. Despite legal protections, transgender South Africans lack access to medical care in the country to aide in transitioning via medical and/or surgical methods. The first dedicated transgender facility in South Africa was opened in 2019, which was opened in part to improve community education and reduce the stigma around transgender people. Of particular concern for these patients is the 49 times higher risk of transgender patients to be infected with HIV, so they require a facility where they feel comfortable while accessing care and avoiding cultural stigma (27)

Recommendations

For the future of transgender people in the United States military currently depends on policy changes or continuations. However, to be the best providers to today's transgender service members, veterans, and families, military medical personnel should start implementing some of the following recommendations:

1.   Dedicated continuing medical education for providers

The transgender transition process requires a multi-disciplinary approach involving the patient's primary care physician, psychiatrist, and possibly endocrinologist and surgeon. As previously mentioned, there is very little education about LGBTQ+ topics. Two surveys of military medical practitioners at separate military sites demonstrated a lack of comfort with LGBTQ+ patients and education about medical concerns for these populations. Only about 5% of practitioners were comfortable asking about same-sex relationships, and 4/5 of those expressed desire for clearer guidance on these topics (26). Standardized training and curriculum for military medical personnel could help close these knowledge gaps (30).

2.   Evidence based guidance for active duty members transitioning

While much of the guidance for transgender transition endorses flexibility and an individualized plan, it also emphasizes the importance of a strong support system in a successful transition (5,8,23). Having clear written policy for transgender service members to come out without risk of discharge could help these members to create a social support system that could help improve mental health outcomes. Additionally, over 66% of active duty soldiers anonymously surveyed endorse support for transgender military personnel (7). Increased transgender inclusion could lead to better readiness and overall health (25).

3.   Connecting with specialists in the military and civilian communities

The lack of formal training that primary care practitioners have on transgender topics creates a knowledge gap. As PCPs are the main contact to the health care system for many military personnel and are sometimes the only provider for a rural duty station, this creates a need for specialty communication to help bridge this knowledge gap (28). This would help provide more comprehensive care for transgender patients.

Conclusion

The United States Military is the largest employer in the nation, and estimates show that transgender people are twice as likely to join, making it the largest employer of transgender people in the country (31). The current transgender ban on service members has a negative impact on soldiers' overall health and well-being. Requiring transgender people to serve only in their biological sex could negatively affect mental and physical well-being of service members and veterans and lower military retention rates. To address the medical concerns of transgender service members, there should be a dedicated multi-disciplinary medical curriculum, support for transgender service members, and communication with specialists in the area.

Disclaimer: The opinions and assertions expressed herein are those of the author and do not reflect the official policy or position of the Department of Defense.

References:

1. Armed Forced Health Surveillance Branch. (2020). Update: Sexually transmitted infections, active component, U.S. Armed Forced, 2011-2019. *Medical Surveillance Monthly Report, 27*(03), 2–11.

2. Belkin, A. (2015). Caring for Our Transgender Troops—The Negligible Cost of Transition-Related Care. *New England Journal of Medicine, 373*(12), 1089–1092. https://doi.org/10.1056/NEJMp1509230

3. Carroll, A. (2016). *State Sponsored Homophobia: A World Survey of Sexual Orientation Laws: Criminalisation, Protection, and Recognition* (11th Edition; p. 193). International Lesbian, Gay, Bisexual, Trans, and Intersex Association.

4. Carter, A. (2016). *DoD Instruction 1300.28: In-Service Transition for Transgender Service Members*. Office of the Under Secretary of Defense for Personnel and Readiness. https://dod.defense.gov/Portals/1/features/2016/0616_policy/DoD-Instruction-1300.28.pdf

5. Cartwright, L., & Weis, M. (2015, September). *Emerging Transgender Issues and the Law: Medical and Legal Update.*

6. Collins, S. (2017, October 10). *The Splendor of Gender Non-Conformity In Africa*. Mediume. https://medium.com/@janelane_62637/the-splendor-of-gender-non-conformity-in-africa-f894ff5706e1

7. Dunlap, S. L., Holloway, I. W., Pickering, C. E., Tzen, M., Goldbach, J. T., & Castro, C. A. (2020). Support for Transgender Military Service from Active Duty United States Military Personnel. *Sexuality Research and Social Policy*. https://doi.org/10.1007/s13178-020-00437-x

8. Elders, M. J., Brown, G. R., Coleman, E., Kolditz, T. A., & Steinman, A. M. (2015). Medical Aspects of Transgender Military Service. *Armed Forces & Society, 41*(2), 199–220. https://doi.org/10.1177/0095327X14545625

9. Engel, K. (2018, April 30). *TGCT-NME Transition Health Care Process* [Powerpoint].

10. Fadus, M. (2019). Mental Health Disparities and Medical Student Education: Teaching in Psychiatry for LGBTQ Care, Communication, and Advocacy. *Academic Psychiatry, 43*(3), 306–310. https://doi.org/10.1007/s40596-019-01024-y

11. Folaron, I., & Lovasz, M. (2016). Military Considerations in Transsexual Care of the Active Duty Member. *Military Medicine, 181*(10), 1182–1186. https://doi.org/10.7205/MILMED-D-15-00559

12. Gates, G. J., & Herman, J. (2014). *Transgender Military Service in the United States*. https://escholarship.org/uc/item/1t24j53h#page-4

13. Guice, K. (2016). *Guidance for Treatment of Gender Dysphoria for Active and Reserve Component Service Members*. Department of Defense.

14. Lindberg, B. M., Fulleborn, S. T., Semelrath, K. M., Lee, R. C., & Nguyen, D. R. (2019). Steps to Improving Sexual and Gender Diversity Curricula in Undergraduate Medical Education. *Military Medicine, 184*(1–2), e190–e194. https://doi.org/10.1093/milmed/usy190

15. Marrian, L. (n.d.). Trans soldiers protected by SA constitution. *PDBY.* Retrieved August 28, 2020, from https://pdby.co.za/trans-soldiers-protected-by-sa-constitution/

16. Matarazzo, B. B., Barnes, S. M., Pease, J. L., Russell, L. M., Hanson, J. E., Soberay, K. A., & Gutierrez, P. M. (2014). Suicide Risk among Lesbian, Gay, Bisexual, and Transgender Military Personnel and Veterans: What Does the Literature Tell Us? *Suicide and Life-Threatening Behavior, 44*(2), 200–217. https://doi.org/10.1111/sltb.12073

17. Mattis, J. (2018). *Department of Defense Report and Recommendations on Military Service by Transgender Persons.* https://media.defense.gov/2018/Mar/23/2001894037/-1/-1/0/MILITARY-SERVICE-BY-TRANSGENDER-INDIVIDUALS.PDF

18. Meadows, S. O., Engel, C. C., Collins, R. L., Beckman, R. L., Cefalu, M., Hawes-Dawson, J., Waymouth, M., Kress, A. M., Sontag-Padilla, L., Ramchand, R., & Williams, K. M. (2018). 2015 Department of Defense Health Related Behaviors Survey (HRBS). *RAND Corportation.* https://www.rand.org/pubs/research_reports/RR1695.html

19. Newport, F. (2018, May 22). In U.S., Estimate of LGBT Population Rises to 4.5%. *Gallup.Com.* https://news.gallup.com/poll/234863/estimate-lgbt-population-rises.aspx

20. Norquist, D. (2019). *Directive-Type Memorandum-19-004: Military Service by Transgender Persons and Persons with Gender Dysphoria.* Department of Defense.

21. Equal Employment Opportunity in the Federal Government, 11478 Executive Order (2014).

22. Okros, A., & Scott, D. (2014). Gender Identity in the Canadian Forces: A Review of Possible Impacts on Operational Effectiveness - Alan Okros,

Denise Scott, 2015. *Armed Forces & Society*. http://journals.sagepub.com/
doi/10.1177/0095327X14535371

23. *Part 3: Clinical Skills for the Care of Transgender Individuals.* (2013, July
11). https://www.youtube.com/watch?v=RM8MTuMTeSk&feature=yo
utu.be

24. Pitasi, M. A., Kerani, R. P., Kohn, R., Murphy, R. D., Pathela, P.,
Schumacher, C. M., Tabidze, I., & Llata, E. (2019). Chlamydia, Gonorrhea,
and Human Immunodeficiency Virus Infection Among Transgender
Women and Transgender Men Attending Clinics that Provide Sexually
Transmitted Disease Services in Six US Cities: Results From the Sexually
Transmitted Disease Surveillance Network. *Sexually Transmitted
Diseases, 46*(2), 112–117. https://doi.org/10.1097/OLQ.0000000000000917

25. Polchar, J., Sweijs, T., Marten, P., & Galdiga, J. (2014). *LGBT Military
Personnel: A Strategic Vision for Inclusion.* The Hague Center for
Strategic Studies.

26. Rerucha, C. M., Runser, L. A., Ee, J. S., & Hersey, E. G. (2017). Military
Healthcare Providers' Knowledge and Comfort Regarding the Medical
Care of Active Duty Lesbian, Gay, and Bisexual Patients. *LGBT Health,
5*(1), 86–90. https://doi.org/10.1089/lgbt.2016.0210

27. *SA gets first transgender healthcare facility.* (n.d.). ENCA. Retrieved
August 28, 2020, from https://www.enca.com/life/wits-opens-door-
healthcare-trans-people

28. Schvey, N. A., Blubaugh, I., Morettini, A., & Klein, D. A. (2017). Military
Family Physicians' Readiness for Treating Patients With Gender
Dysphoria. *JAMA Internal Medicine, 177*(5), 727–729. https://doi.
org/10.1001/jamainternmed.2017.0136

29. *Sexually Transmitted Diseases.* (2020, August 18). Healthy People 2020.
https://www.healthypeople.gov/2020/topics-objectives/topic/sexually-
transmitted-diseases

30. Shrader, A., Casero, K., Casper, B., Kelley, M., Lewis, L., & Calohan,
J. (2017). Military Lesbian, Gay, Bisexual, and Transgender (LGBT)

Awareness Training for Health Care Providers Within the Military Health System. *Journal of the American Psychiatric Nurses Association, 23*(6), 385–392. https://doi.org/10.1177/1078390317711768

31. Sosin, K. (2019, January 23). *The Defense Dept. Is About to Fire More Than 13,700 Trans People.* https://www.advocate.com/transgender/2019/1/23/defense-dept-about-fire-more-13700-trans-people

32. Stahlman, S., Javanbakht, M., Cochran, S., Hamilton, A. B., Shoptaw, S., & Gorbach, P. M. (2014). Self-Reported STIs and Sexual Risk Behaviors in the U.S. Military: How Gender Influences Risk. *Sexually Transmitted Diseases, 41*(6), 359–364. https://doi.org/10.1097/OLQ.0000000000000133

33. Surveillance and Data Management Branch. (2019). *Sexually Transmitted Disease Surveillance 2018.* Centers for Disease Control and Prevention

Health Disparities Faced by Women Who Have Sex with Women and Recommendations.

Kohl, Mitchell

Introduction

There is a portion of our population who may be afraid to address their sexual practices based solely on the fear of how their healthcare provider will react. I will be focusing on women who have sex with women. "Women who have sex with women focuses on the behavioral aspects of sexuality for women who have sex with other women. The term women who have sex with women includes women who may identify themselves as lesbian, heterosexual, gay, straight, bisexual, queer, or may prefer to not identify with any sexual identity" (Harvey, 2014). These women are of every race, age and socioeconomic class.

According to the Institute of Medicine, more than 2 million women self-identify as lesbian, yet there is reason to believe that this number does not cover all of the women who have sex with women. 7.5% of women report having same-sex sexual attraction or desires (Hutchinson, 2006). While in the United Kingdom 1% of their population consider themselves lesbian (Spiegelhalter, 2015). A large portion of the population fit the description of women who have sex with women, and it is important to understand the specific issues that these women face and what can be done to mitigate the effects.

One of the first things that affects the quality of healthcare is the disclosure of sexual practices. This is not of significant importance when the complaint is a broken toe, but this becomes an issue when there are gynecological complaints or complaints that could be related to cancer. "16% of lesbians delayed seeking health care because they feared discrimination based on sexual orientation. Likewise, 74% of lesbians who experienced discrimination in a physician's office believed the discrimination resulted from sexual orientation" (Harvey, 2014). The disclosure of sexual practices is important because about 30 percent of lesbians did not know or believe that Human Papillomavirus (HPV) can be transmitted between women (Harvey, 2014). This is a dangerous way of thinking because HPV can lead directly to certain types of cervical cancer, and more than 27,000 Americans are diagnosed with a cancer related to HPV every year (What is HPV?, 2015).

The misconceptions regarding transmission of HPV and other sexually transmitted infections (STI) are just one of the reasons that proper disclosure of sexual practices is important. If a woman feels that the disclosure that she has sex with women will lead to discrimination or a reduced quality healthcare, the healthcare provider needs to create and environment in which the woman feels comfortable to divulge such. By fully understanding a person's sexual orientation and practices, it allows healthcare providers to ask questions that are directly related to a fully formed differential diagnosis.

Once the patient tells a healthcare provider that she has sex with women, it is the provider's duty to understand their own biases and work to be mindful of their biases. A recommendation that I believe would help gather further information is a questionnaire given to women who identify as women who have sex with women. The questionnaire would be designed to ask specific questions that avoid the heteronormative attitudes of some providers. It could be designed to gauge the patient's attitudes towards STIs. By understanding the specific attitude of the patient, the provider could then focus their further questioning based on the results. For example, if the questions revealed that the woman believed it was less likely for her to receive HPV or other STIs from another woman, it would be a great educational opportunity that should not be overlooked.

Other factors affect the health disparities women encounter if they have sex with women. They are more likely to smoke and to consume alcohol (Cochran, 2000). This, combined with the increase in obesity that is present with women who have sex with women, leads to increased incidences of cardiovascular disease (White, 1997). Women who have sex with women are also at greater risk of breast cancer, possibly as great as one in three (Roberts, 1998). This increased incidence is a major public health issue and as such it is important to create an environment free of either actual or perceived judgment. An environment where all patients feel as though their quality of treatment is not dependent on their sexual practices and that their provider considers "normal".

One of the aspects that can be important to focus on is that women who have sex with women are in need of the same screening practices that heterosexual women receive. In some cases, due to their null parity, there may be cases whereby she needs special education as to her increased risks of certain cancers.

One of the reasons that there exists a health disparity and thus a public health issue with women who have sex with women is that the information and language used assumes heterosexuality (Stevens, 1995). This assumption makes it necessary for the women seeking care to go out of their way, in a way that may make themselves uncomfortable to make sure that their provider understands their sexual practices. For example, the patient questionnaire that most receive upon a first visit to a new providers office, when asking for relationship status can list: single, married or widowed (Mollon, 2012). For some women this may not fit their situation. To remedy this issue in a non-obstructive manner, these questionnaires could be modified to include "in a relationship" and should include a question about sexual identity and practices with the option for the patient to add in their own identification. Adding this simple element would allow for more information to be available to the healthcare providers and would help to make disclosure of such information less risk for discrimination. Increasing disclosure to their providers is associated with increased health care utilization among lesbians (Bergeron, 2003).

It is natural that those women who have sex with women would seek providers that they believe will have a more positive view of their sexuality. Also, it has been found that if a patient views their healthcare provider in a more positive light, they are then more likely to follow through on the treatment plan and will then be more likely to return for a follow up visit (Stevens, 1996). A good way to manage chronic diseases is with consistent care managed by a provider that is intimately aware of the patients wants, desires, and needs. If it is possible to increase a patient's trust and comfort with their providers, it is something that needs to be addressed. An example of the power that greater patient comfort and understanding can lead to is, women who let their provider know their sexual orientation were more likely to have received a Pap smear within the last two years and were more likely to seek out preventive care (Hutchinson, 2006).

There exist a few things that healthcare providers can do to increase the inclusive non-judgmental attitudes that emanate from their offices and clinics. It is important to change provider's attitudes away from the heteronormative thinking that is pervasive. The best way to do this is to focus on the training aspect. If there was more awareness of the disparities and public health issues that exists in the Lesbian, Gay, Bisexual, Transgender, and Queer (LGBTQ) community, then the level of comfort with treating these populations will increase. This is important because, healthcare providers have reported that they are less comfortable treating homosexuals when they are not familiar with gay culture (Schwanberg, 1996). If training and awareness exposure can reduce the level of discomfort, it is going to translate into greater patient comfort. We all have been in situations in which we can tell that another person is not comfortable, the hospital or clinic is no different.

It will be important to increase the amount and quality of training, as 68 percent of medical students believe that their training of lesbian health issues is lacking (McGarry, 2002). If we can make more providers comfortable, it will be the first step to reducing the disparities. To combat this, after meeting with Dr. Mark Goodman MD, I am suggesting that standardized patients be utilized. These actors already do a great deal to allow for future physicians to learn how to build rapport and to become comfortable with many different types of patients. These actors should also be used to increase student's level of comfort in discussing a patient's sexuality. This will be especially helpful in helping the student's comfort level in asking the necessary questions of patients with a different sexuality than their own. By becoming more comfortable with the LGBTQ community, the specific issues and inserting into interviewing a part of medical education from the beginning, it will be possible to make these discussions less taboo and more in line with the needs of all providers' patients. With Dr. Goodman, we discussed how important this training would be and how it is one of those suggestions that can be implemented relatively quickly and can help to eliminate and discomfort that some medical students may face.

As a part of preparing for this paper, I watched a seminar put on by Gay and Lesbian Medical Association (GLMA). In this seminar, they noted that the largest fear for those in the LGBTQ community is that there are not enough healthcare professionals that are adequately trained to care for the community (HCHDS, 2012). It is for this reason that I am recommending that more use of standardized patients be used. This will help to add time to the total amount given in medical school to LGBTQ health issues which as of now, averages to only 5 hours in the four years (HCHDS, 2012). As a part of making the health community more attuned to the health issues faced by LGBTQ persons, increasing the exposure to these health disparities and developing changes to curriculum will help to make the providers and the patients more comfortable discussing important health issues.

It will also be important to redesign the questionnaires and the patient information material to reflect an openness and acceptance of women who have sex with women. By providing a nonjudgmental atmosphere within the environment, by the staff and providers, the patients will feel more comfortable and be more likely to follow up on treatment recommendations. I recommend that providers seek out continuing medical education that focuses on women who have sex with women and how to better serve their needs, as well as those faced by other members of the LGBTQ community. According to the GLMA seminar, the brochures should focus on safe sexual practices, HIV/AIDS and screening procedures. When these women are treated, it is important to keep cognizant of the screening recommendations and to dispel myths that the patients may have, just the same as the provider would for any of their patients.

In conclusion, women who have sex with women face health disparities that are part of the pervasive myths that need to be addressed. Then the healthcare field can implement education regarding the spread of HPV and the discrimination that these women feel when they seek healthcare. Some of these women believe that disclosure of their sexual practices will lead to substandard healthcare and are therefore the topic is never broached and the provider assumes heterosexuality. Sexual orientation is not what puts the woman at an increased risk, but it is their sexual practices (Hutchinson, 2001). Due to this, it is important for a provider to make sure that their patients feel comfortable disclosing their sexual practices in a way in which will not bring about feelings of judgment. Providers can start by providing questionnaires for new patients that give respondents more options than the current assumption of heterosexuality. Allow the patients to describe in their own words if necessary, their sexual orientation and practices. It will also be necessary to increase medical education exposure during training directed at issues faced in the LGBTQ community, with focus on making patients truly feel as though they will suffer no ill will because of their sexual practices. This can be reinforced through the provider's continuing medical education on this issue throughout the provider's career. With a focus and effort, the disparities that women who have sex with women face can be eroded.

References:

1. Bergeron, S., & Senn, C. (2003). Health care utilization in a sample of Canadian lesbian women: Predictors of risk and resilience. *Women & Health*, **37**, 19-35.

2. Cochran, S., Keenan, C.,Schober, C., & Mays, V. (2000). Estimates of alcohol use and clinical treatment needs among homosexually active men and women in the U.S. population. *Journal of Consulting and Clinical Psychology*, **6**, 1062-1071.

3. Harvey, V.L., & Housel, T.H. (2014). *Health care disparities and the LGBT population*. Lanham: Lexington Books.

4. HCHDS (2012, December 20). *Part 2: Creating a welcoming and safe environment for LGBT people and families* Retrieved from https://www.youtube.com/watch?v=e8KJ8uKVQj0&feature=youtu.be

5. Hutchinson, M., Sosa, D., &Thompson, A. (2001).Sexual protective strategies of late adolescent females: More than just condoms.*Journal of Obstetrical, Gynecological and Neonatal Nursing*, **30**, 429-438.

6. Hutchinson, M. K., Thompson, A. C. and Cederbaum, J. A. (2006), Multisystem Factors Contributing to Disparities in Preventive Health Care Among Lesbian Women. Journal of Obstetric, Gynecologic, & Neonatal Nursing, 35: 393–402. doi:10.1111/j.1552-6909.2006.00054.x

7. McGarry, K., Clarke, J., Cyr, M., & Landau, C. (2002). Evaluating a lesbian and gay health care curriculum. *Teaching and Learning in Medicine*, **14**, 244-248.

8. Mollon, L. (2012, February). The Forgotten Minorities: Health Disparities of the Lesbian, Gay, Bisexual and Transgendered Communities. *Journal of Health Care for the Poor and Underserved, 23(1), 1-6. Doi:10.1353/ hpu.2012.0009*

9. Roberts, S., Dibble, S.,Scanlon, J., Paul, S., & Davids, H. (1998).Differences in risk factors for breast cancer: Lesbian and heterosexual women. *Journal of the Gay and Lesbian Medical Association*, **2**, 93-101.

10. Schwanberg, S. (1996). Health care professionals' attitudes toward lesbian women and gay men. *Journal of Homosexuality*,**31**, 71-83.

11. Spiegelhalter, D. (2015, April 05). Is 10% of the population really gay? Retrieved November 10, 2016, from https://www.theguardian.com/society/2015/apr/05/10-per-cent-population-gay-alfred-kinsey-statistics

12. Stevens, P. (1996). Lesbians and doctors: Experiences of solidarity and domination in health care settings. *Gender & Society*, **10**, 24-41.

13. Stevens, P. (1995). Structural and interpersonal impact of heterosexual health care clients. *Nursing Research*, **44**, 25-30.

14. What is HPV? (2015, December 28). Retrieved November 06, 2016 from http://www.cdc.gov/hpv/parents/whatishpv.html

15. White, J.C. & Dull. V.T. (1997) Health risk factors and health-seeking behavior in lesbians. *Journal of Women's Health.* 6(1). 103-112

Barriers Faced by the Transgender Community in Seeking OB/GYN Care

Salinas Calma, Rei Christian

Introduction

Individuals of the LGBT community have a growing presence in all aspects of society, especially as healthcare patients. As the prevalence of non-heterosexual individuals arise, the status quo must adjust to better accommodate the growing needs of the LGBT community. This is especially palpable in the field of Obstetrics and Gynecology (OB/GYN) and transgender individuals. Transgender is defined as "people who have a gender identity that differs from their assigned sex", and they have reached 1.4 million in number in the United States alone as of 2016 (Hoffman, 2016). This is opposed to a natal individual, which refers to someone whose biological gender is syntonic with his or her sexual identity. As the number of sex reassignment surgery correspondingly rises, especially in the United States, the medical community has begun to face numerous questions that it has not yet faced prior. This paper explores the current state of medical care regarding provided by healthcare professionals in general, and for OB/GYNs, in particular for transgender individuals who pursue sex reassignment surgery (SRS). Specifically, it will identify the kind of care that is appropriate for individuals who have transitioned from male-to-female or female-to-male once completing their gender reassignment surgery. I will then expand my findings to the current state of transgender care on a global health perspective and the implications this has on public health. In my review, I will also identify barriers to care that healthcare professionals may initially be unaware of, such as current stigma, lack of medical education, and paucity of existing data. Finally, I will identify areas of improvement we must focus on as a medical community so that we may better provide care for the transgender community.

Background

Under the spectrum of the LGBT community, the transsexual individual is one that is relatively new, and therefore, poses new challenges to healthcare workers, especially those in the field of OB/GYN. As compared to the transgender patients, transsexual patients are "individuals who desire to achieve reassignment and have committed to transitioning to their desired sex," meaning they have completed SRS (Coleman, 2017).

The screening criteria a patient must pass before undergoing SRS is rigorous and not completely standardized. A transgender patient who is seeking SRS requires both a diagnosis of gender dysphoria and a desire to undergo SRS. From the time of diagnosis, it is standard practice to establish continued care with a psychiatrist for 12 months, at minimum, so that the psychiatrist may better assess the severity of gender dysphoria, taking special note as to how much the patient will benefit from SRS (WPATH, 2018). Additionally, most surgeons who perform SRS require two letters of recommendation that speak to the patient's need for said procedure (WPATH, 2018). During this period, most patients also undergo a "real-life test," during which the patient lives completely as the gender he or she identifies (WPATH, 2018). This "real-life test" may last as long as one year. Many patients also choose to initiate hormone therapy during this time so that their appearance will be congruent with their desired sex.

Once a transgender patient has undergone SRS, such patients often seek care from an OB/GYN. However, current data regarding the size of the transsexual community is incredibly lacking; there is no level-1 evidence for routine health care maintenance (Unger 2014). Nevertheless, some guidelines have been developed. For example, regarding osteoporosis, transgender men (referring to a biologically female individual who has undergone SRS) should be screened for osteoporosis beginning 10 years after initiating testosterone therapy and every 10 years thereafter. Likewise, transgender women only need to be screened every 10 years after age 65 or 10 years after the patient has stopped hormone therapy (Unger, 2014). These, however, are simply extrapolations and are not part of official U.S. Preventive Task Force (USPTF) recommendations.

Once SRS is completed, transgender males and females often seek care from an OB/GYN. Transsexual male often pursue this for several reasons, including affirmation of their new gender. Transsexual females may choose to do this for continued care with their already established OB/GYN (Unger, 2014). For both transsexual males and females who receive care from an OB/GYN, the OB/GYN is often responsible for hormone therapy maintenance in addition to general woman's health.

Global Perspective

The LGBT community faces disparity not only in the United States but also on a global scale. Though data exist regarding LGBT status and health outcomes, it is, however, not standardized, making it nearly impossible to make any inferences. Nevertheless, it is estimated that there is a prevalence of 0.3 – 0.5%, though this number is presumed to be underreported (The Williams Institute, 2014).

Utilizing the existing data, it is interesting to note that LGBT individuals from countries outside the United States face different problems than what we face within our own country. From a health perspective, almost all countries surveyed showed an increased prevalence of HIV infections and suicidal behavior (Reisner, 2016). In Mexico, HIV-infected transgender men were shown to have an increased prevalence of diabetes (Alvarez-Wyssmann, 2013). Data from the Netherlands also suggest transgender patients suffer from increased cardiovascular mortality, all-cause mortality, mortality from malignant neoplasm, AIDS, external causes, illicit drug use, and suicide (Asscheman, 2013).

Thailand, in particular, has a rich history of LGBT rights. Though Thailand is known as a haven for LGBT tourists, the local LGBT community has faced unequal discrimination (Bangkok Post Public Company Limited, 2013). For example, the definition of rape did not include male or transgender victims until the year 2007 (Sanders, 2011). Even after this expansion of the definition of rape, the practice of corrective rape, which is the practice of raping a non-heterosexual individual with the goal of converting said individual, was still widely practiced in 2016 (Bangkok Post Public Company Limited, 2016). Regarding transsexual care, Thailand has been an established destination for SRS since 1975 (Gale, 2015). Just as in the United States, transsexuals in Thailand also face discrimination when seeking employment. This occurs despite the seemingly wide acceptance of transsexuals in popular Thailand culture (Bangkok Post Public Company Limited, 2013).

Public Health Concerns

As an underserved group, LGBT individuals innately have a deficit in access to education, healthcare, and housing: only 30-40% of transgender receive routine care (Bockting, 2010). Of the factors that most contributed to poor access to care, the most common include the following: lack of insurance (64%), inability to pay (46%), provider insensitivity or hostility to transgender individuals (32%), and fear of transgender status revealed (32%) (Xavier, 2000).

From a mental health standpoint, the LGBT community has universally faced high rates of suicide and suicidal ideation (Proctor, 1994). This is only compounded by the fact that LGBT individuals already have lower access to healthcare than the general population.

The most studied public health concern regarding the LGBT community is that of sexually transmitted infections. Despite this, my research findings suggest there continues to be a lack of data due to several reasons. For one, the LGBT community as a whole is one that is still highly stigmatized. It is probable that the stigma associated with being LGBT would result in underreported numbers of individuals. Most strikingly is the transmission of HIV. Of the new cases of HIV in the United States in 2015, 68% were due to men who have sex with men and bisexual men (CDC, 2015). Of these men, the most affected groups included black male-to-male sexual contact and Hispanic/Latino male-to-male sexual contact (CDC, 2015).

With this data, it is fair to categorize the LGBT community within the United States as one as a group that has less access to healthcare than the general population. The reasons for this are rooted in an inability to pay for care, as well as social stigma. Preventable causes of death and disease such as suicide and HIV are especially prevalent in the LGBT community, and that fact that the LGBT community has limited access to care only worsens this. However, not all is bleak. Medicare and Medicaid have since been expanded in 2014 to include SRS (Green, 2014).

Research Findings

In researching OB/GYN care for the transgender patient, I found the lack of data and lack of standardization of data to be incredibly troubling. My review of existing literature suggests this is due to several reasons. For one, surveys designed to capture health disparity often use language that exclude non-heterosexual individuals (Reisner, 2016). The fact that LGBT members may feel hesitancy in stating their sexual preference further compounds their underrepresentation in data sets. Definitions of the LGBT subcategories may also be confusing by both patients as well as survey designers, leading to a miscategorization of patients (Unger, 2014).

Regarding barriers for transgender patients in receiving OB/GYN care, my research suggests these obstacles are primarily due to health insurance coverage. Prior to the Affordable Care Act, being transgender was considered a "pre-existing" condition for which patients could be denied coverage unless they deny their gender identity (Learmonth, 2018). Even after the passage of the ACA, transgender individuals face limited options that are suboptimal at best in addressing their healthcare needs, especially regarding fertility. Take, for example, a transsexual male (a biological female who has transitioned into a male). The patient is identified by insurance companies as a male, and plans targeted towards males do not include stipulations for fertility issues such as egg preservation (Learmonth, 2018). Even if a transgender patient is able to attain coverage, electronic health records are often inflexible in their linking of a patient's registered sex with presumed organs. This, unfortunately, results in patients being denied for appropriate screening, such as the case of a transgender male who retains his cervix (Learmonth, 2018).

Researching the topic in my own community of Omaha, Nebraska, I found the lay public is speedily becoming LGBT friendly. "I was able to find a physician pretty easily, and I honestly never felt awkward speaking to healthcare professionals about my issues. My insurance covered the bulk of the cost, too. I don't know, I guess we're lucky to be alive when we're alive," stated A.J., a homosexual male whom I interviewed regarding his experience procuring HIV-prophylaxis medication in Omaha, NE (Calma, 2018). The medical community itself is making transitions, albeit slowly. Dr. Shanahan, an OB/GYN who practices in my community, mentioned in an interview that she still does not see many LGBT patients, even less so who are transgender or transsexual. She even affirmed she faced a common problem I came across my own research, which is when transgender patients are denied coverage for medical services that do not match their gender at birth. Specifically, she cited an example of a transsexual male who would not receive insurance coverage for a pap smear. According to Dr. Shanahan, however, steps have been made to address these issues. For example, Epic, an electronic health record software used in my community, was just recently updated to allow add or remove a patient's recorded organs regardless of the patient's listed gender. This will allow for transgender and transsexual individuals to receive coverage when the previously would have been denied (Calma, 2018).

Recommendations

As society becomes more accepting of LGBT individuals, healthcare professionals must learn to better service the particular needs of such individuals. This is especially true for the specialty of OB/GYN where a provider may see patients that range from natal females to transsexual men and women.

Several barriers exist that prevent healthcare professionals from providing comparable care to the LGBT community to that of natal men and women. The growing number of LGBT individuals is a relatively new phenomenon. Accordingly, many healthcare professionals have not received adequate training on using inclusive language regarding sexuality and care. Furthermore, some healthcare providers may be morally opposed to caring for LGBT individuals. This is especially precarious in communities that are already lacking access to healthcare. I propose a two-fold solution to this problem. At this moment, healthcare providers are able to deny care to patients, even for personal reasons. If this is so, however, then such providers must be able to refer care to an LGBT-friendly provider. Secondly, I suspect the newer generations of physicians will be more accepting of the LGBT community. I foresee that opposition to the care of LGBT patients will decrease as time passes.

Though many providers may be LGBT-inclusive in spirit, they may not realize their clinic uses vocabulary that excludes non-heterosexual individuals. For example, a physician may assume his 30-year-old female patient is having regular menses, when his or her patient is actually a transsexual female. Clinics can address this by beginning conversation with inclusive language. For example, healthcare providers should ask how the patient identifies sexually in the first office visit. The provider should also further differentiate between the patient's biological gender and identified gender. These questions can even be completed by form so as to be less awkward for the patient and healthcare provider.

The number of transsexual individuals is ever increasing, and it is imperative that OB/GYNs develop a greater expertise in hormone replacement therapy for both transsexual males as well as transsexual females. As stated previously, transsexual males and females often seek OB/GYN providers to serve as their primary care provider. Though some OB/GYNs receive training in hormone replacement therapy for menopausal women, they seldom receive training for hormone replacement therapy in the context of transsexual males and females. This should be incorporated in all OB/GYN residency programs so that care can be provided, even to patients in rural settings, where an endocrinologist may not be present.

Regarding insurance coverage of the LGBT, efforts must be undertaken so that as many LGBT individuals as possible may receive coverage. Likewise, software developers who are responsible for designing and updating electronic health records should allow room to better describe a patient's gender and said patient's corresponding organs. Insurance companies would likewise need to be more understanding to transgender individuals. They can do this by making stipulations that allow patients who have an unconventional pairing of genitalia and gender to more easily gain coverage. Likewise, insurance companies should also consider bundling health insurance that is specific for the transsexual patient so that said patient could receive better targeted care. Accomplishing such changes requires advocacy from a vocal & credible body, and the American Congress of Obstetricians and Gynecologists is in an excellent position to accomplish this.

Global LGBT care is in its infancy. In the current state, we can only make inferences at best between one culture and another. Pursuing any targeted global LGBT health initiative at this moment is not feasible. Rather than focus efforts outward, a more productive approach would be for healthcare providers to master best practices within their own community first. Over time, practitioners should strive to mature in their treating the LGBT regarding inclusivity, the development of a common vocabulary, and increased access to care. It is when this is achieved that physicians should look to global LGBT care, potentially even using their own practices as standards of care.

As for education, I suggest LGBT knowledge be incorporated into schooling, as early as grade 6, which is the beginning of middle school. I foresee that this will initially be met with some opposition. Nevertheless, I think that over time this will normalize LGBT status and also contribute to an environment that is more inclusive regarding LGBT care.

For my colleagues in the healthcare profession, I suggest that we take time to recognize we face our own intrinsic biases. Though we may be LGBT-inclusive in spirit, healthcare professionals often exclude non-heterosexual individuals without even realizing it. Thus, it is imperative that we, as a community be aware of when this happens and make adjustments accordingly.

Conclusion

Despite the obstacles faced by the LGBT community, the future is bright for these individuals from a healthcare perspective. Medicare has begun including SRS since 2014, and insurance companies have only increased care since that point. Despite the ever-changing landscape of LGBT care, medical schools and residency programs have gone through enormous efforts to incorporate LGBT education into the curriculum. The LGBT community is one that is young and is developing in tandem with future generations of physicians. In time, I foresee these two communities growing in a complimentary fashion, making adjustments as necessary as new problems inevitably arise, until one day soon there will be no difference in the care between the LGBT and natal patients.

References:

1. Alvarez-Wyssmann, V. (2013). Diabetes prevalence and factors associated among patients at an outpatient HIV clinic in Mexico City. Journal of the International AIDS Society, 16(Suppl 1). doi:10.7448/ias.16.2.18664. Accessed 22 Jun 2018.

2. Asscheman, H., Giltay, E. J., Megens, J. A., Ronde, W. D., Trotsenburg, M. A., & Gooren, L. J. (2011). A long-term follow-up study of mortality in transsexuals receiving treatment with cross-sex hormones. European Journal of Endocrinology, 164(4), 635-642. doi:10.1530/eje-10-1038. Accessed 22 Jun 2018.

3. Bangkok Post Public Company Limited. (2013). Katoey face closed doors. Retrieved from https://www.bangkokpost.com/opinion/opinion/355011/katoey-face-closed-doors. Accessed 22 Jun 2018.

4. Bangkok Post Public Company Limited. (2013). The two faces of Thai tolerance. Retrieved From http://bangkokpost.com/news/

investigation/368584/the-two-faces-of-thai-tolerance. Accessed 22 Jun 2018.

5. Bangkok Post Public Company Limited. (2013). We need to fight homophobia at home. Retrieved from https://www.bangkokpost.com/opinion/opinion/1009557/we-need-to-fight-homophobia-at-home. Accessed 22 Jun 2018.

6. Bockting, W. (2010). Stigma, Mental Health, and Resilience Among the U.S. Transgender Population. PsycEXTRA Dataset. doi:10.1037/e609762010-001. Accessed 22 Jun 2018.

7. Calma, RC. (2018). Interview with an OB/GYN [Personal interview]. (2018, June 22).

8. Calma, RC. (2018). LGBT in Omaha, NE [Personal interview]. (2018, June 22).

9. Center for Disease Control. (2015). HIV in the United States: At A Glance. https://www.cdc.gov/hiv/statistics/overview/ataglance.html. Accessed 22 Jun 2018. Center for Disease Control. (2016). Gay and Bisexual Men's Health. https://www.cdc.gov/msmhealth/stigma-and-discrimination.htm. Accessed 22 Jun 2018.

10. Clements-Nolle, K. (2001). HIV prevalence, risk behaviors, health care use, and mental health status of transgender persons: Implications for public health intervention. American Journal of Public Health, 91(6), 915-921. doi:10.2105/ajph.91.6.915. Accessed 22 Jun 2018.

11. Coleman, E. (2017). Standards of Care for the Health of Transsexual, Transgender, and Gender-Nonconforming People. Principles of Gender-Specific Medicine, 69-75. doi:10.1016/b978-0-12-803506-1.00058-9. Accessed 22 Jun 2018.

12. Gale, J. (2015, October 26). How Thailand Became a Global Gender-Change Destination. Retrieved from https://www.bloomberg.com/news/features/2015-10-26/how-thailand-became-a-global-gender-change-destination. Accessed 22 Jun 2018.

13. Green, J. (2014). Transsexual Surgery May Be Covered By Medicare. LGBT Health, 1(4), 256-258. doi:10.1089/lgbt.2014.0076. Accessed 22 Jun 2018.

14. Hoffman, J. (2018, January 20). Estimate of U.S. Transgender Population Doubles to 1.4 Million Adults. Retrieved June 28, 2018, from https://www.nytimes.com/2016/07/01/health/transgender-population.html. Accessed 22 Jun 2018.

15. Hughto, J. M., Reisner, S. L., & Pachankis, J. E. (2015). Transgender stigma and health: A critical review of stigma determinants, mechanisms, and interventions. Social Science & Medicine, 147, 222-231. doi:10.1016/j.socscimed.2015.11.010. Accessed 22 Jun 2018.

16. Khan, Shivananda (February 2005). "Assessment of sexual health needs of males who have sex with males in Laos and Thailand" (PDF). Naz Foundation International. Accessed 22 Jun 2018.

17. Learmonth, C., Viloria, R., Lambert, C., Goldhammer, H., & Keuroghlian, A. S. (2018). Barriers to insurance coverage for transgender patients. American Journal of Obstetrics and Gynecology. doi:10.1016/j.ajog.2018.04.046. Accessed 22 Jun 2018.

18. Light AD, Obedin-Maliver J, Sevelius JM, Kerns JL. Transgender men who experienced pregnancy after female-to-male gender transitioning. Obstet Gynecol 2014;124:1120-7. Accessed 22 Jun 2018.

19. Mott, S. (2017, November 03). Does Medicare Cover Gender Reassignment Surgery? Retrieved from https://medicare.com/coverage/does-medicare-cover-gender-   reassignment-surgery/. Accessed 22 Jun 2018.

20. Proctor, C. D., & Groze, V. K. (1994). Risk Factors for Suicide among Gay, Lesbian, and Bisexual Youths. Social Work, 39(5), 504-513. doi:10.1093/sw/39.5.504. Accessed 22 Jun 2018.

21. Reisner, S (2016). Global health burden and needs of transgender populations: A review. (2016, June 17). Retrieved from https://www.sciencedirect.com/science/article/pii/S014067361600684X. Accessed 22 Jun 2018.

22. Sanders, D (2011). Queer Bangkok: twenty-first-century markets, media, and rights. Aberdeen, Hong Kong: Hong Kong U Press, 2011. Print. Accessed 22 Jun 2018.

23. Unger, C. A. (2014). Care of the transgender patient: The role of the gynecologist. American Journal of Obstetrics and Gynecology, 210(1), 16-26. doi:10.1016/j.ajog.2013.05.035. Accessed 22 Jun 2018.

24. Unger, C. A. (2015). Care of the Transgender Patient: A Survey of Gynecologists Current Knowledge and Practice. Journal of Womens Health, 24(2), 114-118. doi:10.1089/jwh.2014.4918. Accessed 22 Jun 2018.

25. The Williams Institute. (2014). Best Practices for Asking Questions to Identify Transgender and Other Gender Minority Respondents on Populati on-Based Surveys. Retrieved from https://williamsinstitute.law.ucla.edu/wp-content/uploads/geniuss-report-sep-2014.pdf. Accessed 22 Jun 2018.

26. WPATH. (2018). Standards of Care version 7. Retrieved from https://www.wpath.org/publications/soc. Accessed 22 Jun 2018.

27. Xavier, J. (2000). The Washington Transgender Needs Assessment Survey. Retrieved from http://www.glaa.org/archive/2000/tgneedsassessment1112.shtml. Accessed 22 Jun 2018.

Transgender in Omaha: Disparities in Mental Health Care

Kiblinger, Sana

Introduction

The inclusion of homosexuality and gender identity disorder in the *Diagnostic and Statistical Manual of Mental Disorders* shaped transgender patients' interactions with the health care system and providers until 1973. *Stigma,* defined as an inferior status or negative regard toward individuals or groups associated with various conditions or attributes, continues to influence the experience of transgender patients in the health care system to date. (Institute of Medicine, 2011) Studies have found a significantly higher suicide attempt rate (approximately 40%) among transgender person (Moody and Smith, 2013) The health disparities that result from societal stigmas lead to obstacles in mental health care, higher rates of mental illness, or poorer outcomes. This paper discusses the mental health disparities affecting transgender patients, the positive direction of change, and the future steps necessary to support this community.

Background

According to national survey data from 2015, 1.6% of respondents identified as being gay or lesbian. (National Center for Health Statistics, 2018) National population-based surveys in the U.S.—such as the American Community Survey and the National Health Interview Survey— track demographics, health, and well-being of residents; however, they do not yet measure gender identity. The only available data is currently at the state level. A 2016 report based on Center for Disease Control (CDC) state-level data estimates that about 0.6% of the U.S. population (an estimated 1.4 million adults) identify as transgender. This data estimates 0.39% (or 5,400 people) in Nebraska identify as transgender. Similar to the NHIS findings, younger adults (age 18-24) are more likely to identify as transgender. (Flores et. al., 2016) It is important to note these surveys rely on self-identification as transgender, which varies greatly geographically.

What is the Disparity?

In the United States 18.5% of adults suffer from mental illness at a given time. (NAMI, 2018) An estimated 1.9-8.7% of adults in the U.S. have attempted suicide at some point in their lives. Studies with sizable convenience samples of transgender youth report the majority of these youth are well-adjusted and do not exhibit mental health problems. Many studies showing a high prevalence of mental illness in the transgender population were conducted over 20 years ago. However, several more recent studies have again found higher risk of suicidal ideation or suicidal plans in transgender subjects. These studies are consistent with associated variables affecting LGBT youth, including higher rates of "depression, substance use, early sexual initiation, not feeling safe in school, cigarette smoking, and inadequate social support." (Institute of Medicine, 2011)

Given the lack of large data sets measuring how many people identify as transgender, data on suicidal behavior and prevalence of mental illness is also lacking in this group. A 2010 study examining the life course of 571 transgender females aged 19-59 years found similar themes related to major depression and attempted suicide in 15-20% of subjects. (Institute of Medicine, 2011) The National Transgender Discrimination Survey recently surveyed 6,456 self-identified transgender and gender non-conforming individuals in the U.S. and found that 41% of them reported attempting suicide at least once in their life. (Moody and Smith, 2013) With such variable data and concerns for poor mental health care outcomes in transgender patients, it becomes important to evaluate the causes of these disparities.

Why Does the Disparity Occur?

Structural Barriers

Structural stigma is the manifestations of stigma within the institutions of society. For instance, a Health Maintenance Organization (HMO) that provides care for employees' opposite-sex partners or spouses, but not their same-sex partners essentially downgrades the status of sexual minorities. A similar major structural barrier is lack of recognition of same-sex partners or transgender partners as a couple in hospital systems, preventing providers from updating or allowing visitation by those spouses during hospital admission. (Institute of Medicine, 2011, p. 66)

In evaluating other barriers to mental health care for transgender patients, a discussion of personal health insurance benefits cannot be avoided. In "Access to Care Ranking" from 2011 to 2014, change over time revealed state-level policy changes (compared with federal changes) had the greatest impact on access to mental health care. The largest improvement in access occurred in states making aggressive policy changes. For instance, Nebraska took a huge fall from the 7th best state for mental health care access in 2011 to the 32nd best state in 2014. Meanwhile, states like California (who passed the aggressive policy changes in implementing the Mental Health Services Act) rose from 39th best state to 25th best state for mental health care access. In response to the gaps in coverage, Medicaid expansion under the Affordable Care Act played a huge role in improving access to mental health care. Uninsured adults with a mental illness make up 19% of the population in states that did not expand Medicaid; meanwhile in states that did expand Medicaid, only 13% of adults with a mental illness are underinsured. ("2017 State of Mental Health Care", 2017) The reason for Nebraska's major fall in mental health care access could be attributed to lack of Medicaid expansions. Nebraska is one of 18 states that chose not to expand Medicaid coverage under the Affordable Care Act. On a positive note, on November 6, 2018, Nebraskans finally voted to expand Medicaid (against the wishes of their Governor, Pete Ricketts). On November 13, 2018, the Health and Human Services secretary announced that states will now be able to seek Medicaid waivers to cover mental health treatment lasting greater than 16 days; these payments had previously been denied.

A relevant and equally important discussion is the structural barrier that occurs when health care providers are not properly trained in the health needs of transgender patients. Without cultural competency, patient-provider communication is disrupted, resulting in lower likelihood of patient follow-up, barriers to sharing their mental health struggles and stresses, with resulting increases in adverse health behaviors. According to the Association of American Medical Colleges, "Particularly for transgender patients, access to providers who are knowledgeable about transgender health issues is critical… [yet] it is rare for medical students to receive any training in transgender health." (Institute of Medicine, 2011, p. 86)

Individual Barriers

The Institute of Medicine (2011) emphasizes the role of stigma as a barrier to transgender patients' healthcare access. *Enacted stigma* are explicit behaviors that express an individual's stigma, which could include verbal expressions, violence, shunning, and other forms of overt discrimination. Transgender patients can experience this from individual providers or other health care staff. *Felt stigma* is the awareness of the possibility that stigma could be enacted in a given situation. This often results in transgender patients feeling the need to protect themselves from stigma by hiding their gender identity even from their health care provider. *Internalized stigma* can be seen in heterosexuals who may internalize and accept society's negative regard for transgender patients. These providers may feel uncomfortable providing care to transgender patients and therefore provide substandard care. Although it appears 40% of surveyed physicians admitted to feeling uncomfortable treating transgender patients in the 1980s, a repeat survey in 2007 reported 18% of physicians admitting to this discomfort. (Institute of Medicine, 2011)

Family/Social Support

Family rejection due to sexual orientation may be associated with increased risk of suicidality, as studied in 2005 in over 500 LGBT youth. Increase in parental efforts to discourage gender-atypical behavior were associated with increased risk of suicide attempts. A similar 2006 study found that family connectedness, adult caring, and safety in school were protective factors against suicidal ideation or attempt. (Institute of Medicine, 2011) A 2013 survey found "[trans individuals] who reported high levels of family connectedness had almost half the odds of suicidal ideation and attempts than youth who reported lower levels of family connectedness." (Moody and Smith, 2013) To extrapolate these findings to mental health care access, we could connect a higher degree of social and family support to a greater likelihood the transgender individual would feel comfortable reaching out for treatment. No recent studies have yet examined this specific scenario.

Identification of Protective Factors

It is important to distinguish between two different focuses of studies regarding transgender patients and positive mental health outcomes. A large number of earlier studies have focused on factors associated with positive outcomes of sex reassignment surgery and hormonal therapy. These include prior psychological adjustment, family support, psychological treatment, and good surgical outcomes. It is these studies that have influenced the Endocrine Society guidelines regarding endocrine treatment of transsexual persons. (Institute of Medicine, 2011, p. 222) As part of the evaluation of a transsexual person seeking a hormone regimen, "a mental health professional (MHP) must recommend endocrine treatment and participate in ongoing care throughout the endocrine transition and decision for surgical sex reassignment." (Hembree et. al., 2009)

Psychologists in Montreal collected data in a secure survey platform to determine suicide protective factors in transgender individuals. (Moody and Smith, 2013) "Reasons for living" were operationalized in 1983 by a group of researchers as "life-oriented beliefs and expectations that might mitigate against committing suicide." Of the reasons for living, "child-related concerns" had the highest negative correlation with suicide attempt. The study also evaluated the all-important variable of social support, which has long been studied as a protective factor in mental health and in navigating a society where stigma against transgender individuals exists. Dispositional optimism, a trait that reflects a person's favorable expectancies for their future, is another factor considered protective for transgender patients. (Moody and Smith, 2013)

Recommendations

Resilience

The discussion of resilience is an important one in evaluating the progress of the LGBT community as a whole over the last decades. The HIV/AIDS epidemic, though a devastating time for the community, also brought a response of resilience and growth in the form of community-based organizations, advocating organizations, stronger bonds among the LGBT people, and new models of care including support physically, psychologically, and socially. These structures, created in response to the disease in the 1970s, continue even today. (Institute of Medicine, 2011, p. 70)

Moody and Smith (2013) surveyed self-identified transgender subjects in Montreal with the Suicide Resilience Inventory 25 (SRI-25), a 25 item self-report used to assess defense against suicidal ideation and behavior. Essentially, three sub-scales assessed subjects' positive perceptions of their social support, their emotional stability, and their internal satisfaction with themselves and their life overall. Their study found that emotional stability was a very important protective factor against suicidal behavior. Of interest, the value in this sample was lower than prior studies in 2004 and 2008, which indicates that this sample of transgender people could benefit from delivery of interventions aimed to increase suicide resilience and emotional coping techniques through cognitive behavioral therapy. (Moody and Smith, 2013)

Local Resources

In Omaha, the Professional Transgender Resource Network (PTRN) serves as an inter-disciplinary coalition of professionals (established in 2009) to educate and advocate for transgender individuals seeking health care. This group includes a gynecologist specializing in hormone therapy, social workers, sociologists, attorneys, psychotherapists, and a public relations expert. (PTRN, 2018) Nebraska Medicine has a Transgender Clinic geared toward providing support and care for people of all ages and genders in their transition. The Heartland Center for Reproductive Medicine offers fertility preservation for transgender persons. The Open Arms Trans Social Group provides a safe and welcoming environment for transgender youth, children, and their families in Omaha, primarily geared toward supporting and connecting people going through similar experiences. The Proud Horizons youth group provides Omaha residents aged 13 to 23 with a community for GLBT and allies. Heartland Pride, PFLAG, River City Gender Alliance, and Families of Gender Expansive Youth are more family-geared support networks in Omaha. In general, other social structures, such as families, schools, workplaces, churches, and community groups influence transgender peoples' mental health and health care accessibility. These groups should be supported both at the local and national level.

Future Directions

From an early stage, transgender patients are at risk of discrimination due to their orientation and gender status. As summarized in a number of research studies, social and community support is vital in improving mental health as well as health care access for transgender patients. Thus, we need to support legislation and public policy that advocates for LGBTQ individuals and for anti-bullying, safe schools at the state and federal level. Regulations to eliminate inequities based on sexual orientation or gender identity are important. As a group we need to advocate for improved mental health services access through expansion of health insurance. Population based data on LGBT community (tracking sexual orientation and gender preference data) through federal benchmark surveys allows for transgender patients' needs to be adequately evaluated and resourced each fiscal year. (Haas et. al., 2011) Catholic Health Initiatives is in the process of developing and implementing a survey of their patients that includes gender identity and sexual orientation data. Much of the transgender mental health care access issue occurs due to stigma, which is best battled by increasing awareness. Battling for equal rights at the legislative level is the best way to improve access for these patients.

Conclusion

Transgender individuals are more likely to experience mental illness and also less likely to have adequate access to mental health care providers. National survey data lacks gender preference questions, research on mental health care in this population is still lacking, and current data is variable. The most significant studies on the transgender population consistently show a role of stigma; both internalized by transgender patients and thus inhibits their comfort in sharing with their physician, and stigma even among health care providers as they, too, feel uncomfortable treating this population. As multiple studies have demonstrated, the best way to improve transgender patients' outcomes and access to mental health care is through robust community support and legislative action to protect the rights of each individual.

Author Experience

As I watched the LGBT introduction video, I found myself becoming aware of a bias I have not consciously identified before. I felt myself tense as I listened to the story of the *genderqueer* individual and to the frustrations of a male-to-female transgender patient. I realized much of this discomfort is from a lack of familiarity with this group. Where there is misunderstanding and miscommunication, there is some subconscious distrust. I felt that in order to eliminate these fears, I needed to understand this group. Mental health care is very important to me and I recalled— from the "It Gets Better" campaign during my college years— that an access problem exists for the LGBT community. From meeting with Dr. Goodman, I became aware of the prevalence of transgender patients in Omaha. I also became aware of the surprisingly large number of resources Omaha has to offer the transgender community.

Though I did not have a chance to interview a patient who self-identifies as transgender, I listened to several podcasts and YouTube videos by "Gigi Gorgeous", arguably one of the most well-known male-to-female transsexuals. She first became famous on YouTube as she shared her journey of transitioning, using the platform as a diary and gaining support from a large community of followers. I was particularly struck by her recent experience of going to the doctor to talk about fertility and conception with her lesbian partner. She described the difficulty she had bringing up the subject of her being genetically male. The doctor saw them together and immediately began talking about all the options for a lesbian couple to conceive, without realizing that she was genetically male. During that first consultation, she did not have the courage to discuss her desire to be the sperm donor for her wife. I realized that I, too, frequently make assumptions about an individual's gender identity or sexual orientation status. (YouTube, 2018)

As I spoke with a friend who is pursuing a PhD in a field of psychology, I became aware of an opportunity for us medical students. When she was preparing to be a teaching assistant in a statistics class at her University, she had to go through "Safe Space Training". Part of this training involved a panel of students from diverse backgrounds, specifically LGBTQ. These students talked about their experiences in a classroom and ways to make them feel comfortable. On the first day of class, every teaching assistant was required to introduce themselves and make a statement to the class about the safe space and the expectations to uphold.

Writing this paper has been a very eye-opening experience, but I am not yet ready to be "finished" yet. I hope my next steps involve more patient care interactions with LGBTQ patients. I have so much yet to learn about this population and their needs. I would like to hone my skills in taking care of these patients' health needs by hearing from them.

Glossary

Gender identity:

an individual's personal and subjective inner sense of self as belonging to a particular gender (e.g. being a boy/man, girl/woman, genderqueer, transmasculine spectrum, transfeminine spectrum).

Gender nonconforming:

a person who does not conform to prevailing gendered behaviors or roles within a specific society. People who are gender nonconforming may not take part in activities conventionally thought to be associated with their assigned gender. For example, a gender nonconforming male child might wish to dress in girls' clothing and to play exclusively with girls. The term gender variant has been used synonymously.

Genderqueer:

an umbrella category for people whose gender identities are something other than male or female. People who are genderqueer may identify as: having an overlap or indefinite lines between gender identity and sexual and romantic orientation; being two or more genders; being without a gender; or moving between genders or having a fluid gender identity.

Transgender:

individuals who have gender identities that do not align with the gender labels they were assigned at birth.

Transsexual:

historically a term used to refer to a person who has undergone what today are called gender-affirming interventions.

References

1. 2017 State of Mental Health in America - Access to Care Data. (2017, November 15). Retrieved November 11, 2018, from http://www.mentalhealthamerica.net/issues/2017-state-mental-health-america-access-care-data

2. Eisenberg, M. E., & Resnick, M. D. (2006). Suicidality among Gay, Lesbian and Bisexual Youth: The Role of Protective Factors. *Journal of Adolescent Health, 39*(5), 662-668. doi:10.1016/j.jadohealth.2006.04.024

3. Flores, A.R., Herman, J.L., Gates, G.J., & Brown, T.N.T. (2016). *How Many Adults Identify as Transgender in the United States?* Los Angeles, CA: The Williams Institute.

4. Gay and Lesbian Medical Association and LGBT health experts. Healthy People 2010 Companion Document for Lesbian, Gay, Bisexual, and Transgender (LGBT) Health. San Francisco, CA: Gay and Lesbian Medical Association, 2001.

5. Gorgeous, G. (2014, August 20). Retrieved November 14, 2018, from https://www.youtube.com/watch?v=F_waToC5l5M

6. Haas, A. P., Eliason, M., Mays, V. M., Mathy, R. M., Cochran, S. D., D'Augelli, A. R., Silverman, M. M., Fisher, P. W., Hughes, T., Rosario, M., Russell, S. T., Malley, E., Reed, J., Litts, D. A., Haller, E., Sell, R. L., Remafedi, G., Bradford, J., Beautrais, A. L., Brown, G. K., Diamond, G. M., Friedman, M. S., Garofalo, R., Turner, M. S., Hollibaugh, A., ... Clayton, P. J. (2011). Suicide and suicide risk in lesbian, gay, bisexual, and transgender populations: review and recommendations. *Journal of homosexuality, 58*(1), 10-51.

7. Hembree W, Cohen-Kettenis PT, Delemarre-van de Waal HA, et al Endocrine Treatment of Transsexual Persons: An Endocrine Society Clinical Practice Guideline J Clin Endoc Metab, 2009; 94(9): 3132-3154

8. Interview with Claire Shah [Personal interview]. (2018, November 10).

9. IOM (Institute of Medicine). 2011. *The Health of Lesbian, Gay, Bisexual, and Transgender People: Building a Foundation for Better Understanding.* Washington, DC: The National Academies Press.

10. Moody, C., Fuks, N., Pelaez, S., & Smith, N. G. (2013). Protective Factors Against Suicide Among Transgender Adults. *PsycEXTRA Dataset, 5*(42). doi:10.1037/e617502013-001

11. NAMI. (2018). Retrieved November 11, 2018, from https://www.nami.org/Learn-More/Mental-Health-By-the-Numbers

12. National Center for Health Statistics. (2018, November 08). Retrieved November 11, 2018, from https://www.cdc.gov/nchs/nhis/index.htm

13. The Professional Transgender Resource Network (PTRN). (n.d.). Retrieved November 11, 2018, from http://www.ptrnnebraska.com/about-us/)

Mental Health Professionals and PrEP for the LGBTQIA Community

Bosi, Theodore

Introduction

LGBQTIA youth are an at-risk group for homelessness, mental illness, and HIV infection (CDC, 2018), (Durso, 2012), & (Mustanski, 2010). Durso and Gates in 2012 found that 40% of youths in group home, street outreach programs, and other programs for homeless youth identified as LGBQTIA. One third of LGBQTIA people were found to meet the criteria of one or more mental illnesses (Mustanski, 2010), compared to the one fourth of people in the general population. Many of these outreach programs that interact with homeless youth employ social workers, therapists, and other mental health professionals, many of which go on to have a long-term relationship with these providers. Mental health providers whether it be a licensed therapist or a psychiatrist on average spend more time with patients than the average primary care doctor does per visit; therefore, these mental health professionals are uniquely positioned to understand patients' sexual practices, counsel, and treat members of the LGBQTIA community that are at risk for HIV infections.

1.1 million Americans live with a diagnosis of HIV, and in 2016, another 38,500 people became HIV positive (CDC, 2018). The majority, 26,200, were men who had sex with men (CDC, 2018). 68% of new cases of HIV occur in males who have sex with males even though studies estimate that population only makes up 8.2% of Americans (Gates, 2011). Men who have sex with men are the most vulnerable group when it comes to contracting HIV infection. This is why a multitude of practices have been employed in the public health sector to help reduces these rates. A relatively new HIV prevention strategy is pre-exposure prophylaxis or PrEP.

PrEP is a term used for anti-viral medication that can be used to protect individuals from HIV infections (US Public Health Service, 2014). As of now, there is one FDA approved PrEP therapy, which is the Gilead Sciences product Truvada (tenofovir/emtricitabine), but other PrEP are in development. Truvada is a once daily oral medication that has been shown to be effective at preventing HIV infections. Taken as directed, PrEP is 92% effective at preventing HIV infections (Jiang et. Al, 2014). PrEP is FDA approved for the following individuals: Men who have sex with men that are not in a monogamous relationship, a man or woman who is at increased risk for an HIV infection, or anyone who has used IV drugs in the past 6 months (US Public Health Service, 2014). There is also post exposure prophylaxis (PEP) that is a two-drug regiment to be taken at within 72 hours after possible exposure to HIV taken once or twice daily for 28 days. The regiment has been shown to reduce the risk of HIV infection by 81% (Roland et. Al, 2005). There are multiple PEP medications and none have been shown to be better than others.

Background

Out of pocket, Truvada costs $8,000-$14,000 per year (Project Inform, 2018). Although, the company Gilead Sciences has also offered free coverage for some uninsured individuals and co-pay programs for others (Gilead, 2018). There have been a few generic formulations of Truvada that bring the cost down to $50 per year available outside of the United States in some endemic areas, and as of June 2018 there is a FDA approved generic formulation of Truvada available in the U.S., which will be at the very least 80% cheaper than its name brand (Project Inform, 2018). This will further increase access to PrEP throughout the United States.

As far as mental health is concerned, PrEP has no known drug-drug interaction between PrEP and any psychotropic medications (anti-depressants, anti-psychotics, mood stabilizers, etc.) (Ashley, 2018). There are not any contraindications for use of PrEP in those individuals receiving pharmaceutical treatment of substance use disorders. It also has not been shown to cause any worsening in any psychiatric condition, making PrEP overall a safe addition to anyone's medication regiment for mental health conditions (Ashley, 2018).

Public Health

A 2015 meta-analysis of PrEP found that the side effect profile of PrEP to be comparable to aspirin, demonstrating the safety of the drug for the general population (Kojima, 2016). Side effects that were found included changes in fat distribution, nausea, unintentional weight loss, lowering of the white blood cell count, and renal dysfunction (Kojima, 2016). The number needed to harm for a decrease in white blood cell count was 68 with PrEP whereas the number needed to harm for aspirin for moderate gastrointestinal bleed was 123 and 15 for any bruising or non-gastrointestinal bleed (Kojima, 2016). PrEP has only been available for a few years so long term safety has yet to be assessed.

Overall, the incidence of HIV in the United States, decreased by 19% from 2005 to 2014 (Sangaramoorthy, 2017). Although the total numbers are on the decline, pockets with increased rates of infection are popping up in rural and underserved communities, especially in the south which had 52% of new HIV infections in 2015 (Sangaramoorthy, 2017). Increase rates in the south can be contributed to increased poverty and restrictive access to care. 41% of the population in the south lives below the national poverty level, leaving many at risk for being without access to appropriate medical care. Southern states have some of the strictest eligibility for Medicaid. Alabama, the worst offender, only covering individuals below 11% of the national federal poverty line and Mississippi the worst for pharmaceutical plans, only covering a maximum of 5 medications (Sangaramoorthy, 2017). These issues were only exacerbated by these states denying the Medicaid expansion in 2010. The few community-based programs that have tried to fight against the rising rates of

HIV infections in these Southern rural areas have been ineligible for federal funding due to their rural location. In North Carolina, 63% of HIV positive people live outside of these funded areas (Sangaramoorthy, 2017). Policies such as these it makes access to a simple doctor's visit seem like a luxury let alone access to PrEP.

A 2017 10-city survey asked primary care physicians about familiarity and comfortability with PrEP. Of the 525 physicians, 76% had heard of PrEP, whereas only 17% had ever prescribed it before. The most common responses the survey team received when asked why so few felt comfortable with PrEP most common responses were time constraints, dealing with insurance, and lack of knowledge of PrEP, and feeling uncomfortable discussing patients' sexual practices. (Petroll et. al., 2017). This survey gathered physician practices and attitudes 5 years after the approval of PrEP and surveyed physicians in 10 major U.S. cities. Many of these cities have employed multimillion dollar public health initiatives to curb the spread of HIV. If this is the pervasive attitude of physicians in the most densely diverse communities, how can we hope to put a dent in the rising increase in transmission in rural American communities?

A 2018 study tested medical students' abilities to effectively and efficiently find individuals who are most at risk for HIV and decide whether to prescribe PrEP (Calabrese et. al., 2018). The 854 participants were current medical students enrolled in northeastern American medical schools. The study found that these medical students were more hesitant to prescribe PrEP for those who were most at risk for HIV infections but were more than willing to prescribe for those who demonstrated safe sex practices (Calabrese et. al., 2018). It seemed that the students believed that prescribing PrEP to patients with risky sexual behavior condoned their practices, which only hurt patients that would most benefit from intervention. Additional education is clearly necessary to help ameliorate any prejudice notions students have towards the LGBQTIA community. Most medical schools only spend 5 hours of their total curriculum on LGBQTIA health disparities and other unique health issues (Obedin-Maliver J, et al., 2011). Spending appropriate time educating students before they are practicing physicians should improve interactions and interventions for the LGBQTIA community.

Global Perspective

Outside of the United States, a number of countries are working towards solutions to work within their communities. In the United Kingdom, a study titled "Pre-exposure Option for reducing HIV in the UK: immediate or Deferred" reviewed the efficacy of PrEP in the UK in high risk males. The trial found that PrEP reduced the risk of HIV infection by 86% (Dolling, et. al., 2016). Another study, the TDF2 study PrEP effectiveness in Botswana heterosexual couples. Their results were 63% reduction and 84% compliance (Thigpen, et. al., 2012). Each country adopts their own guidelines for how PrEP should be used. As of now some countries do not fully embrace LGBQTIA needs or will help ameliorate their unique health risks. Fortunately, PrEP has been embraced around the globe, so we may see a global reduction in HIV infection. As of 2018, the following governments have outlined their own guidelines for PrEP: Botswana, Canada, European Union, Kenya, Lesotho, South Africa, Uganda, the United Kingdom, Zambia, and Zimbabwe.

Research

In the Omaha community, there are many individuals that are on PrEP. A local provider Dr. Mark Goodman, an HIV specialist, confirmed information of the affordability of PrEP. The quoted figures of $8,000-$14,000 a year are nowhere near what his patients pay for PrEP. Thanks to insurance covering the bulk of the expenses as well as coupons from Gilead, the average out of pocket cost can be as low as $50 a month. He has not seen one patient has been unable to afford PrEP. Dr. Goodman did mention that some patients did seek him out specifically for PrEP when their primary care physicians were unwilling to prescribe it themselves. Other patients heard about his services through the Nebraska AIDS project; a community group that has helped connect patients with HIV or those at risk of HIV with providers that can reduce the risk and spread of HIV. Dr. Goodman has works closely with mental health providers on cases that need additional help managing HIV medications, but has not had a referral for PrEP from any of his mental health colleagues. It is something that he would be willing to assist with if needed. Communication between providers could aid in the risk reduction of the spread of HIV in the Omaha community.

Recommendations

Awareness, access, and affordability are the biggest hurdles in providing care adequate care to the LGBTQIA community, especially when it comes to utilization of PrEP. Emory University has created an interactive map for patients and health care providers to find providers that can prescribe PrEP and PEP for those who are uninsured or underinsured. So even if the current provider cannot offer appropriate intervention due to the cost to the patient, they can refer out to a center that is able to give them the appropriate intervention, providing adequate care regardless of insurance.

A reason many primary care providers claim they do not prescribe PrEP is that the time it would take to adequately have informed patients would take longer than they have per visit (Petroll et. al., 2017). Mental health professionals take exhaustive histories of patient's social and sexual history along with many other factors which would help determine a patient's risk of contracting HIV. Mental health providers also have more time to discuss the risks and benefits of PrEP and can help reduce other risk factors of contracting HIV. It is already common for mental health professionals to screen patients for HIV, going one step further in HIV prevention with PrEP will make a difference to LGBQTIA members at risk for HIV.

Conclusion

40,000 people a year contract HIV, most of which are men who have sex with men. Many cities have employed public health strategies to reduces these numbers with HIV screenings, treatment of those infected, and prevention for those who are at risk. With advancements in access and affordability in PrEP therapy, one of the biggest barrier to care has been awareness. Mental health professionals have a unique relationship with individuals in their care and may be able to get to know individual's sexual practices and counsel them on whether PrEP therapy would be right for them. Some mental providers can prescribe PrEP themselves while others can refer to physicians that can, especially thanks to Emory's PrEP map that shows the closest locations to providers that can provide PrEP regardless of insurance status. With the addition of mental health providers informing patients at-risk patients about PrEP, many overlooked individuals, especially those in the LBGQTIA community will get the care they need.

References

1. Allday, E. (15 September 2017). "Aggressive prevention pays off as new HIV infections in SF hit a record low". SFGate.com. Retrieved 15 December2017.

2. Ashley, K. (2018). Mental Health Clinical Care - Use of Pre-Exposure Prophylaxis (PrEP) for Clients at High Risk of HIV | SAMHSA Knowledge Network. [online] Knowledge.samhsa.gov.

3. Calabrese, S., Earnshaw, V., Underhill, K., Krakower, D., Magnus, M., Hansen, N., Mayer, K., Betancourt, J., Kershaw, T. and Dovidio, J. (2018). Prevention paradox: Medical students are less inclined to prescribe HIV pre-exposure prophylaxis for patients in highest need. 2018 Jun; 21(6): e25147.

4. CDC Estimated HIV incidence and prevalence in the United States, 2010–2015. HIV Surveillance Supplemental Report 2018;23(1).

5. Cochran SD, Sullivan JG, Mays VM. Prevalence of mental disorders, psychological distress, and mental health services use among lesbian, gay, and bisexual adults in the United States. J. Consult. Clin. Psychol. 2003;71:53–61

6. Dolling DI, Desai M, McOwan A, Gilson R, Clarke A, Fisher M, et al. (March 2016). "An analysis of baseline data from the PROUD study: an open-label randomised trial of pre-exposure prophylaxis"

7. Durso LE, Gates GJ. Serving Our Youth: Findings from a National Survey of Service Providers Working with Lesbian, Gay, Bisexual, and Transgender Youth who are Homeless or At Risk of Becoming Homeless. Williams Inst. True Colors Fund, Palette Fund; Los Angeles, CA: 2012

8. Emory University. "PrEP Locator". Emory University PrEP Locator. Emory University. Retrieved 15 December 2017.

9. Gates, GJ. (April 2011). "How many people are lesbian, gay, bisexual, and transgender?". Williams Institute, University of California School of Law.

10. Gilead.com. "TRUVADA FOR PREP MEDICATION ASSISTANCE PROGRAM." (2018). Truvada for PrEP Medication Assistance Program. [online] Available at: http://www.gilead.com/responsibility/us-patient-access/truvada%20for%20prep%20medication%20assistance%20program [Accessed 9 Aug. 2018].

11. Jiang J, Yang X, Ye L, Zhou B, Ning C, Huang J, Liang B, Zhong X, Huang A, Tao R, Cao C, Chen H, Liang H (2014-02-03). "Pre-exposure prophylaxis for the prevention of HIV infection in high risk populations: a meta-analysis of randomized controlled trials". PLOS One. 9 (2): e87674.

12. Kojima N., Klausner J.; Is Emtricitabine-Tenofovir Disoproxil Fumarate Pre-exposure Prophylaxis for the Prevention of Human Immunodeficiency Virus Infection Safer Than Aspirin?, Open Forum Infectious Diseases, Volume 3, Issue 1, 1 January 2016, ofv221, https://doi.org/10.1093/ofid/ofv221

13. Mustanski BS, Garofalo R, Emerson EM. Mental health disorders, psychological distress, and suicidality in a diverse sample of lesbian, gay, bisexual, and transgender youths. Am. J. Public Health. 2010;100:2426–32. Obedin-Maliver J, Goldsmith ES, Stewart L, et al.

14. Petroll AE, Walsh JL, Owczarzak JL, McAuliffe TL, Bogart LM, Kelly JA. PrEP awareness, familiarity, comfort, and prescribing experience

among US primary care providers and HIV specialists. AIDS Behav. 2016;21:1256–67.

15. Project Inform. (2018). The FDA Has Approved Generic PrEP—but Access May Remain Difficult - Project Inform. [online]

16. Roland ME, Neilands TB, Krone MR, et al. Seroconversion following nonoccupational postexposure prophylaxis against HIV. Clinical Infectious Diseases 2005;41(10):1507-13.

17. Sangaramoorthy, T. and Richardson, J. (2017). Why the South still has such high HIV rates. [online] The Conversation. Available at: https://theconversation.com/why-the-south-still-has-such-high-hiv-rates-76386 [Accessed 2 Aug. 2018].

18. Thigpen MC, Kebaabetswe PM, Paxton LA, Smith DK, Rose CE, Segolodi TM, et al. (August 2012). "Antiretroviral preexposure prophylaxis for heterosexual HIV transmission in Botswana". The New England Journal of Medicine. 367 (5): 423–34.

19. US Public Health Service. "PREEXPOSURE PROPHYLAXIS FOR THE PREVENTION OF HIV INFECTION IN THE UNITED STATES - 2014" (PDF). Centers for Disease Control.

Medicine and Law: End of Life Care Considerations for Lesbians, Gay Bisexual and Transgender Patients

Saffold, Joseph

Background

Where medicine and the law intersect, it can make caring for patients complicated. Reflecting on End-of-Life care, new legislation, red tape and hospital policy can make common-sense decisions more complicated. With the national climate changing regarding rights and anti-discrimination policies towards lesbian, gay, bisexual and transgender (LGBT) individuals, new laws have been passed to afford this community equal rights. Barriers to quality healthcare are being addressed at the medical school level up to some healthcare organizations. The American Association of Medical Colleges (AAMC) has pushed to increase the lecture time dedicated to teaching about LGBT patients and their unique needs that extends further than the conversation about HIV and AIDS (Rubin, 2015). In a recent survey of all 176 allopathic and osteopathic medical schools, the median time spent teaching about LGBT topics was 5 hours, with 9 schools having no dedicated class time on these topics. When considering clinical hours, the number increases to 44 schools having no dedicated clinical hours dedicated to LGBT topics (Rubin, 2015). Over the past 10 years, laws have been passed legalizing same-sex marriages (ACLU, 2018), granting same-sex couples visitation protection in hospitals (GLAAD, 2016) and increasing access to healthcare through the Affordable Care Act. This is a step in the right direction for equality for the LGBT community; however, these laws can quickly change and be dismantled depending on the members of congress, the president or the Supreme Court. This reality can cause anxiety especially in LGBT patients whose lives may be greatly impacted by these decisions.

In light of this reality, healthcare providers should be mindful when treating patients. A great starting place is realizing that LGBT patients don't necessarily require special treatment. They require equal treatment which is the same treatment given to heterosexual patients (Higginson, 2009). When considering end of life care (including hospice and palliative care) there has been limited research examining disparities in care given or provided to LGBT patients. However, there have been a few cases that have had national impact and brought about action of the president of the United States in ensuring that same sex couples receive equal rights pertaining to visitation and end of life care. This paper sets out to examine how medicine and the law intersect, how it can cause problems with honoring same sex patients' end of life wishes and give suggestions to providers to empower patients to skillfully navigate through this ever-changing topic.

End of Life Care

Mental health and suicide are common areas of research exploration for the LGBT community. The changing national climate and laws granting same sex couples the right and marry have had a positive impact on the mental health of LGBT people (Raifman, et al., 2018). Comparatively, the change in the laws have not shown to have the same impact on the mental health of heterosexual couples. It is important to keep this in mind when treating patients especially those that identify as LGBT. A study in 2010 showed that the legalization of same sex marriages at the state level in Massachusetts correlated with a 7% risk reduction in suicide among LGBT high school students (Raifman, 2017). LGBT patients in states with laws permitting denial of services to LGBT individuals are associated with a 46% increase mental distress (Raifman, et al.,

2018) versus heterosexual patients. The positive and negative impacts of laws pertaining to same sex rights need further study.

For years, end of life care in relation to the LGBT community focused mainly on men that have sex with men (MSM) and AIDS related deaths (Higginson, 2009). In many of these cases, the prognosis was known months to years in advance and was shared by a trusted, caring and competent health care provider. With the luxury of time, the patient's wishes were able to be discussed, planned and honored. Partners had the opportunity to play a major role in navigating the difficult decisions that lay ahead (Higginson, 2009). When time is not a luxury, LGBT patients and their partners can run into red tape and in some cases be prohibited from seeing their partner or children while dying. This is what happened to lesbian couple, Janice Langbehn and Lisa Pond in Florida (Parker-Pope, 2009). While boarding a cruise ship, Lisa collapsed with a brain aneurysm and was rushed to the hospital. Janice, Lisa's partner of 18 years, was prohibited by hospital staff from seeing or being at her bedside for eight hours. When she was finally allowed in Lisa has slipped into a coma and subsequently died (Parker-Pope, 2009). The guilt felt by Janice is still something she struggles with today (Parker-Pope, 2009). This case claimed the national spotlight and helped bring about a new memorandum signed by then President Barack Obama,

"According to today's announcement, the memorandum directs the Secretary of Health and Human Services (HHS) to promulgate a regulation requiring all hospitals that receive federal Medicare and Medicaid funding – nearly every hospital in America – to allow patients to designate who may visit them and prohibiting discrimination in visitation based on several factors, including sexual orientation and gender identity. In addition, the memorandum calls on the Secretary to issue new guidance and provide technical assistance to hospitals to help them comply with existing federal regulations that require them to respect individuals' advanced healthcare directives and other documents establishing who should make healthcare decisions for them when they are unable to do so. Finally, the memorandum directs HHS to conduct a larger study of the barriers LGBT people and their families face in accessing healthcare." (GLAAD, 2016).

This memorandum cleared up some of the red tape and helped patients by giving their voice power into these decisions. It is important to point out that although this memorandum affects most hospitals, private hospitals that do not receive federal Medicare and Medicaid funding are exempt from these changes.

End of life and hospice care can present unique challenges for LGBT patients. The pain of the loss of a loved one can have a lasting impact on the patient's partner, children, family and caretakers.

"The bereaved person's perception of the circumstances surrounding the death has been shown to be related to bereavement outcomes. Poor bereavement outcomes, such as depression, are associated with caregiver perceptions of poor quality end-of-life care for the person, and perceived inadequacy of informational, instrumental, social and psychological support for themselves" (Higginson, 2009).

The distress can be compounded for those patients whose sexual orientation has not been disclosed to those close to them or not openly acknowledged by healthcare professionals. Navigating end of life care for same sex couples should focus on providing the patients equal rights and respecting their wishes regarding who they want around and who can be involved in making healthcare decisions on their behalf. (Higginson, 2009). When relationships are not recognized, bereaved partners and friends miss out on the social support necessary for coping with grief (Blevins, et al., 2006). For gay and lesbian patients, failure by family members and health professionals to acknowledge the appropriate decision-maker at the end of life causes additional grief, loss of dignity and loss of property upon the death of same-sex partners.

For transgender people, the lack of recognition of their chosen gender identity, or the humiliation of having to explain that they are transgender, can cause issues (Cartwright, et al., 2016). As LGBT patients grow older, the social support around them can become smaller and smaller. LGBT patients and couples that do not have adult children can be left with less social support as they age. Children can play an important role in advocating for their parents and caring for their parents as they age and towards the end of their lives. This can be a unique challenge faced by LGBT patients that impacts their end of life care.

Family can also complicate end-of-life care and decisions. Fortunately, the law has changed by granting same sex couples the right to marry and the benefits afforded married couples. The legalization of same sex marriage has made it easier for same sex spouses to visit, be informed about patient progress and be proxies in the case of an incapacitated spouse. Although same sex couples now have the right to marry, some may choose not to, even though they are in a committed relationship. This can complicate end of life considerations and have an impact after the patient has died. A sad example of this was shared by Dr. Goodman about a same sex couple that had been together for many years. The couple lived together and had built a life together. Sadly, one of the partners became sick and subsequently passed away. Amid dealing with the pain of losing a loved one, the patient's family, which lived out of town, arrived and told the partner that they needed to immediately move out of the house the two had shared (Goodman, 2018). Due to the laws at that time, the family was able to step in where the partner should have been in being updated on progress, increased visitation and the role of surrogate decision maker for the patient if needed. The couple had not been able to marry, legally leaving the property and assets to the family of the deceased.

Recommendations

Healthcare providers can help ease or add to patient distress in navigating the intersection of medicine and law at it relates to LGBT issues. This is without regard to what the law says or the national climate in relation to same sex couples. All patients should be treated with respect and dignity, especially those dealing with terminal illnesses and the ending of life. It should be the goal of all health care providers to ease distress during this difficult time. Healthcare professionals can either ease the distress of the bereavement journey through sensitive caring for the couple or exacerbate the distress by thoughtless practice or comments (Higginson, 2009).

As health care providers we should take time to get to know our patients and work with them to achieve their health goals, including their end of life wishes. All primary care providers should have a conversation with every adult patient about end of life wishes, advanced directives, powers of attorney for healthcare and proxies for decision making. This is particularly important for LGBT patients due to how quickly the law can change. Having the proper documentation can give you peace of mind regardless of the changes in the law. In a survey of 575 gay and lesbian people in the US, Stein and Bonuck (2001) found that, despite high levels of knowledge about health care proxies (72%) and advance health care directives (90%), only about half of the participants had completed these documents. Reasons given included: not necessary now (28%); not knowing who to appoint (25%); hard to think about (20%); don't know where/how to do it (18%); and haven't found the time (18%). These reasons are comparable to other studies in the general population (Cartwright et al. 1998; Fagerlin and Schneider 2004; Steinberg et al. 1997) Having these conversations can also give health care providers insight and perspective. Advance care planning can assist patients to plan for the treatment they will or will not receive during the dying process, and to appoint a substitute decision-maker to ensure that their wishes are respected (Cartwright, et al., 2012).

It can be easy for heterosexual individuals to be ignorant to the changes in laws pertaining to same sex couples because they do not have much impact on their daily lives. The research has shown that many of the laws that affect same sex couples also affect their mental health and utilization of health care. (Raifman, 2018) and suicide attempts (Raifman, 2017).

Global Impact

Many of the concerns shared in this paper are echoed globally. As the international attitude changes towards the LGBT community, increasing numbers of countries are legalizing same-sex marriage and passing anti-discrimination laws. Fear of discrimination and bias was a major barrier to accessing healthcare by LGBT peoples in a study done in Australia (Cartwright, et al., 2012). With the law now giving more support and rights to LGBT individuals, hopefully, many of these barriers and concerns will be less frequently experienced by any patient. Support for same-sex marriage has continued to increase across Latin America with many Latin American countries legalizing same-sex marriage and affording these couples protection under the law (Lodola, 2010).

Conclusion

When same-sex and other important relationships are communicated to and recognized by families and health professionals, and when advance care planning is well organized and communicated to significant people, it is possible for LGBT people to experience appropriate end-of-life care and to die with dignity. It is important to recognize the barriers to care and eliminate them with the goal of creating a safe supportive environment for LGBT patients. Discrimination, bias and health care provider ignorance can stand in the way of LGBT patients seeking out a care provider and at times delaying life saving care. (Cartwright, et al., 2012). A top down approach aimed at improving care given to LGBT patients includes examining and potentially revising organizational policy all the way down to healthcare providers reflecting on their own biases and obstacles that prevent them from delivering quality care. Fostering a supportive environment that empowers patients to be actively involved in their healthcare decisions helps achieve better outcomes for patients and providers. Establishing rapport and an open relationship with patients can ease the difficulty of broaching difficult subjects such as end of life arrangements. Although death is unpleasant to think about, it is important to talk with patients and their families about end of life care and arrangements. These conversations can help give the provider an opportunity to learn more about the patient's support system and offer referrals to programs and social services prior to an emergency or the end of the patient's life. Staying current on laws that affect LGBT patients, understanding the role healthcare providers play in patient's healthcare decisions, and cultivating a relationship that empowers patients to ask difficult questions so they can be involved in their care are just a few easy ways to help improve care given to LGBT people and create more competent health care providers

References

1. ACLU. (2016). *Past Anti-LGBT Religious Exemption Legislation Across the Country.* Retrieved from American Civil Liberties Union: https://www. aclu.org/other/past-anti-lgbt-religious-exemption-legislation-across-country?redirect=anti-lgbt-religious-refusals-legislation-across-country

2. Blevins, D. a. (2006). End-of-life issues for LGBT older adults. In Lesbian, gay, bisexual and transgender aging: Research and clinical perspectives, ed. D. *New York: Columbia University Press.*, 206-26.

3. Cartwright CM, H. M. (2012). End-of-life care for gay, lesbian, bisexual and. *Culture, Health & Sexuality: An International Journal for Research, Intervention and Care*, vol. 14, no. 5, pp. 537-548.

4. Cartwright, C. (2012). Ethical Challenges in End-of-Life Care for GLBTI Individuals. *Bioethical Inquiry*, 9:113-114.

5. GLAAD. (2011, September 14). *GLAAD Applauds Presidential Memorandum Adding Hospital Visitation Protections for Same-Sex Couples.* Retrieved from GLAAD: https://www.glaad.org/2010/04/16/ glaad-applauds-presidential-memorandum-adding-hospital-visitation-protections-for-same-sex-couples/

6. Goodman, M. (2018, June 21). Personal Conversation. Omaha, NE.

7. Higginson, A. &. (2009). Sculpting the distress: easing or exacerbating the grief experience of same-sex couples. . *International Journal Of Palliative Nursing,*, 15(4), 170-176.

8. Lodola, G. C. (2010). *Support for Same-Sex Marriage in Latin America.* Retrieved from Insights Vanderbilt University: https://www.vanderbilt. edu/lapop/insights/I0844.enrevised.pdf

9. Parker-Pope, T. (2009, May 18). *Kept From a Dying Partner's Bedside.* Retrieved from The New York Times: https://www.nytimes.com/2009/05/19/health/19well.html

10. Raifman J, M. E. (2017). Difference-in-Differences Analysis of the Association Between State Same-Sex Marriage Policies and Adolescent Suicide Attempts. *JAMA Pediatrics,* 171(4):350–356.

11. Raifman J, M. E. (2018, May 23). *Association of State Laws Permitting Denial of Services to Same-Sex Couples With Mental Distress in Sexual Minority AdultsA Difference-in-Difference-in-Differences Analysis.* Retrieved from JAMA Psychiatry. : doi:10.1001/jamapsychiatry.2018.0757

12. Rubin, R. (2015, June 24). Minimizing Health Disparities Among LGBT Patients. *JAMA,* 313(1):15–18. Retrieved from JAMA: doi:10.1001/jama.2014.17243

A Literature Review and Discussion of the Incidence and Prevalence of Mental Health Issues in the LGBTQIA Community

Clark, Tiffany

Introduction

There has been increasing attention given to closing the Health Disparities Gap affecting various marginalized groups of people within the United States. The Health Disparities Gap is not only leading to detrimental health outcomes, but the gap is attributing to rising healthcare costs. Over the recent years, extensive research has been done focusing on the increasing health care gap affecting patients based on race and ethnicity. However, there has been very little research done examining patients' sexual orientation and how sexual preference and/or gender identification can impact healthcare outcomes.

The Lesbian, Gay, Bisexual, Transgender, Transsexual, Queer, Questioning, Intersex, Intergender, Asexual/Aromantic (LGBTQIA) community is often overlooked in the context of health disparities. The associated terms used to describe the community can become complex for the lay person, therefore, it is important to provide clarification when referencing these terms used as self-identifiers. The language used to describe each individual compromising this group is located in the LGBTQIA terminology section of the paper.

In one of the largest, single study of the distribution of the lesbian, gay, bisexual and transgender population in the United States, 3.4% of adults said "yes" when asked if they publicly identify as a member of the LGBT community (Gates & Newport, 2012). Unfortunately, social stigma and cultural influences may have influenced participants' disclosure; therefore, the percentage may actually be higher among the individuals surveyed. Additionally, the national survey results demonstrate that there is a higher rate of identification as a LGBT member among African Americans, Hispanics and Asians compared to the Caucasian population (Table 1). The increasing trend of individuals identifying with the LGBTQIA community, prompted a more thorough examination of the health disparities affecting this group, especially regarding mental health. This paper will address the occurrence of mental illness among this community and disclose contributing factors, in an effort to provide conscious resolutions to deal with such critical issues.

Table 1

Do you, personally, identify as lesbian, gay, bisexual, or transgender?

	Yes %	No %	DK/Ref %
Non-Hispanic white	3.2	93.9	2.8
Black	4.6	90.1	5.3
Hispanic	4.0	90.2	5.8
Asian	4.3	92.0	3.7

Gallup Daily tracking
June 1-Sept. 30, 2012

GALLUP

Gender Dysphoria Disorder:

Gender Dysphoria, previously named Gender Identity Disorder (GID) in the Diagnostic and Statistical Manual of Mental Disorders – Fourth Edition

(DSM –IV), is a condition in which someone is intensely uncomfortable with their biological gender and strongly identifies with, and wants to be, the opposite gender (1994). Furthermore, the disagreement between birth gender and personal identification must cause the individual distress. The classic estimate for prevalence of GID comes from the DSM-IV, which reported 1:30,000 natal males and 1:100,000 natal females (1994). One study suggests that between 0.5%-2% of the population have strong feelings of being transgender and between 0.1%- 0.5% actually take steps to transition from one gender to another (Conway,2002). However, the true prevalence is likely to be underestimated due to societal and cultural stigmatization that could lead to a lack of disclosure to health care providers.

The distress of feeling uncomfortable in one's own body and outside the gender norms can majorly impact one's mental psyche. Atypical gender expression in childhood has been correlated with more experiences of abuse and mental health problems in childhood and adolescence. In a two year longitudinal study of 528 lesbian, gay and bisexual youth, the effects of the youth's nonconforming gender identity and sexual orientation on their mental health was examined. Nearly 80% reported verbal victimization, 11% physical victimization and 9% sexual victimization with males reporting significantly more victimization. Post Traumatic Stress Disorder (PTSD) was found in 9% of the youth and was associated with past physical victimization (D'Augelli, Grossman & Starks, 2006).

Additionally, the study highlighted the issue of victimization and stigma within one's own family. Nearly 30% of LBGT youth considered gender atypical by parents reported parental efforts to discourage gender nonconforming behaviors: 53% were told to change their behavior, 12% were punished or restricted in their activities and 8% were sent to counseling. (D'Augelli et al., 2006). The possibility of harsh family rejection and harassment not only contributes to an unhealthy internalization of emotions by LGBTQIA members, but strained family relationships can further complicate financial and housing stability. According to the National Transgender Discrimination Survey, a large percentage of Transgender survey respondents reported experiencing housing insecurity due to their gender identity, with 26% having to find a different place to sleep for a short period of time and 19% became homeless (2009).

Victimization, familial stigma and the denial of basic human rights are harsh realities for many members of the LGBTQIA struggling with gender identity issues and serve as major barriers when attempting to seek medical treatment for associated mental health issues. It is important for society and health care professionals to become educated about the issues that affect the LBGTQIA community so they may be addressed, in order to promote health and well-being among this community of individuals.

Suicide

The unique challenges the LGBTQIA community faces, as mentioned above, can create vulnerability within an individual. This vulnerability along with a lack of familial and/or social support can lead to isolation and feelings of helplessness for an individual struggling with his or her sexual identity and/ or gender identity. The most susceptible appear to be LBGTQIA youth, who are two to three times more likely to attempt suicide than other young people and might compose of up to 30% of youth suicides annually (Gibson, 1989). Additionally, according to data from a Minnesota Student Survey of 21,927 LBGTQIA 9th and 12th grade students, over half of the students had "thought about" suicide and 37.4% reported a "suicide attempt" (Eisenberg & Resnick, 2006). One of the most important protective factors used to guard against suicide among LGBTQIA youth is school safety. In fact, more recently, there has been more attention on suicide ideation and attempts among LBGTQIA youth due to an increase in the rate of bullying at schools. In 2010, there was a call for stronger anti-bullying laws in Indiana after 15 year old Billy Lucas hung himself from the rafters of his barn due to constant bullying by his peers on the basis of his sexual orientation. In May 2015, there was a call for more proactive measures against bullying in Wisconsin when 15 year old Cameron Langrell, committed suicide just days after announcing to friends and classmates that she identified as a transgender girl on Facebook.

In addition to school safety, family connectedness and having a caring adult present in one's life are additional protective factors that guard against suicide. Among those that attempted suicide based on the Minnesota Student Survey mentioned above, almost half of the participants reported that their fathers were intolerant or rejecting of their sexual orientation, compared with approximately one-quarter among those that had never attempted suicide (Eisenberg & Resnick, 2006). Untreated mental illness among LGBTQIA youth influences suicide ideation and should be considered as one of the strongest motivators to commit suicide. Combining results from 25 international adolescent and adult studies, researchers found depression, anxiety disorders, and substance use disorders to be 1.5 times more common in LGBT people than in comparable heterosexual individuals (King, et. El, 2008). In a personal interview with Hussein, the medical student Founder of Creighton University's School of Medicine LGBTQIA student organization, he commented on the issue of mental illness: " There is a lot of depression, substance abuse and suicidal ideation among members of the LBGTQIA community regardless of socioeconomic status, because people are internalizing their emotions about being queer and not accepted by society, which not only manifests itself as self-hate, but encourages risky behavior" (2016).

Health Care's Impact on Addressing Health Disparities among the LGBTQIA Community

Discrimination and Barriers to Care:

In a survey conducted by Lambda Legal, out of the 4,916 survey respondents, 56% of the LGBT respondents experienced at least one of the following types of discrimination in healthcare: being refused needed care, health care professionals refusing to touch them or using excessive precautions; health care professional using harsh or abusive language; being blamed for their health status; or healthcare professionals being physically rough or abusive (2010). Even more appalling, almost 8% of LGBT respondents reported that they had been denied needed health care outright and almost 27% of transgender and intergender individuals reported being denied care Due to their discriminatory experiences, survey respondents reported a high degree of anticipation and belief that they would face discriminatory care, which may impair their decision to seek future care. Overall, 9% of LGBT respondents and over half of transgender and gender-nonconforming respondents shared the concern about being refused medical services when they needed them (Legal Lambda, 2010).

The perceived discrimination is a major barrier that many LGBTQIA members not only have to endure when receiving care, but the discrimination also prevents them from seeking care, which is a major contributing factor for the health disparity gap among the marginalized group. For instance, it has been found that lesbian and bisexual women may use preventive health services less frequently than heterosexual women, consequently, it appears as though LGBTQIA adults may experience more mood and anxiety disorders, such as depression and suicidal ideation and attempts compared with heterosexual adults (National Academics Press, 2011). A study done in the United States found that lesbians and bisexual women who were " out" (of the closet) experienced more emotional stress as teenagers and were 2 to 2.5 times more likely to experience suicidal ideation in the past 12 months than heterosexual women. According to a report published by the U.S. Department of Health and Human Services: Substance Abuse and Mental Services, lesbian and bisexual women who were not "out"(of the closet) were more likely to have attempted suicide than heterosexual women. (2012). Although, there is a lack of extensive research on the prevalence of mental illness among the LGBTQIA community, it is evident that the negative attitudes and behaviors of health care providers towards this community can have long lasting and detrimental effects.

Further Recommendations:

- -Create a LGBTQIA friendly and welcoming environment such as, providing LGBTQIA magazines in the waiting room, visible support symbols for LGBTQIA community, etc.

- -Elimination of discriminatory sexual orientation and gender semantics used in medical terminology (ex. Gender Identity Disorder)

- Develop an anonymous physician evaluation system for patients to assess their sensitivity towards LGBTQIA issues.

- Develop a national database of healthcare providers that are competent and comfortable treating LBGTQIA patients that is readily accessible to patients.

- Expand public and private funding for research on the most prominent issues the LGBTQIA community deals with.

Culturally Competent Training & Education:

In order to address the issues affecting the LGBTQIA community, one has to first be aware of the issues. Hussein shared his experience as a member of the LBGTQIA community and medical student, in which he experienced insensitive remarks made by professors in class, in addition to poorly worded, inconsiderate test questions regarding issues affecting the LGBTQIA community. The nonchalant attitude carried over to his fellow students, who would make comments about the insignificance of LGBTQIA issues, because they did not think they would have encounters with these types of patients in their future careers.

The AAMC has taken the lead in addressing the gap in cultural competent education regarding LGBTQIA issues. In 2014, the organization released the first guidelines for training physicians to care for people of the LGBTQIA community. The guidelines identify 30 competencies that physicians must master that fall under eight domains of care critical to training physicians, including: patient care, knowledge for practice, practice-based learning and improvement, interpersonal and communication skills, professionalism, systems-based practice, interprofessional collaboration, and personal and professional development. Furthermore, the AAMC convened an Advisory Committee on Sexual Orientation, Gender Identity, and Sex Development to develop a set of consensus-driven educational goals to directly address issues of sex, sexuality, and gender-related clinical care. In 2012, the committee introduced *Implementing Curricular and Institutional Climate Changes to Improve Health Care for Individuals Who Are LGBT, Gender Nonconforming, or Born with DSD: A Resource for Medical Educators.*

Further Recommendations:

- Continue to develop strong guidelines for the treatment of LGBT patients in all disciples as appropriate

- Discourage "Othering" In Medical School Curriculum: Move Away from thinking about LGBTQIA patients as separate from general population

- Ensure that medical school educational curriculum and residency training offers educational materials related to LGBTQIA mental health needs and suicide risk

- Encourage student-led and student organized school clubs that promote safe, welcoming and accepting school environment for LGBTQIA members

Patient Sexual Orientation Self-Disclosure

Primary care physicians are in many cases the first people that LGBTQIA individuals confide in about their sexual orientation and/or gender identity preference. There is evidence that when lesbians do come out it, it is often only after trust is established with a healthcare provider and that can happen long into the relationship (Harvey & Housel, 2014). Therefore, it is important that physicians are prepared to handle such a sensitive topic when the issues arise. In an enlightening interview with Hussein, he described his experience "coming out" to his health care provider: " My provider was really encouraging and gave me great advice. She instructed me to first "come out" to a close friend and when I was ready to come out to my parents, she suggested that I should have a back-up plan for an alternative place to stay in case it didn't go well".

Even if a patient does not readily introduce the "coming out" conversation to healthcare providers, the physician can encourage disclosure by establishing routine sexual health and orientation inquires for patient encounters. In a study examining the effects of routine sexual health questioning, all of two participants said they came out to a physician during routine questioning or in some cases when the physician asked a heteronormative question and participants didn't want to lead the physician down a wrong path (Harvey & Housel, 2014). As noted previously in the paper, there is a clear link between the internalization of emotions about sexual orientation and mental illness. When physicians demonstrate compassionate concern about patients' sexual orientation and sexual health, patients feel comfortable in verbalizing the negative emotions they have internalized, which if go unchecked can manifest into deeper mental health issues.

Further Recommendations:

- Implement Routine Sexual Health Questioning into Clinical Encounters with Patients
- Avoid language that suggest an assumed gender identity and/or sexual orientation
- Patient-Physician Confidentiality Policies should be visible to patients during healthcare encounters
- Provide more inclusive options in regards to relationship/relation status on screening questionnaires prior to physician encounters
- Increase training and education in regards to the four elements of a "coming out" conversation and learning the appropriate response (Practice Conversation, Safety Plan, etc.)

Conclusion:

Healthcare providers play a more pivotal role than imagined in caring for the LGBTQIA community. The office or hospital setting can either a safe space to talk about their concerns or a place where they continue to be victimized and discriminated against. After extensive literature review and conversations with LGBTQIA community members and healthcare providers, I have gained a deeper appreciation for my role in helping to facilitate a discussion about sexual orientation and/or gender identity concerns with the patients I will encounter.

It is not enough to be familiar with the "coming out" conversation patients might introduce, but I need to learn how to respond in a responsible, competent manner to ensure the safety and intact mental health of my patients. Moreover, there are additional steps I can take to create a welcoming atmosphere for patients, such as showing visible support for the human and civil rights of the LGBTQIA community and being more cognizant of my personal and professional affiliations that have in the past, historically discriminated against the LBGTQIA community. Hippocrates once said, " The life so short, the craft so long to learn". This quote is a great reminder that there is much work to do regarding LGBTQIA health disparities and I intend to sharpen my craft by learning how to better address this community's issues with the tools and knowledge I gain along the way.

LGBTQIA Terminology

Lesbians and Gay people are individuals who are romantically and/or sexually attracted to and/or sexually active with people of the same gender. Lesbian refers exclusively to women, while gay can refer to either women or men.

Bisexual people are attracted to and/or sexually active with people regardless of gender. Transgender is a word commonly used to describe people who live in a gender different from the one assigned to them at birth, similar to the term Transsexual.

A Transsexual, which is an older tem that originated in the medical and psychological communities, is an individual who emotionally and psychologically feels that they belong to the opposite sex.

Queer is an identity used by people who reject conventional categories such as "LGBT" or may include heterosexuals who embrace non-normative or counter-normative sexual identity.

Intersex is a general term used for a variety of conditions in which a person is born with the reproductive or sexual anatomy that doesn't seem to fit the typical definitions of female or male. The older tem hermaphrodite was replaced by intersex.

Intergender is a gender identity between, among, or in the midst of the binary genders of male/masculine and female/feminine.

An Asexual/Aromantic person is an individual who is not interested in or does not desire sexual activity, either within or outside of a relationship.

References:

1. Conway, L. How Frequently Does Transexualism Occur? Web-published document, 2002. {Accessed: May 2, 2016] Available from http://ai.eecs. umich.edu/people/conway/TS/Tsprevalence.html.

2. D'Augelli ARGrossman AHStarks MT Childhood gender atypicality, victimization, and PTSD among lesbian, gay, and bisexual youth. *J Interpers Violence* 2006;21 (11) 1462- 1482

3. *Diagnostic and statistical manual of mental disorders: DSM-IV.* (1994). Washington, DC: American Psychiatric Association.

4. Eisenberg M. E., Resnick M. D. Suicidality among gay, lesbian and bisexual youth: The role of protective factors. Journal of Adolescent Health. 2006;39:662–668.

5. Gates, G., & Newport, F. (2012). *Special Report: 3.4% of U.S. Adults Identify as LGBT* (Rep.). Washington, D.C.: Gallup.

6. Gibson P. Gay male and lesbian youth suicide. In: Alcohol, Drug Abuse, and Mental Health Administration. Report of the Secretary's Task Force on Youth Suicide, Volume 3: Prevention and Interventions

in Youth Suicide (DHHS Pub No. (ADM)89-1623). Washington, DC: Superintendent of Documents, US Government Printing Office, 1989.

7. Harvey, V. L., & Housel, T. H. (2014). *Health care disparities and the LGBT population.* Lanham, MD: Lexington Books.

8. Health Disparities & Healthcare Among the LBGTQIA Community [Personal interview]. (2016, May 28).

9. *Implementing Curricular and Institutional Climate Changes to Improve Health Care for Individuals Who Are LGBT, Gender Nonconforming, or Born with DSD: A Resource for Medical Educators.* (pp. 1-306, Rep.). (2014). Washington, DC: AAMC. doi:www.aamc.org/publications

10. King M., Semlyen J., Tai S. S., Killaspy H., Osborn D., Popelyuk D., et al. A systematic review of mental disorder, suicide, and deliberate self-harm in lesbian, gay, and bisexual people. BMC Psychiatry. 2008, August 18;8:70. Retrieved May 1, 2009, from http://www.ncbi.nlm.nih.gov/pmc/articles/PMC2533652

11. *When Health Care Isn't Caring: Lambda Legal's Survey of Discrimination Against LGBT People and People With HIV* (pp. 1-26, Publication). (2010). New York City, NY: Lambda Legal.

12. *National Transgender Discrimination Survey* (pp. 1-4, Rep.). (2009). Washington, DC: National Center for Transgender Equality and National Gay and Lesbian Task Force.

13. Substance Abuse and Mental Health Services Administration, *Top Health Issues for LGBT Populations Information & Resource Kit.* HHS Publication No. (SMA) 12-4684. Rockville, MD: Substance Abuse and Mental Health Services Administration, 2012.

14. *The Health of Lesbian, Gay, Bisexual and Transgender People: Building a Foundation for Better Understanding* (pp. 1-368, Rep.). (2011). Washington, DC: National Academics Press.

An Exploration of Health Disparities in LGBTQ American Indian/Alaska Natives

Bahe, Brianna

Introduction

Few groups are so marginalized and overlooked as Lesbian, Gay, Bisexual, Transgender, and Queer/Questioning (LGBTQ) communities and American Indian/Alaska Native (AI/AN) communities. While more research is being done on LGBTQ communities, still little is known about the intersection of the LGBTQ and AI/AN communities. Few studies have been done on those who identify as LGBTQ and who are part of an AI/AN tribe. Further complicating matters is the enormous diversity of AI/AN tribes and cultures. There are over 500 federally recognized AI/AN tribes and each of these has their own rich histories and cultures (Indian Health Services, 2019). These weave together to shape the experience of those individual tribe members who also identify as LGBTQ, as some tribes are accepting of such individuals and some are not. Historically, both groups have experienced healthcare inequities so it stands to reason that those individuals at the intersection of these two groups may experience at least as many inequities as each individual group, if not more. This paper seeks to explore the healthcare disparities among LGBTQ Natives and to give recommendations about how we, as healthcare providers, can combat these inequities.

A quick note on terminology: the many rich histories and cultures of AI/AN tribes also means that there are many different opinions on what members of AI/AN tribes should be called. Older generations are accustomed to referring to themselves as "Indians," as English speakers historically have referred to the indigenous tribal members here (Yellow Bird, 1999). Official US documents such as the census still refer to these individuals as "American Indians/Alaska Natives." However, younger generations of the tribes often prefer the term, "Indigenous" or "Native," (Yellow Bird, 1999). For simplicity, in this paper, we will refer to individuals as "Natives" and collectively as "American Indian/Alaska Natives" or AI/AN for consistency with the terminology of other papers and with legal documents.

Along the same lines, the experiences of LGBTQ-identifying individuals are also incredibly diverse and varied. These groups of individuals get lumped together under the umbrella term "LGBTQ." Some preliminary reading on the topic also reveals, much like with Natives, there is no consensus on what LGBTQ-identifying individuals should be called. Some prefer the term, "queer," while others prefer "LGBT" or their individual identity, such as "lesbian" or "gay," (National LGBT Health Education Center, 2016). Furthermore, these terms are also constantly evolving as we find new ways to express the beautiful diversity in sexual identity and expression. Similarly, to our reasoning above, we will use the terminology "LGBTQ-identifying individuals" or "LGBTQ communities" for simplicity and inclusivity, as past documents and articles refer to these individuals as such.

Background

A quick search online quickly yields several studies, large and small, about the healthcare inequities consistently experienced by LGBTQ-identifying individuals. According to the Centers for Disease Control (CDC):

Members of the LGBT community are at increased risk for several health threats when compared to their heterosexual peers. Differences in sexual behavior account for some of these disparities, but others are associated with social and structural inequities, such as the stigma and discrimination that LGBT populations experience. (Centers for Disease Control, 2014).

Furthermore, mental health issues and suicide continue to be huge issues facing these populations, especially among transgender individuals (Clements-Noelle et al, 2006).

The CDC has also conducted studies on Native healthcare disparities. They wrote, "American Indians/Alaska Natives (AI/AN) have a lower life expectancy, a lower quality of life, and a higher prevalence of many chronic conditions," (Centers for Disease Control, 2018).

Public Health

An entire paper could be written on public health implications for both LGBTQ communities and AI/AN communities individually. According to the American Public Health Association, public health, "promotes and protects the health of people and the communities where they live, learn, work and play," (American Public Health Association, 2020). Public health plays an extremely important role in the health and wellness of both these communities as it addresses potential barriers to healthy living or receiving adequate healthcare.

Three major issues affecting both LGBTQ and AI/AN communities at higher rates than others are mental health issues, suicide, and violence. According to the Indian Health Services (IHS) statistics, Natives are 2.1 times more likely die from homicide and 1.7 times more likely to die from suicide compared to their non-Native counterparts (Indian Health Services, 2019). In a 2006 study on interpersonal violence in AI/AN women published in the American Journal of Public Health, 64.5% of women surveyed endorsed experiencing a period of depression in their lifetimes (Evans-Campbell et al, 2006). In that same study, 65.5% of respondents endorsed experiencing at least one instance of interpersonal violence in their lifetime (Evans-Campbell et al, 2006). The implications of the statistics is summarized best in this statement from the Substance Abuse and Mental Health Services Administration (SAMHSA);

For American Indians and Alaska Natives, multiple factors influence health outcomes, including historical trauma and a range of social, policy, and economic conditions such as poverty, under-employment, lack of access to health care, lower educational attainment, housing problems, and violence.

These disparities have consequences. Suicide is the second leading cause of death among American Indian and Alaska Native youth ages 8 to 24. Also, while there is general awareness that Native Americans experience higher rates of alcohol and substance use, the scope of these behavioral health problems is not fully understood.

Native communities face service delivery issues that are complicated by personnel shortages, limited health care resources, and distances to obtain services. There also are other issues that inhibit access to appropriate behavioral health services such as referrals from school, detention, court, housing, primary care, child welfare, and other systems (Substance Abuse and Mental Health Services Administration, 2020).

Furthermore, several studies have established that LGBTQ youth and adolescents are more likely to experience bullying, depression, and have suicidal ideation compared to their non-LGBTQ peers (Baams et al, 2018, 2019, Kelleher, 2009, Hafeez et al, 2017, Centers for Disease Control, 2019). Alarmingly, according to FBI statistics, hate crimes directed against LGBTQ individuals based on their sexual identity have been increasing over the past few years (U.S. Department of Justice, 2018). These crimes target gay men and transgender women (U.S. Department of Justice, 2018). There is further data that indicates that the FBI's statistics underestimate the frequency of anti-LGBTQ crimes (Oudekerk, 2019).

Little research has been done on specifically LGBTQ Natives but one study found that LGBTQ individuals who are also considered minorities in ethnicity and/or race experience higher rates of discrimination in the workplace, in housing, and in other arenas (Whitfield et al, 2016). While it did not specifically address Native LGBTQ individuals, it provides valuable insight into some of the challenges faced by these individuals.

A study by Sutter et al in 2016 showed increased rates of suicidal ideation among LGBTQ persons of color, including Black, Latinx, and Natives, compared to their White counterparts (Sutter et al, 2016). This study has important implications for clinicians and states:

...[C]ounseling psychologists who work with this population... may benefit from focusing on how experiences with both LGBTQ-based discrimination and racism play into presenting mental health problems... [It] may be beneficial to focus on how LGBTQ-based discrimination may lead to suicidal ideation, especially if this occurs in the context of one's own family or racial/ethnic group (Sutter et al, 2016).

Regarding interventions to address specifically LGBTQ health disparities, a 2018 study showed that integrating an LGBTQ education and awareness curriculum into medical school education resulted in students reporting, "increased awareness and understanding of health disparities specific to the LGBTQ population," (McNeil et al, 2018). This study indicates that intervening at the level of the medical student helps future medical professionals to feel more comfortable addressing health disparities within the LGBTQ population.

Global Perspective

Because of the unique histories and statuses of sovereign nations of AI/AN tribes in this country, it is difficult to draw good comparisons globally. However, in the Journal of Lesbian Studies, an interesting article was published in 2016 examining the historical and contemporary attitudes regarding "Two-Spirit" individuals. "Two-Spirit" does not exactly correspond to our current notions of "lesbian," "gay," "bisexual," or "transgender," but rather refer to individuals in various First Nations (Canada's indigenous tribes collectively) who do not conform to their cultural norms of male or female (Lang, 2016). Interestingly, in some First Nations tribes, Two-Spirit individuals traditionally held places of honor and were revered as having great wisdom, being neither wholly male nor wholly female (Lang, 2016). This view is not necessarily shared among all Canadian or American Natives, but it is certainly an interesting perspective, one that many healthcare providers, especially Americans, may not be aware of. At the very least, this exemplifies the great diversity in views among the different North American Native Peoples, illustrating that we should tread carefully in trying to lump all Native tribes together into one collective.

Research

In the Omaha area, the Nebraska Urban Indian Health Coalition (NUIHC) is a valuable resource for LGBTQ Natives. According to Dr. Donna Polk, Chief Executive Officer of NUIHC, there are several resources for patients such as access PrEP therapy if they are at high risk of acquiring HIV. The healthcare providers at the NUIHC clinics also receive training in treating transgender/transitioning patients to better understand their healthcare needs and risks. In the past, the healthcare providers have also received training in cultural awareness, as well as training to screen for sexual abuse and/ or trafficking.

NUIHC also has several treatment programs, both inpatient and outpatient for Natives battling addiction. These treatment programs serve Natives from the Nebraska area, as well as those from surrounding states.

Recommendations

First and foremost, as evidenced by this paper, there are very few studies that investigate LGBTQ AI/AN populations specifically. This group could be considered a minority within a minority. Due to the complex nature of the cultures from whence these individuals come, it is very important that we gather more information on this specific group.

While it can still be helpful to investigate healthcare disparities in AI/AN tribes as whole, it would be more useful to investigate the different tribes individually in order to understand the special challenges faced by LGBTQ

Natives within the context of their own background cultures. An individual who is Native and LGBTQ and who comes from a cultural background where their sexual identity is not fully accepted likely has different needs from a healthcare provider than the LGBTQ Native whose culture is accepting of their sexual identity. Partnering with individual tribes to address their specific needs and the specific needs of the LGBTQ individuals within that community would likely be incredibly helpful.

Furthermore, given healthcare professionals' frontline vantage point, it is imperative that we ensure that these professionals not only avoid perpetuating disparities for these groups but actively seek to remedy them. McNeil's study in 2016 showed us that educating medical students about LGBTQ healthcare disparities helped those students to feel more comfortable in addressing health considerations specific to LGBTQ-identifying individuals.

Lastly, as medical professionals, it is our duty to care for our patients and as we learn more about the social determinants of health such as education, housing, nutrition, and the like, the more we should feel comfortable working towards remedying any healthcare disparities that stem from social determinants. Working towards eradicating such healthcare disparities requires more than just being mindful of the disparities, but rather requires us, as medical professionals, to advocate for these patients in legislature, in society at large, and in ensuring there are adequate community resources for those who need them. In general, the American people as a whole are trusting of physicians, with 69% of the 2013 Gallup poll respondents stating that they considered physicians to be of "high" or "very high" ethical standards (Blendon et al, 2014). Utilizing this trust, physicians in particular can utilize the trust placed in them to advocate for their patients at a legislative and community level.

Conclusion

In conclusion, little is known about the specific healthcare disparities faced by Native individuals who also identify as LGBTQ. These individuals may face discrimination due to their race as well as their identity, and this may be two pronged, coming from their tribal communities as well as the larger American society. These patients may be hesitant to seek care from providers who they feel will not understand their cultural background or who they fear will judge them for their sexual identities. While this paper is far from comprehensive, it serves as a starting point for further inquiry into more specifics of LGBTQ Native healthcare. The healthcare professional has a unique vantage point and has can have valuable influence on societal perceptions and legislation. At the end of the day, we are bound to do what's best for our patients and this includes advocating for them in the larger society. Do not forget your Native patients and your LGBTQ patients and the particular considerations of their healthcare.

References

1. American Public Health Association (2020). *What is Public Health.* APHA. https://www.apha.org/what-is-public-health

2. Baams, L. (2018). Disparities for LGBTQ and Gender Nonconforming Adolescents. *Pediatrics* 141 (5) e20173004; DOI: https://doi.org/10.1542/peds.2017-3004

3. Baams, L., Wilson, B. and Russell, S. (2019). LGBTQ Youth in Unstable Housing and Foster Care. *Pediatrics 143* (3) e20174211; DOI: https://doi.org/10.1542/peds.2017-4211

4. Blendon, R., Benson, J., and Hero, J. (2014). Public Trust in Physicians – U.S. Medicine in International Perspective. *New England Journal of Medicine 131;17,* 1570-1572. DOI: 10.1056/NEJMp1406707

5. Centers for Disease Control (2014, March 24). *About LGBT Health.* Lesbian, Gay, Bisexual, and Transgender Health. https://www.cdc.gov/lgbthealth/about.htm

6. Centers for Disease Control (2019, December 20). *Health Disparities Among LGBTQ Youth.* Adolescent and School Health. https://www.cdc.gov/healthyyouth/disparities/health-disparities-among-lgbtq-youth.htm

7. Clements-Nolle, K., Marx, R., & Katz, M. (2006). Attempted suicide among transgender persons: The influence of gender-based discrimination and victimization. *Journal of homosexuality, 51*(3), 53–69. https://doi.org/10.1300/J082v51n03_04

8. Evans-Campbell, T., Lindhorst, T., Huang, B., and Walters, C. (2006).

9. Interpersonal Violence in the Lives of Urban American Indian and Alaska Native Women: Implications for Health, Mental Health, and Help-Seeking *American Journal of Public Healt*, 96, 1416-1422, https://doi.org/10.2105/AJPH.2004.054213

10. Hafeez, H., Zeshan, M., Tahir, M. A., Jahan, N., & Naveed, S. (2017). Health Care Disparities Among Lesbian, Gay, Bisexual, and Transgender Youth: A Literature Review. *Cureus, 9*(4), e1184. https://doi.org/10.7759/cureus.1184

11. Indian Health Services (2019). *Disparities.* Indian Health Services Fact Sheets. https://www.ihs.gov/newsroom/factsheets/disparities/

12. Kelleher, C. (2009). Minority stress and health: Implications for lesbian, gay, bisexual, transgender, and questioning (LGBTQ) young people, *Counselling Psychology Quarterly*, 22:4, 373-379, DOI: 10.1080/09515070903334995.

13. Lang, S. (2016) Native American men-women, lesbians, two-spirits: Contemporary and historical perspectives, *Journal of Lesbian Studies*, 20:3-4, 299-323, DOI: 10.1080/10894160.2016.1148966

14. McNiel P., Elertson K. (2018). Advocacy and Awareness: Integrating LGBTQ Health Education Into the Prelicensure Curriculum. *J Nurs Educ.* 57(5) 312-314. doi:10.3928/01484834-20180420-12 [link]

15. National LGBT Health Education Center (2016). *Glossary of LGBT Terms for Healthcare Teams.* https://www.lgbtqiahealtheducation.org/wp-content/uploads/LGBT-Glossary_March2016.pdf

16. Oudekerk, B. (2019). *Hate Crime Statistics: Briefing prepared for the Virginia Advisory Committee, U.S. Commission on Civil Rights.* Bureau of Justice Statistics. https://www.bjs.gov/content/pub/pdf/hcs1317pp.pdf

17. Owens, D. (2017). *Medical Bondage: Gender, Race, and the Origins of American Gynecology.* University of Georgia Press.

18. Substance Abuse and Mental Health Services Administration. (2020). *Tribal Affairs.* https://www.samhsa.gov/tribal-affairs

19. Sutter, M., & Perrin, P. B. (2016). Discrimination, mental health, and suicidal ideation among LGBTQ people of color. *Journal of Counseling Psychology, 63*(1), 98–105. https://doi.org/10.1037/cou0000126

20. U.S. Department of Justice – Federal Bureau of Investigation. (2018). *Incidents and Offenses.* 2017 Hate Crime Statistics. https://ucr.fbi.gov/hate-crime/2017/topic-pages/incidents-and-offenses

21. Wahab, S., & Olson, L. (2004). Intimate Partner Violence and Sexual Assault in Native American Communities. Trauma, Violence, & Abuse, 5(4), 353–366. https://doi.org/10.1177/1524838004269489.

22. Whitfield, D., Walls, N., Langenderfer-Magruder, L., and Clark, B. (2014). Queer Is the New Black? Not So Much: Racial Disparities in Anti-LGBTQ Discrimination, *Journal of Gay & Lesbian Social Services,* 26:4, 426-440, DOI: 10.1080/10538720.2014.955556

23. Yellow Bird, M. (1999). What We Want to Be Called: Indigenous Peoples' Perspectives on Racial and Ethnic Identity Labels. *American Indian Quarterly, 23*(2), 1-21. doi:10.2307/1185964

Suicide in Queer Adolescents

Giancola, Nicholas

Introduction

Suicide is one of the great epidemics facing the world, with more than 800,000 people dying every year, according to the World Health Organization (WHO 2019). As an understanding of mental health has begun to permeate into popular culture, so has the discussion of suicide, a previously unspeakable topic. Despite the stigma that remains, many have begun to address how to prevent suicide, particularly among the youth. Mental health issues, including suicide, are also notably present in queer-identifying youth (Haas 2011, Cover 2019). It is the duty of health practitioners to advocate for patients such as queer adolescents, who not only face discrimination but undesired health outcomes. A comprehensive understanding of suicide in queer adolescents requires a biopsychosocial perspective, with which one can begin to address the root causes, contributing factors, and possible prevention tactics.

Background

The word "queer" has a myriad of definitions that mirrors its multifaceted and metareferential use. Merriam Webster features a total of nine distinct definitions for the adjective form of the word. Most relevantly, these include "of, relating to, or characterized by sexual or romantic attraction that is not limited to people of a particular gender identity or sexual orientation" as well as "of, relating to, or being a person whose sexual orientation is not heterosexual and/or whose gender identity is not cisgender." These are modern definitions, as many still understand queer in its more primitive forms, that of an epithet for homosexual men. While this definition is also included in the dictionary, the word queer has exploded in recent years as an appropriate, albeit ambiguous term in describing those who do not subscribe to traditional heteronormativity, particularly in reference to sexuality. In this sense, queer is paradoxically both specific and broad – it stands as its own identity, while also encompassing other non-heterosexual identities including, gay, lesbian, and bisexual. Still, it is important to recognize that there is still much discussion and controversy with respect to queer terminology.

The intersection of queer sexuality and psychiatric disease is one fraught with misunderstanding and complexity. It was not until the 1970s that the American Psychological Association and the Diagnostic and statistical manual of mental disorders (DSM) removed homosexuality from its classification as a psychiatric pathology. Still, a questionable connection remains between the risk of mental illness and queer identities, which is not necessarily due to the identities themselves but the circumstances and contexts in which these identities exist. Many agree that minority stress theory is the overarching framework for the relationship between queerness, psychiatric illness, and suicide by proxy (McDermott 2018). In this sense, discrimination and victimization of queer individuals can prompt a distressing emotional and psychological state that begets depression, and potentially suicidality (McDermott, 2019). However, the diversity within the queer population is a reminder that there is rarely a "one-size-fits-all" theory or solution that encompasses all queer psychopathology. Individual idiosyncrasies as well as cultural, racial, and sociological intersections must be considered, though they can be difficult to accurately capture in the scientific canon.

Public Health

Approximately 6-7% of cisgender males and 13-15% of cisgender females self-identify as non-heterosexual (e.g., homosexual or bisexual) in the United States (McCabe et. al. 2011). The non-heterosexual, i.e. queer community is a significant, albeit vulnerable, minority group that faces specific issues with respect to suicidality. There is extensive literature from the Western world describing the association of suicide and queer adults and adolescents, who collectively make up a significant, albeit vulnerable minority group (Hall 2017, Wozolek 2019, Lytle 2018). Studies cite different numbers that overwhelmingly indicate that there is a statistically significant, and clinically relevant increase in risk for suicide among queer-identifying patients, including suicidal attempts and completed suicide. A metanalysis from 2008 revealed a two-times increase in suicide attempts made by lesbian, gay and bisexual people, as well as a 1.5 times as likely risk for depression and anxiety disorders, and lifetime prevalence of suicide attempt risk ratio of 2 in both cisgender men and women, ranging alarming high in queer men up to 4 (King, et. al 2008). This phenomenon has been explicitly in the adolescent/pediatric population as well, one study reporting LGBQ youth were approximately three times more likely to have suicidal ideation and have suicidal intent with a plan, and approximately five times more likely to have attempted suicide itself (Kann et al., 2016; Garofalo, 1999). The Center for Disease Control similarly reports that nearly one-third (29%) of LGB youth had attempted suicide, in comparison to 6% of their heterosexual peers (Kann et al., 2016). However, a positive school environment has been shown to be a protective factor, specifically those that prohibit bullying provide support groups like gay-straight alliances (Hatzenbuehler 2014; Saewcy 2014). In the same vein, a positive home environment, characterized by family acceptance, has also been shown to be protective, while a parental rejection is associated with depression as well as substance use in teenagers (Ryan 2010, Puckett 2009). Further research is necessary to better identify specific, effective, home and school interventions for preventing suicidality in queer adolescents, as many of the studies are relatively recent – essentially all within the past ten years.

Global Perspective

It is imperative to recognize that a large majority of the literature regarding queer adolescent suicide is Euro/Western-centric. This paradigm exists across many disciplines and not only limits the generalizability of the current canon but misrepresents and reduces the global queer population. While it is documented that queer youth of color are disproportionally affected in multiple domains related to mental health, including suicidality (Lardier et. al. 2020), just recently there has been a growing attitude towards correcting some of the ethnocentrism evident in the literature regarding queer health (Moe et. al. 2020). Still, a large paucity of data exists in non-developed nations, as there is a lack of research comparing queer populations of different nations. Further education and international collaboration are necessary for a better, more comprehensive picture of the queer experience, particularly as related to depression and/or suicide. Queerness is one of many personal identities that plays a role in how adolescents live their lives, and an intersectional lens is critical to properly understand the relationship between queerness, youth, mood disorders, and suicidality.

Research

I interviewed a Chicago-based clinical psychologist and psychotherapist who has been working with patients, including LGBTQIA-identifying children and adults, for more than a decade. His clinical interests in adolescent challenges and family therapy have provided him valuable anecdotal experience with queer adolescents that helps uncover some of the reasons why suicide is such an issue for this population. While he has not had any queer adolescent patients commit suicide, the clinical psychologist does endorse that suicidality is certainly discussed explicitly in his sessions with his patients and does come up more often with queer-identifying patients than their heterosexual peers. He frames his work with this population stating,

In general, adolescence is a time of identity formation and confusion so when something as important as sexuality arises [...] something that will eventually be visible to others, it's a big process that can be confusing [...] and if you feel that your sexuality prohibits you from fitting in, that can be incredibly distressing.

While he asserts that an adolescent, queer or otherwise, who is actively suicidal, should be treated in an inpatient setting with a team of clinicians contributing to their care, though suicidality is certainly addressed in his practice. He adds that, "*There are so many more processes and dynamics when you're the minority of anything, including sexuality, and thus interacting with less power.*" In this sense, he addresses the topic of powerlessness often intertwined within discussions of suicide, particularly in reasons why certain patients may think about or attempt it. The psychologist believes that these systems of power and privilege are keenly at play when considering suicidality in queer adolescents. Furthermore, when asked what he believes are the biggest protective factors against suicide in queer adolescents, he firmly states "*acceptance from peers and acceptance from family.*"

The psychologist's expertise in working with adolescents also provides insight into specific actions clinicians can take in order to best treat patients struggling with suicidality, specifically in a queer context. When working with a queer child or teen, he explains that he finds it is helpful and most productive to take a more bottom-up, inductive approach, which is explicitly distinct to the more philosophical top-down deductive way of thinking that is commonly exercised in interpersonal types of therapy. He says this is particularly important when working with queer patients because it forces the practitioner to better see the world through their eyes; again, harkening back to the roles in which intersectionality influence a person's experience. Moreover, he contends that looking at queer adolescents through a developmental framework is critical, being that a significant, substantial piece of their identity – queerness – can be complicated and confusing for patients to fully appreciate. He adds that this technique allows for a more comprehensive and authentic understanding of the patient and their subsequent feelings that may be contributing to a mood disorder and or suicidality. Furthermore, one of the most important things he considers when treating adolescents, regardless of sexuality, is the therapeutic relationship itself. This is particularly challenging when one considers teenagers' general "*ambivalence about connecting with adults, as well as them [teens] being characteristically bad historians.*" Again, it is evident that feeling supported in their relationships is an alleviating factor when considering suicidality in queer adolescents.

The psychologist also stresses the importance of adolescents feeling like they belong within a group to avoid depression suicidality. He explains that this feeling of belonging is also related to the significance of self-identification and terminology saying, *"sometimes they don't have the language necessary to define themselves or provide more nuanced descriptions of themselves."* Finding a label that feels authentic can be stress-reducing, though not all queer adolescents will choose to label themselves and might change their label over time especially in the framework of sexual fluidity. Still, he asserts that dynamics of belonging is why, in his opinion, group therapy could be an actionable, explicit clinical asset for queer adolescents struggling with suicidality and underlying mood disorders. He continues that "so much of the experience of adolescence is about being part of a group [...] to be able to have others to relate to and a space where they can fully be themselves would be extremely powerful." While he has not facilitated group therapy specific for queer adolescents, he has seen success in other group therapy settings, and feel that this population could greatly benefit.

Recommendations

It is overwhelmingly evident that there is an important, positively correlated relationship between suicidality and queerness in adolescents. Just as a multifaceted approach is necessary for an accurate understanding of queerness and suicidality, a similarly multidisciplinary approach is required to properly address and prevent suicide in this population. Cultural, political, and medical interventions are all necessary, as is further research.

First, a cultural shift in approach to queerness must be mediated in order to properly address the root causes for suicide in queer adolescents. Along the lines of minority stress theory, queer adolescents will continue with increased risks of suicide if they continue to feel ostracized or othered by their larger communities. While we know that anecdotally, adolescents do better when they feel a part of a group, and when they feel accepted, further studies are needed to properly document the significance and protective nature of acceptance from peers and family. A cultural shift in the conversation surrounding depression and suicidality is also required, as these topics lend themselves to taboo discussions with layers of shame seeming to compound already existing shame that often plague those struggling with depression. While it seems that many are trying to reduce the stigma associated with mental health and psychiatric illness more broadly, there is still a massive area for improvement in the acceptance and explicit support of those who face these challenges.

Furthermore, policy changes should reflect explicit support for queer adolescents in order to reduce suicidality. Legal protections against discrimination help reduce the victimization of queer adults and adolescents alike and can help mitigate feelings of rejection. The legal status of same-sex marriage also represents an overall attitude towards homosexual or queer individuals that permeates through society and can be either hopeful or disheartening to queer-identifying youth. Along the lines of depression, queer youth may lack hope for the future if they see they may not be able to experience and succeed in the seemingly omnipresent, problematic goal of finding a spouse. There must also be institutional protections for queer individuals in schools, as bullying is both an anecdotally and documented aggravating or risk factor for mood disorders and suicide, especially in this population.

There are also specific action items that should be taken by clinicians to address this issue. From physicians, social workers, and therapists, an intersectional, inductive approach can help foster authentic, and honest therapeutic relationships with their patients. As the psychologist I interviewed explained, the therapeutic relationship provided by a clinician can be an incredibly powerful protective factor for queer adolescents, through providing support and validation. As mentioned previously, acceptance from others has been shown to be a protective factor against suicide, and a physician's cultivation of a healing, accepting environment is crucial in caring for queer patients. Similarly, early intervention and detection of mood disorders and warning signs is necessary in order to prevent exacerbation of depression or anxiety, which often precedes suicide. Many of the clinical decisions made by physicians are unfortunately limited by the available resources, which is again why public policy and public advocacy are crucial for addressing this issue. Similarly, medical schools should make a concerted effort to integrate authentic queer patient experiences into educational materials, particularly regarding clinical science. A more organic inclusion of the queer perspective into curriculums will provide more sustainable changes within the medical community rather than the current trend of isolated courses focused on minority health groups specifically, such as this one. Medical licensing boards may also begin to require a cultural competency component for physicians that would provide explicit incentive to have an adequate understanding of the queer patient. Physicians are able to directly impact their queer patients through advocating for legal protections for LGB-identifying people, domestic and abroad.

Further research is critical for a better characterization of the relationship between queer adolescents and suicide. The body of literature concerning the specifics of this issue is sparse, particularly with respect to interventions and geographical differences. Specific areas in need of investigation include geographical differences in queer suicide, as well as culturally specific studies that can perhaps shed light on differences and similarities among suicide rates in respective locations. Similarly, having more information will provide fodder for determining better interventions for prevention of suicide in this vulnerable population, not only in the United States but around the world.

Conclusion

Suicide in queer adolescents is an unfortunate reality of the world today. Fortunately, there is a growing movement within the scientific community to address this problem. Further research can help clarify the root causes for why queer children and teens choose to end their lives. Queer adolescent suicide is a reminder of the significant burdens that face queer people around the world, and the essential nature of correcting the interpersonal, cultural, political, and healthcare barriers for this population. Queer adolescents are a vulnerable, but resilient population that are entitled to protection and the opportunity to live lives of dignity.

References

1. Cover, R (2013). Conditions of Living: Queer Youth Suicide, Homonormative Tolerance, and Relative Misery, *Journal of LGBT Youth*, 10:4, 328-350, DOI: 10.1080/19361653.2013.824372

2. Garofalo R, Wolf RC, Wissow LS, Woods ER, Goodman E. Sexual Orientation and Risk of Suicide Attempts Among a Representative Sample of Youth (1999). *Arch Pediatr Adolesc Med.* 153(5):487–493. doi:10.1001/archpedi.153.5.487

3. Haas, A. P., Eliason, M., Mays, V. M., Mathy, R. M., Cochran, S. D., D'Augelli, A. R., Silverman, M. M., Fisher, P. W., Hughes, T., Rosario, M., Russell, S. T., Malley, E., Reed, J., Litts, D. A., Haller, E., Sell, R. L., Remafedi, G., Bradford, J., Beautrais, A. L., Brown, G. K., … Clayton, P. J. (2011). Suicide and suicide risk in lesbian, gay, bisexual, and transgender populations: review and recommendations. *Journal of homosexuality*, 58(1), 10–51. https://doi.org/10.1080/00918369.2011.534038

4. Hall, W. (2018) Psychosocial Risk and Protective Factors for Depression Among Lesbian, Gay, Bisexual, and Queer Youth: A Systematic Review, *Journal of Homosexuality*, 65:3, 263-316, DOI: 10.1080/00918369.2017.1317467

5. Hatzenbuehler ML, Birkett M, Van Wagenen A, Meyer IH (2014). Protective school climates and reduced risk for suicide ideation in sexual minority youth. *Am J Pub Health.*;104(2):279-286.

6. Kann, L., Olsen, S., McManus, T., Harris, W., Shanklin, S., Flint, K. H., Queen, B., Lowry, R.,Chyen, D., Whittle, L., Thornton, J., Lim, C., Yamakawa, Y., Brener, N., & Zaza, S. (2016).Sexual identity, sex of sexual contacts and health-related behaviors among students ingrades 9–12–United States and selected sites, *2015.MMWR.* Surveillance Summaries,65,1–201

7. King, M., Semlyen, J., Tai, S. S., Killaspy, H., Osborn, D., Popelyuk, D., & Nazareth, I. (2008). A systematic review of mental disorder, suicide, and deliberate self harm in lesbian, gay and bisexual people. *BMC psychiatry*, *8*, 70. https://doi.org/10.1186/1471-244X-8-70

8. Lardier DT, Pinto SA, Brammer MK, Garcia-Reid P & Reid RJ (2020) The Relationship Between Queer Identity, Social Connection, School Bullying, and Suicidal Ideations Among Youth of Color, *Journal of LGBT Issues in Counseling*, 14:2, 74-99, DOI: 10.1080/15538605.2020.1753623

9. Lytle, M, Silenzio V., Homan CM, Schneider, P & Caine ED (2018) Suicidal and Help-Seeking Behaviors Among Youth in an Online Lesbian, Gay, Bisexual, Transgender, Queer, and Questioning Social Network, *Journal of Homosexuality*, 65:13, 1916-1933, DOI: 10.1080/00918369.2017.1391552

10. McCabe, J., Brewster, K. L., & Tillman, K. H. (2011). Patterns and correlates of same-sex sexual activity among U.S. teenagers and young adults. *Perspectives on Sexual and Reproductive Health*, 43, 142–150. doi:10.1363/psrh.2011.43.issue-3

11. McDermott E., Roen K. (2019) Reframing Queer Youth Suicide and Self-Harm. In: Queer Youth, Suicide and Self-Harm. Palgrave Macmillan, London. https://doi-org.cuhsl.creighton.edu/10.1057/9781137003454_1

12. McDermott E., Hughes E. & Rawlings V. (2018) Norms and normalisation: understanding lesbian, gay, bisexual, transgender and queer youth, suicidality and help-seeking, Culture, *Health & Sexuality*, 20:2, 156-172, DOI: 10.1080/13691058.2017.1335435

13. Moe J, Carlisle K, Augustine B & Pearce J (2020) De-colonizing International Counseling for LGBTQ Youth, *Journal of LGBT Issues in Counseling*, 14:2, 153-169, DOI: 10.1080/15538605.2020.1753625

14. Puckett JA, Woodward EN, Mereish EH, Pantalone DW (2015). Parental Rejection Following Sexual Orientation Disclosure: Impact on Internalized Homophobia, Social Support, and Mental Health. *LGBT Health*; 2(3): 265-9.

15. Queer. (n.d.) In *Merriam-Webster's Dictionary*.

16. Ryan C, Russell ST, Huebner D, Diaz R, Sanchez J (2010). Family acceptance in adolescence and the health of LGBT young adults. *J Child Adolesc Psychiatr Nurs*; 23(4): 205-13.

17. World Health Organization (2019). Suicide. https://www.who.int/news-room/fact-sheets/detail/suicide

18. Saewcy EM, Konishi C, Rose HA, Homma Y (2014). School-based strategies to reduce suicidal ideation, suicide attempts, and discrimination among sexual minority and heterosexual adolescents in Western Canada. *International Journal of Child, Youth and Family Studies*;1:89-112.

19. Wozolek, B., Wootton, L., & Demlow, A. (2017). The School-to-Coffin Pipeline: Queer Youth, Suicide, and Living the In-Between. *Cultural Studies ↔ Critical Methodologies*, 17(5), 392–398. https://doi.org/10.1177/1532708616673659

Approaches to Improve the Knowledge and Skills of Healthcare Professionals about LGBT Community

Anonymous

Abstract

Lesbian, gay, bisexual, and transgender (LGBT) patients often receive substandard care within the healthcare field. This substandard care can partially be attributed to the lack of physician training and knowledge on specific LGBT issues. This paper provides an overview of healthcare disparities and recommendations on how to improve the healthcare gap within the LGBT community. A brief epidemiology of the LGBT community is provided before discussing several of the more prominent health disparities pertaining to the LGBT patient. This paper then discusses changes that must occur in medical schools as well as within the clinical encounter itself in order to provide higher quality care to the LGBT patients. Lastly, continuing education on LGBT issues for current healthcare professionals is explored.

Approaches to Improve the LGBT Knowledge and Skills of Healthcare Professionals

The lesbian, gay, bisexual, and transgender (LGBT) community has made tremendous strides in social acceptance, however these individuals continue to face stigma and discrimination. This discrimination does not evade the healthcare system and as a result, the LGBT population faces multiple health disparities and a lower quality of healthcare. It is crucial that all physicians and healthcare professionals have the knowledge and skills to provide an inclusive environment for LGBT patients in order to achieve the highest quality of care.

Epidemiology

It is estimated that 3.5% of adults in the United States identify as lesbian, gay, or bisexual and 0.3% of adults are transgender (Gates, 2011). These percentages equate to about 9 million LGBT Americans. In addition, there are a larger number of individuals that engage in same-sex sexual behavior. One survey reported that 12.5% of women and 5.2% of men had a history of same-sex sexual contact and 16.1% of women and 6.1% of men reported sexual attraction to members of the same sex (Ard, 2016) Looking at these percentages, it is almost inevitable that physicians and healthcare professionals will treat a patient that is part of the LGBT community at some point during their career. Therefore, it is important that they be aware of how to best care for this population of patients. In order to understand how to offer the best possible care, it is important to recognize the unique health concerns that the LGBT community faces.

Within the healthcare system, there is a long-standing history of anti-LGBT bias that continues to provide barriers to these patients. Up until 1973, homosexuality was listed as a disorder in the Diagnostic and Statistical Manual of Mental Disorder (DSM) and it was not until 2013 that "transgender" was removed as a gender identity disorder in the DSM (Makadon et al, 2015). This historical mindset combined with the continued discriminatory experiences that some LGBT patients experience has led to poorer quality of care. Patients may be reluctant to share their sexual orientation, gender identity, or problems they may be having which can lead to overlooked opportunities to educate and treat the LGBT patient.

Specific Health Disparities

Aside from the long-standing bias that the LGBT community experienced, there are multiple health disparities that exist that partially stem from lack of provider knowledge. Some of the health disparities include higher rates of mental illness, higher rates of HIV and other sexually transmitted infections (STIs), lower rates of mammography and Papanicolaou (Pap) smear screening leading to a higher incidence of cancer, higher rates of substance abuse, and higher rates of smoking (Lee, 2000). Physician's ability to understand these health disparities is the first step to closing the healthcare gap within the LGBT community.

Mental health illnesses are extremely prevalent among the LGBT community, particularly among youths. It is estimated that forty percent of LGBT youths have either attempted suicide or seriously contemplated suicide (Lee, 2000). However, the risk does not disappear with age and LGBT adults face similar risks. In addition to increased rates of depression and suicide, there is also a higher rate of anxiety and substance abuse among LGBT individuals (Ard, 2016). Building a safe environment for patients to share sensitive information provides the opportunity for physicians to screen for mental health illnesses and provide treatment to aid in recovery.

The increased risk of HIV infections in men who have sex with men (MSM) has been well documented. In 2014, there were over 1 million people in the United States living with HIV, and of that 1 million people, MSM accounted for 67%. MSM also accounted for 70% of all newly diagnosed HIV infections (Centers for Disease Control and Prevention [CDC], 2017). Physicians should educate themselves on the proper screening guidelines in place for HIV testing as well as proper treatment guidelines for HIV-positive patients. In addition to HIV, other STIs occur at a higher rate among the LGBT community. These infections include syphilis, human papilloma virus (HPV), gonorrhea, chlamydia, and hepatitis (Substance Abuse and Mental Health Services Administration, 2012). This increased risk of STIs makes assessing sexual activity in the healthcare setting a necessity. Taking a proper history and properly educating patients on safe sex practices can help to lower the rate of transmission.

In addition to mental health illnesses and STIs, there is an increased risk of cancer among the LGBT community. For lesbian, bisexual, and transgender women, the risk for breast and cervical are increased. This increased rate of cancer can partially be attributed to the decreased cancer screening rates among the LGBT population. In one survey, it was reported that 44-57% of lesbian women received a recent pap smear compared to 75-84% of all women (Tracy, Schluterman, Greenberg, 2013). The rate of screening mammography within the LGBT community compared to their heterosexual counterparts is not well established. However, lesbian and bisexual women are less likely to use oral contraceptives, more likely to be nulliparous, and more likely to smoke cigarettes. These are all risk factors that increase to the risk of breast and cervical cancer (Lee, 2000).

MSM are at a higher risk for cancer as well, particularly anal cancer. Risk factors for anal cancer include being infected with HPV, having HIV, having multiple sexual partners, engaging in receptive anal intercourse, and smoking (Lee, 2000). The incidence of anal cancer among HIV-positive MSM was 9 fold higher than HIV-negative MSM, and still the rate of anal cancer among all MSM was higher than the general population (Quinn et al, 2015). Anal cancer is causes by the HPV virus, therefore routine vaccination is currently recommended, and physicians should remain up to date on vaccination guidelines. Anal cancer screening guidelines are not well established, but anal cytological testing and anal anoscopy have been suggested as screening tools in high-risk populations, such as HIV-positive individuals (Ard, 2016). Having a solid understanding of the standard cancer screening guidelines can aid in prevention, diagnosis, and treatment.

Recommendations for Improving LGBT Specific Knowledge and Skills

These mentioned health disparities represent a small sample of the healthcare differences that exist within the LGBT community. The majority of these disparities come from a lack of cultural competency. Cultural competency is an important aspect of healthcare that refers to the set of skills that a physician possesses allowing them to give the highest level of culturally appropriate care to individuals of different cultures (Institute of Medicine [IOM], 2011). With implementation of education and policy changes, it is possible to gain cultural competency and provide LGBT with high quality care. However, there are many changes that must occur for this vision to become a reality.

The current education that medical students receive on LGBT issues is extremely minimal. A recent study showed that medical schools only spend a median of five hours educating students on LGBT issues (Obedin-Maliver et al, 2011). There is currently no requirement from the Accreditation Council for Graduate Medical Education (ACGME) that medical schools or residency programs devote any time to education on LGBT healthcare. In 2014, the Association of American Medical Colleges published recommendation that encourage, but did not require, inclusion of LGBT curriculum in medical schools (Johnson, 2017). It is necessary that medical schools initiate curriculum to include more education on LGBT issues. This should begin within the first year and should include information on definition and concepts related to sexual orientation and gender identity, respectful interviews, and specific health concerns within the LGBT community.

As a student progresses into their clinical years, an effort should be made to build on the knowledge gained in the preclinical years. This might prove to be a challenge in some settings as it is difficult to guarantee certain encounters. However, the clinical setting does allow instructors to provide insight into taking a non-judgmental history, performing a respectful and sensitive physical exam, and discussing care related to sex, sexual orientation, and gender identity, which are topics that are not specific to LGBT patients. In order to get an objective measure of mastery of LGBT-care skills, LGBT related cases should be incorporated into the Objective Structured Clinical Exam (OSCE) setting (Makadon et al, 2015). These additions to the medical school curriculum will provide future physicians with the foundation of knowledge to treat and care for the LGBT patient.

Outside of gaining fundamental understanding about LGBT health issues, creating an inclusive environment is also an important aspect that needs to be addressed. It has been found that LGBT patients search for subtle clues within the environment in order to determine acceptance (Ard, 2016). There are small changes that can be implemented that can make a big difference in providing an affirmative and inclusive environment. Brochures and signs about LGBT health topics should be made readily available. Intake forms should be revised to include sexual orientation and gender identity. All staff members, including receptionists, nurses, and physicians should be trained on how to respectfully interact with an LGBT patient (Makadon et al, 2015). This initial welcoming impression can help LGBT patients feel at ease and may help to facilitate a more open conversation about their health.

The development of an inclusive environment must also extend into the examination room. Poor patient-provider communication has a strong association with adverse health behaviors including decreased level of adherence and decreased rates of satisfaction (IOM, 2011). Non-judgmental social and sexual histories are key to building rapport with the patient. Asking open-ended questions and mirroring terms patients use to describe themselves should be strategies implemented when speaking to any patient. These strategies can help avoid presumptive ideas about a patient's sexual orientation and gender identity.

Within the clinical encounter, physicians also must be respectful of the fact that patients might not have disclosed their sexual orientation or gender identity to friends and family. While each coming out process is unique, a physician should always provide reassurance without influencing the patient's process. Lastly, sensitive and thorough physical exams should be implemented. Of particular importance is the physical exam of transgender patients that have not undergone gender affirmative surgeries (Ard, 2016). A physician must follow the screening guidelines for a patient's assigned sex at birth, while maintaining a respectful environment. Once a patient leaves the office, it is important that the patient be aware of resource available in the community. In addition, the physician should make every effort to ensure that any referrals will maintain the inclusive and respectful environment.

With the lack of education currently in medical schools, it becomes imperative that current physicians educate themselves on various aspects of treating the LGBT patients. In a 2007 survey, 16% of 736 San Diego physicians reported that they were sometimes or often uncomfortable providing treatment of gay patients (Smith, 2007). This level of discomfort can be alleviated with education about various LGBT topics. As a profession, it is important to embody practice-based and life-long learning by continually updating knowledge, skills, and clinical practice behavior based on the needs of one's patients. Each state has different requirements on the number of credit hours of continuing medical education (CME) that each physician must fulfill. However, there is no specific requirement for LGBT issues. Florida is the only state that requires 1 credit hour of HIV/AIDS, which does not fully encompass the health disparities present within the LGBT community (CMEweb, 2016). Making requirements to include CME credit hours on LGBT related issues would ensure that all physicians are receiving education pertaining to LGBT issues.

In addition to CME requirements, having didactics or grand rounds on LGBT topics can help to start building the foundation needed to treat the LGBT patient. In addition, attending webinars and conferences, as well as staying up to date on journal articles can aid in building upon this knowledge. Lastly, it is important to note that the full potential of LGBT-related research can only be achieved with the appropriate dissemination of material in non-LGBT specific settings, such as journals and conferences (Makadon et al, 2015). With these improvements, the knowledge and skill gap that exists among healthcare professionals can start to be closed, and LGBT patients can begin to receive the highest quality care that they long deserved.

References

1. Ard, K. L., MD, MPH. (2016, March). Understanding the Health Needs of LGBT People. Retrieved October, 2017, from

http://www.lgbthealtheducation.org/wp-content/uploads/
LGBTHealthDisparitiesMar2016.pdf

2. CMEweb. (2016, August 17). Retrieved November 07, 2017, from http://
www.cmeweb.com/gstate_requirements.php

3. Gates, G. J. (2011, April). How many people are lesbian, gay, bisexual, and
transgender? Retrieved October, 2017, from https://williamsinstitute.law.
ucla.edu/wp-content/uploads/Gates-How-Many-People-LGBT-Apr-2011.
pdf

4. IOM (Institute of Medicine). 2011. *The Health of Lesbian, Gay, Bisexual,
and Transgender People: Building a Foundation for Better Understanding.*
Washington, DC: The National Academies Press.

5. Johnson, N. (2017, April). LGBTQ Health Education: Where Are We
Now? : Academic Medicine. Retrieved November 07, 2017, from http://
journals.lww.com/academicmedicine/fulltext/2017/04000/LGBTQ_
Health_Education___Where_Are_We_Now_.18.aspx#O2-18-3

6. Lee, R. (2000, June). Health care problems of lesbian, gay, bisexual, and
transgender patients. Retrieved November 05, 2017, from https://www.
ncbi.nlm.nih.gov/pmc/articles/PMC1070935/#ref2

7. Makadon, H. J., Mayer, K. H., Potter, J., & Goldhammer, H. (2015). *The
Fenway guide to lesbian, gay, bisexual, and transgender health* (2nd ed.).

8. Obedin-Maliver J, Goldsmith ES, Stewart L, White W, Tran E, Brenman
S, Wells M, Fetterman DM, Garcia G, Lunn MR. Lesbian, Gay, Bisexual,
and Transgender–Related Content in Undergraduate Medical Education.
JAMA. 2011;306(9):971–977. doi:10.1001/jama.2011.1255

9. Quinn, G. P., Sanchez, J. A., Sutton, S. K., Vadaparampil, S. T., Nguyen,
G. T., Green, B. L., . . . Schabath, M. B. (2015, September). Cancer and
Lesbian, Gay, Bisexual, Transgender/Transsexual, and Queer/Questioning
Populations (LGBTQ). Retrieved November 05, 2017, from https://www.
ncbi.nlm.nih.gov/pmc/articles/PMC4609168/

10. Smith DM, Mathews WC. Physicians' attitudes toward homosexuality and HIV: survey of a C   California Medical Society—revisited (PATHH-II) J Homosex. 2007;52(3-4):1–9.

11. Substance Abuse and Mental Health Services Administration, *Top Health Issues for LGBT Populations Information & Resource Kit*. HHS Publication No. (SMA) 12-4684. Rockville, MD: Substance Abuse and Mental Health Services Administration, 2012.

12. Tracy, J. K., Schluterman, N. H., & Greenberg, D. R. (2013, May 4). Understanding cervical cancer screening among lesbians: a national survey. Retrieved November 05, 2017, from https://www.ncbi.nlm.nih.gov/pmc/articles/PMC3693978

Depression in the Gay and Lesbian Community

Anonymous

Introduction

Depression is one of the most common and serious mental disorders in the United States and can be caused by a combination of genetic, biological, environmental, and psychological factors. Whether a higher prevalence of depression exists in the gay and lesbian community was first brought to light by the flawed logic within earlier debates surrounding classification of homosexuality as a mental disorder. These debates were based on an idea that an increased prevalence of mental disorders in the homosexual community allowed for classification of homosexuality as a disorder itself (Bayer, 1981). Though such classification was removed from the DSM-2 in 1973, the stigmatization of homosexual individuals has continued, perpetuating discrimination towards such individuals and perhaps the distress and greater mental disorder prevalence in this community (Bayer, 1981). Regardless of whether there is a higher prevalence of depression in the gay/lesbian community, more recent looks at this issue make clear the false logic in equating a higher prevalence of depression in homosexuals with homosexuality as a mental disorder itself (Marmor, 1980). The purpose of this paper is to review the research on whether there is an increased risk for depression in homosexual individuals, and if so, to better understand that risk and the factors that aid in ameliorating it, as well as to recount and propose effective methods for prevention and intervention.

Epidemiology with Statistics

The epidemiology of depression has been studied widely as it is a major cause of morbidity and mortality worldwide. The rate of depression within a given population ranges mostly between 2% and 6%. The country with the least depression is Japan, with a diagnosis rate of less than 2.5% and a lifetime prevalence of 3%, whereas the United States has a diagnosis rate of 6.7% and lifetime prevalence of 17% (Ferrari et al., 2013). These rates vary further when comparing between differing sexual orientations, races, age, gender, socioeconomic background, and so forth. For example, elevated rates of depression have commonly been reported in the lesbian and gay community when compared to the heterosexual community, such that homosexuals have a 2-4 times greater likelihood of experiencing depression within their lifetime than their heterosexual counterparts (Zietsch et al., 2011). In the population at large, mental disorders, such as depression, constitute the single greatest risk factor suicidal behavior, and a strong association between mental disorders and suicide attempts is also continually reported by studies on the lesbian and gay community. According to the combined results from 25 international adolescent and adult studies, researchers found depression, anxiety disorders, and substance use disorders to be 1.5 times more common in lesbian and gay people compared to the rates seen within heterosexual individuals (King et al., 2008).

Although there are arguments against the presence of a significant difference in depression rates between homosexuals and heterosexuals, much of this is based on the same flawed logic stated earlier wherein gay-affirmative researchers sought to refute an increased rate of depression for the purpose of disclaiming homosexuality as a mental disorder (Bayer, 1981). More recently, gay-affirmative researchers have advocated the minority stress hypothesis, maintaining that one's social environment can induce adverse health outcomes if it involves chronic exposure to stigma and discrimination (Mays & Cochran, 2001).

This shift in discourse is consistent with evidence from multiple studies showing an increased rate of depression and suicidality in homosexual individuals, proposed to be due to higher levels of hopelessness resulting from high rates of violence and victimization (Marshal et al., 2011). In line with the finding of an increased rate of depression in gay and lesbian individuals are the reports from a number of studies performed in 1999 that showed a substantially higher prevalence of depression and suicide in lesbian and gay people as compared with heterosexual people, similarly suggested to be as a result of homophobia and an adverse social atmosphere (Fergusson, Horwood, & Beautrais, 1999; Herrell et al., 1999). Similar studies throughout the years have continued to report increased rates of suicidality in gay and lesbian individuals, including Paul et al's study (2002) which found that about 12% of adult gay men reported making a lifetime suicide attempt, about three times as likely as their heterosexual counterparts.

Global Perspective and Public Health Impact

Regardless of the factors that influence its development, depression is characterized by severe and distressing psychological as well as somatic symptoms, all of which can affect how one feels, thinks, and manages their daily activities. Depression can also co-occur with other serious medical illnesses, such as diabetes, cancer, heart disease, conditions associated with dementia, and various autoimmune diseases, which are often worse with the presence of depression. Accordingly, it is not difficult to imagine the detrimental effects that depression can have on every aspect of a person's life and the importance of aiming to prevent and intervene with appropriate methods that may be effective. The preference to avoid such manifestations can be aided with increased understanding and recognition of the risk factors for depression. Risk factors of depression include a personal or family history of depression, major life changes, trauma, and stress (Caspi et al, 2003).

Stress is generally conceptualized as involving an individual that experiences external circumstances or events that overwhelm them beyond their capacity and have the potential to induce mental and/or somatic illness (Dohrenwend, 2000). Stressors often cause unpredictable change and require individuals to adapt to the new situation or life circumstance. Commonplace stressors include personal events, such as divorce, job loss, or death of a loved one, as well as even the daily hassles of life (i.e. traffic, losing keys, daily chores). These have been thoroughly studied as varied components of stress with which most people are familiar. However, another component of stress that extends beyond such personal events includes that which is caused by the conditions of one's social environment, such that people belonging to stigmatized groups, including those related to sexual orientation, gender, race/ethnicity, or socioeconomic status, may be strongly impacted by this additional source of social stress. Therefore, similar to the stressors common to all people, social stress brought on by prejudice and discrimination related to homophobia, sexism, racism, or low socioeconomic status, can also induce changes requiring adaptation, adding another layer to the adaptive requirements and energy expenditure of one's life (Pearlin, 1999).

Minority stress is a type of social stress that accompanies stigma, prejudice, and discrimination experienced by members of a minority group, such as those of the gay and lesbian community (Link & Phelan, 2001). The importance of social environment and the effect that being a part of a minority group can have on one's mental health were central to Durkheim's 1951 study of normlessness as a cause of suicide. According to Durkheim, a person of "normlessness" is said to live outside of the standard moral code of society, and thus lacks social control, often leading to suicide due to alienation and unmet social needs (Durkheim, 1951). A more general view of the importance of on an individual's interactions with society is based on the idea that society provides information on the construction of the world and that when this information isn't consistent with a person's experience in the world, health is compromised (Moss, 1973). Such may be more likely said to be the case for a minority person, such as a lesbian or gay individual, in which society has promoted the notion of love and intimacy, yet the social institutions that offer sanction for such have more often been in favor to heterosexual individuals and in contrast condemning to those of the homosexual community (Lazarus and Folkman, 1984).

Just as positive interactions with others can give meaning to one's experiences in life and are arguably important for one's development of sense of self and well-being, negative regard from others, such as the stereotypes and prejudice directed at minority individuals, tend to result in a negative self-regard that can lead to adverse psychological outcomes (Cochran, 2001). Specific processes of minority stress relevant to lesbian and gay individuals have been suggested, which involve external stressful events and experiences (e.g. antigay violence), the expectation from such events and the caution and alertness that comes with it (e.g. expectation of rejection during interactions with others, concealment of identity due to fear of harm), and the internalization of negative societal attitudes (e.g. internalized homophobia) (Meyer and Dean, 1998). These processes would not unlikely encourage a vicious cycle of inner and outer world feelings of negative self-identity.

Personal Research on Individuals Experiencing the Disparity

Throughout my research, I had the opportunity to speak with Dr. MG, MD, a faculty member at Creighton University School of Medicine. He is a leading physician in treating patients of the gay and lesbian community and has presented on topics related to 'Access for LGBT Populations'. Throughout his experiences treating patients of the gay and lesbian community, he has recognized a characteristic set of resilient qualities in these individuals, which he attributes to their ability to overcome adversity. He promotes a focus on the development of such characteristic coping and adaptive mechanisms, as these have aided their ability to buffer the negative impacts of prejudice and stigma and instill a sense of hope and optimism.

Thus, the gay and lesbian community is not only associated with minority stress, but also a characteristic set of important tools and resources that protect these individuals from the adverse health effects of minority stress. Such tools include not only personal coping mechanisms and resilience, but also increased group solidarity and cohesiveness (Clark et al., 1999). Cohesiveness within the gay and lesbian community is built upon the establishment of group structures and values with focuses on empowerment, support, reappraisal, self-acceptance, and identity pride, all of which mediate an enhanced in-group identity and well-being (Crocker and Major, 1989). These findings of counteracting stigma through resilience point to an interaction between stress and coping mechanisms as being able to predict mental disorder. In line with this interaction is the urge for scientists to focus more on the human capacity for adaptation, as it is through such that gay and lesbian individuals have been able to maintain their day-to-day functioning without intrusion due to their minority status (Weinberg and Williams, 1974).

The view described earlier of the homosexual individual as a resilient actor is consistent with the American society values of control and freedom (Hobfoll, 1998). However, in making this contrasted view to that of describing these persons as victims begs the question of whether it may hold danger if weight is taken away from the responsibility of society to stop oppression. The weight of responsibility may be shifted to the individual by implying that all lesbian/gay individuals are expected to have effective coping and failure to do so may be judged as a personal rather than societal failing (Masten, 2001). Regardless, we should stress the importance of both the shifting of society to that of a more accepting, supportive, and empowering one as well as humans' capacity for growth and adaptation. It is also notable to point out that the view of the lesbian and gay individual as a resilient actor acknowledges the strengths of these individuals and reflects their admirable and heroic fight for rights and institutions (D'Emilio, 1983).

Recommendations

The first step in being able to intervene on depression in the lesbian and gay community is to first be able to identify such patients. This process points to the need for a supportive and welcoming environment that encourages an open dialogue between caregiver and patient. We need to recognize the potential for gay and lesbian individuals to feel required to conceal their sexual identity and behaviors or feelings surrounding such. We need to shift away from such a world, especially in the healthcare setting where knowing a patient's full history and background may have vital implications in regards their outcomes. Patients must feel safe disclosing information related to their sexual orientation, stressors, and any other component that involves indications for intervention or prevention methods, and in taking on a similar attitude to that of the resilient actors in the homosexual population, we can aid in the fight for such. Mandatory training and workshops for all those involved in patients' healthcare might be helpful in aiding in more effective communication and in creating a more welcome environment to patients, with specific training for care of minority groups, such as those of the gay and lesbian community.

Such interventions may include not only one-on-one talk therapy, which can instill tools for coping and empowerment, but also encouragement towards community support groups, which have shown to be instrumental in one's sense of in-group identity and well-being. A step further would be to implement and lead such a support group within one's facility or community if it doesn't already exist. The effects of such support groups may be monumental in perpetuating a sense of acceptance and empowerment throughout the community and society at large. Following this, future research should seek to better understand the relationship between depression, health, and the key life events within the gay and lesbian community, which can continue to glean insight on effective multidimensional interventions and preventions within our increasingly heterogeneous society.

Conclusion

In summary, there is extensive and growing evidence to support an increased risk for depression in the gay and lesbian community, with a common theme of being influenced by the minority stress accompanying frequent stigmatization, discrimination, and hostility in one's environment. This risk is counteracted by the development of vital tools and resources for coping and empowerment seen in these resilient individuals. By recognizing the increased risk for development of depression in gay and lesbian individuals and the subsequent effects it can have on their lives and well-being, health professionals should use and build on the knowledge of the ameliorating mechanisms and encourage development and use of such.

References

1. Caspi A, Sugden K, Moffitt TE, Taylor A, Craig IW, Harrington H, McClay J, Mill J, Martin J, Braithwaite A, Poulton R (July 2003). "Influence of life stress on depression: moderation by a polymorphism in the 5-HTT gene". Science. 301 (5631): 386–89. Bibcode:2003Sci...301..386C. doi:10.1126/science.1083968. PMID 12869766.

2. Bayer, R. Homosexuality and American psychiatry: The politics of diagnosis. New York: Basic Books; 1981.

3. Marmor, J. Epilogue: Homosexuality and the issue of mental illness. In: Marmor, J., editor. Homosexual behavior: A modern reappraisal. New York: Basic Books; 1980. p. 391-401.

4. Ferrari AJ, Charlson FJ, Norman RE, Patten SB, Freedman G, Murray CJ, et al. (2013) Burden of Depressive Disorders by Country, Sex, Age, and Year: Findings from the Global Burden of Disease Study 2010. PLoS Med 10(11): e1001547. https://doi.org/10.1371/journal.pmed.1001547

5. Zietsch, B. P., Verweij, K. J., Heath, A. C., Madden, P. A., Martin, N. G., Nelson, E. C., & Lynskey, M. T. (2011). Do shared etiological factors contribute to the relationship between sexual orientation and depression?. Psychological medicine, 42(3), 521-32.

6. King M., Semlyen J., Tai S. S., Killaspy H., Osborn D., Popelyuk D., et al. A systematic review of mental disorder, suicide, and deliberate self harm in lesbian, gay, and bisexual people. BMC Psychiatry. 2008, August 18;8:70. Retrieved June 8, 2009, from http://www.ncbi.nlm.nih.gov/pmc/articles/PMC2533652/ [PMC free article] [PubMed]

7. Dohrenwend BP. The role of adversity and stress in psychopathology: Some evidence and its implications for theory and research. Journal of Health and Social Behavior 2000;41:1–19. [PubMed: 10750319]

8. Pearlin, LI. The stress process revisited: Reflections on concepts and their interrelationships. In: Aneshensel, CS.; Phelan, JC., editors. Handbook of the sociology of mental health. New York: Kluwer Academic/Plenum; 1999. p. 395-415.

9. Link BG, Phelan JC. Conceptualizing stigma. Annual Review of Sociology 2001;27:363–385.

10. Durkheim, E. Suicide: A study in sociology. New York: Free Press; 1951.

11. Moss, GE. Illness, immunity, and social interaction. New York: Wiley; 1973.

12. Lazarus, RS.; Folkman, S. Stress, appraisal, and coping. New York: Springer; 1984.

13. Cochran SD. Emerging issues in research on lesbians' and gay men's mental health: Does sexual orientation really matter? American Psychologist 2001;56:931–947. [PubMed: 11785169]

14. Meyer, IH.; Dean, L. Internalized homophobia, intimacy, and sexual behavior among gay and bisexual men. In: Herek, GM., editor. Stigma and sexual orientation: Understanding prejudice against lesbians, gay men, and bisexuals. Thousand Oaks, CA: Sage; 1998. p. 160-186.

15. Clark R, Anderson NB, Clark VR, Williams DR. Racism as a stressor for African Americans: A biopsychosocial model. American Psychologist 1999;54:805–816. [PubMed: 10540593]

16. Crocker J, Major B. Social stigma and self-esteem: The self-protective properties of stigma. Psychological Review 1989;96:608–630.

17. Weinberg, MS.; Williams, CJ. Male homosexuals: Their problems and adaptations. New York: Oxford University Press; 1974.

18. Mays VM, Cochran SD. Mental health correlates of perceived discrimination among lesbian, gay, and bisexual adults in the United States. American Journal of Public Health 2001;91:1869–1876. [PubMed: 11684618]

19. Marshal, M. P., Dietz, L. J., Friedman, M. S., Stall, R., Smith, H. A., McGinley, J., Thoma, B. C., Murray, P. J., D'Augelli, A. R., ... Brent, D. A. (2011). Suicidality and depression disparities between sexual minority and heterosexual youth: a meta-analytic review. The Journal of adolescent

health : official publication of the Society for Adolescent Medicine, 49(2), 115-23.

20. Fergusson DM, Horwood JL, Beautrais AL. Is sexual orientation related to mental health problems and suicidality in young people? Archives of General Psychiatry 1999;56:876–880. [PubMed: 10530626]

21. Paul J. P., Cantania J., Pollack L., Moskowitz J., Canchola J., Mills T., et al. Suicide attempts among gay and bisexual men: Lifetime prevalence and antecedents. American Journal of Public Health. 2002;92(8):1338-1345. [PMC free article] [PubMed]

22. Herrell R, Goldberg J, True WR, Ramakrishnam V, Lyons M, Eisen S, Tsuang MT. Sexual orientation and suicidality: A co-twin control study in adult men. Archives of General Psychiatry 1999;56:867– 874. [PubMed: 10530625]Hobfoll, 1998).

23. Masten AS. Ordinary magic: Resilience processes in development. American Psychologist 2001;56:227– 238. [PubMed: 11315249]

24. D'Emilio, J. Sexual politics, sexual communities: The making of a homosexual minority in the United States, 1940–1970. Chicago: University of Chicago Press; 1983.

Eating Disorders and Disordered Eating Behaviors among Sexual Minorities in Adolescents

Anonymous

Introduction

Eating disorders have long been associated with both physical and mental health problems particularly in the female and obstetric gynecology patients (Johnson et al, 2001). However, a growing body of evidence demonstrates that sexual minorities – especially adolescent and young adult males – are at increased risk of developing eating disorders and disordered eating behaviors compared to their heterosexual counterparts.

Sexual minority (SM) is an umbrella term and is often used interchangeably with LGBTQIA; SM refers to those who identify as gay, lesbian, and bisexual, those who are unsure of their sexual orientation, and/ or those who have sexual contact with the same sex or both sexes (Kann et al, 2016). The term attempts to be more inclusive: it does not restrict individuals to a label of "gay," "lesbian," or "bisexual," and has been used to describe those who identify as intersex, transgender, gender non-conforming, genderqueer, and individuals with attraction to gender-diverse people. SM has also been a preferred term over MSM (men who have sex with men) and WSW (women who have sex with women) because it does not undermine the self-identification or self-labeling as gay, lesbian, and bisexual (Young & Meyer, 2005). SM best reflects the variation and fluidity of sex, gender, and sexuality

– all of which are rooted in complex social dimensions and realities of human behavior. Lastly, SM is more appropriate terminology in youth who are still developing identities.

Eating disorders are a clinical diagnosis made with the DSM-V (APA, 2013), while disordered eating is characterized by unhealthy behaviors to control weight such as skipping meals, fasting for more than 24 hours, vomiting, and misuse of diet pills and laxatives (Croll et al, 2002). Patients with these conditions present a medical and public health challenge because of the associated disability, functional impairment, and co-occurring psychopathology and physical illness; additionally, these individuals rarely seek treatment and are frequently under-treated (Hudson et al, 2007). It is hypothesized that sexual minorities are at increased risk due to several psychosocial factors unique to these individuals. Much remains to be studied and done to prevent eating disorder symptoms and illnesses in these vulnerable populations, especially in youth when they are forming identities and behaviors that impact their immediate and future health.

Epidemiology

Eating disorders have been classically associated with adolescent females in the general population and often present with other co-morbid conditions. In the U.S., females have twice the prevalence rate as males: females ages 13-18 have a rate of 3.4-4.2% of eating disorders while males of the same age have a rate of 1.2-1.8% (Merikangas et al, 2010). These disorders positively correlate with mood, anxiety, impulse-control, and substance use disorders, adding to further impairments in social, work, and school functionality. In addition to mental health concerns, eating disorders are associated with physical health problems. Patients with anorexia nervosa have a prevalence rate of 15.6% for a BMI less than 18.5, and patients with binge eating disorder have a prevalence of 42.4% for a BMI greater than 30 (Merikangas et al, 2010). These patients at either ends of the BMI spectrum suffer from the health issues related to under-nutrition and obesity.

With recent interest in the unique health concerns of sexual minorities, emerging data demonstrate that this population has increased rates of eating disorders. In a study of college students with a median age of 20, more than 280,000 students were surveyed from more than 220 schools (Diemer et al, 2015). While data show cisgender heterosexual males have a low prevalence rate of 0.55% of a past-year formal diagnosis of an eating disorder, the data for cisgender SM males and transgender individuals show rates of 2.06% and 15.82% respectively. Transgender students are at significantly greater odds of developing eating disorders (OR, 4.62) when compared to cisgender heterosexual women, cisgender SM men were also at increased odds (OR, 1.45), and cisgender heterosexual men were at the lowest odds (OR, 0.27). While this data is evident for transgender and cisgender SM males, data for cisgender SM females is mixed – previous studies have shown that rates for cisgender SM females are comparable or increased to cisgender heterosexual women (Diemer et al, 2015).

These increased prevalence rates are also similar for disordered eating behaviors that do not meet a formal, clinical diagnosis in all SM groups. In a study of high school students in 4 cities and 5 states, more than 24,000 students were surveyed regarding unhealthy weight-control behaviors. Data showed that both SM males and SM females are at increased odds of engaging in self-induced vomiting, misuse of laxatives, and misuse of diet pills than their heterosexual counterparts. When controlled for ethnicity, 1 in 3 lesbian and bisexual females reported these unhealthy behaviors compared to 1 in 10 heterosexual females, while 1 in 5 gay and bisexual males engaged in these behaviors compared to 1 in 20 heterosexual males (Austin et al, 2013). Overall, it is estimated that more than 30% of SM youth engage in weight control behaviors (Hadland et al, 2014).

In addition to eating disorders and unhealthy behaviors, SM individuals also suffer from poor body image. Both SM male and female adolescents are more likely to have inaccurate perceptions of their weight status. For example, gay adolescent males were more likely to report that they feel overweight but were not (OR, 3.13) when compared to exclusively heterosexual males. Interestingly, lesbian adolescent females were twice as likely to misperceive themselves as healthy weight or underweight but were overweight compared to their exclusively heterosexual female peers. However, female adolescents who identified as bisexual or heterosexual with previous same-sex partners were more likely to report feeling overweight despite a normal weight status (Hadland et al, 2014).

Risk Factors

A current prevailing theory to explain this disparity in the sexual minority population in general is the Minority Stress Model. This theory posits that minority populations have an excess of stressors due to stigma and prejudice leading to mental and physical adverse effects (Meyer, 2003). Meyer suggests several stressors: prejudice events, expectations of rejection and discrimination, concealment of sexual identity, and internalized homophobia. Prejudice events are overt acts of discrimination. SM youth have been known to face acts of discrimination, rejection, and antigay violence within schools (Garofalo et al, 1998). This victimization increases the susceptibility to mental health illnesses. Stigmatization, or the expectations of rejection and discrimination, have been well-known to manifest as problems in mental health and social functioning (Link, 1987). Concealment of an individual's sexual identity causes considerable cognitive burden consciously and unconsciously; this inner experience has been described as a "private hell" (Smart & Wegner, 2000). Internalized homophobia, the inner negative self-perception due to outside social stressors, has been shown to be related to self-harm behaviors including eating disorders (Williamson, 2000). These stressors, unique to the sexual minority population, can present as threats to health and safety and are damaging to the psyche, making an individual more susceptible to effects on health.

A significant risk factor that contributes to eating disorders specifically are high levels of body dissatisfaction. As discussed above, poor body image is more prevalent in SM youth. In SM adults, the issue of body dissatisfaction is well-characterized and is shown to be far more pervasive in gay males than their heterosexual counterparts. In a study of homosexual men, body dissatisfaction rates were much higher than those of heterosexual men (Russell & Keel, 2002). While the body ideal in females is to be thin, the ideal in males is to be thin as well as muscular. Though homosexual men did not differ significantly with their BMIs when compared to heterosexual men, homosexual men had sizeable increases of expressed desires and drives for more muscularity and thinness; furthermore, these measures also correlated highly with disordered eating behaviors (Yelland & Tiggemann, 2003).

Factors that are related to body dissatisfaction are BMI and peer pressure. In the study by Hospers & Jansen, higher BMIs and higher levels of peer pressure were strongly correlated with body dissatisfaction among homosexual males (2005). It is hypothesized that this is due to increased social pressures within the gay community to be attractive and achieve an ideal masculine body (Harvey & Robinson, 2003). Interestingly, when controlling for sexual orientation and peer pressures, body dissatisfaction was demonstrated to be the main variable contributing to eating disorder symptoms; body dissatisfaction, not homosexuality, is central to predicting disordered eating behaviors (Hospers & Jansen, 2005).

Discussion & Recommendations

Data show that SM youth suffer more from eating disorders and symptoms than their heterosexual peers. It is significant in SM males and seems to be mixed in SM females. Emerging research shows that transgender youth have alarmingly high rates of this morbidity and signals the urgency to protect the health of this vulnerable population. It is also important to note that this does not trivialize nor minimize the fact that eating disorders still disproportionately impact female youth; rather, this research broadens the discussion of who is adversely affected by eating disorders and demonstrates the need for more understanding of these diverse populations. Research, public prevention efforts, and healthcare approaches are all required to address this need.

Whereas current research shows the prevalence of eating disorders and unhealthy behaviors, more work needs to be done to better understand the risk factors and long-term sequelae. The assessment of the causes and effects of eating disorders in SM youth have not been extensively examined in the same way as they have been in gay adult men. Questions to study are what specific risk factors exist in each sexual minority group among youth, whether gay youth suffer from the same body dissatisfaction as gay adults, whether SM females suffer more from disordered eating behaviors than their heterosexual peers, and what – if any – are the effects into adulthood from these disordered behaviors. Furthermore, research is needed to study eating disorders in transgender youth. Though studies in this population have been small, it is disturbing that the rates are so high.

As the research in sexual minority youth unfold, prevention programs can be enacted to decrease the prevalence in this population. School-based programs have targeted female youth, focusing on risk factors associated with disordered eating as well as other mental health issues. Educational interventions have proven to be successful in long-term changes in self-perceived body image and attitudes toward eating, even at 12 months (O'Dea & Abraham, 2000). Dissonance-based interventions have been shown to be the "gold standard" in prevention programs in adolescent females (Mine et al, 2017). This intervention relies on dissonance, or inconsistent cognitions, which motivates people to change behaviors due to psychological discomfort; this has been applied successfully to smoking, substance use, and diabetes management (Stice et al, 2008). These same approaches can be applied to gay and SM youth. If body dissatisfaction is in fact a risk factor in the development of eating disorders in SM youth, a change in attitudes and cognitions in SM communities can decrease disordered eating behaviors and ultimately the burden of disease. Awareness campaigns can also be implemented to target SM communities. Similar to HIV awareness and PrEP advertising, campaigns to prevent and encourage treatment of eating disorders can be focused on the SM population. Many companies and public health institutions use social media platforms for this purpose. Promotion of body positivity in SM youth can mitigate the body dissatisfaction that is so pervasive within these communities.

Increasing visibility of these issues encourage young people to be more aware of disorders affecting them and their community.

In addition to public health research and societal prevention efforts, much needs to be done within the healthcare sphere. In a personal discussion with Dr. Martin Harrington, the Medical Director of the Eating Disorders Program at Children's Physicians in Omaha, NE, he asserts that SM adolescents should be "treated with respect and acceptance." Currently there is a lack of research in the psychiatric and medical management for eating disorders in SM youth specifically. However, there are other interventions that can be implemented immediately to improve the quality of healthcare delivery. Examples that Dr. Harrington discussed are diversity training for healthcare staff and creating environments that are welcoming to all.

Diversity and cultural competency training can help to establish and maintain therapeutic relationships with patients. For instance, Dr. Harrington noted the importance of using the preferred gender pronouns with which patients identify. This respect and acceptance for an individual's identity is necessary to build trust. A barrier to care, which has been common for transgender patients, is the lack of knowledge among providers (Safer et al, 2016). Training is important for all healthcare personnel – such as front desk staff, nurses, therapists, and physicians – to properly serve patients of different backgrounds, decrease the stigma, and promote access to care. Another way to create welcoming environments is to promote safe spaces. Simply displaying signs in a lobby or on a website to say individuals of all sexual orientations and all genders are welcome there can have lasting impact. This signals to the SM population that they can receive treatment without fear of judgement and threats to safety. Healthcare systems should aspire to be open and knowledgeable to SM youth.

Conclusion

Eating disorders and their associated unhealthy behaviors pose a risk to both mental and physical health. These disorders are prevalent in adolescents especially among sexual minorities during a critical time in their development. This presents an urgent need for intervention in both medical, educational, and public health strategies. With an evolving obesity epidemic and body image issues pervasive among youth, much research remains to be done to better understand the causes and effects of eating disorders. If we are to achieve health equity and ensure all individuals of diverse backgrounds to be physically and mentally healthy, we must address eating disorders and unhealthy eating behaviors early with school-based programs and awareness campaigns within SM communities. Healthcare systems also play a unique role: as direct providers to SM patients, healthcare staff can help to create therapeutic environments so patients of all backgrounds can safely receive care.

References

1. Allen, K. L., Byrne, S. M., Oddy, W. H., & Crosby, R. D. (2013). DSM–IV–TR and DSM-5 eating disorders in adolescents: Prevalence, stability, and psychosocial correlates in a population-based sample of male and female adolescents. *Journal of Abnormal Psychology*, 122(3), 720.

2. APA. (2013). *Diagnostic and Statistical Manual of Mental Disorders*, 5th Edition: DSM-5. Washington, DC: American Psychiatric Association.

3. Austin, S. B., Nelson, L. A., Birkett, M. A., Calzo, J. P., & Everett, B. (2013). Eating disorder symptoms and obesity at the intersections of gender, ethnicity, and sexual orientation in US high school students. *American Journal of Public Health*, 103(2), e16-e22.

4. Boroughs, M., & Thompson, J. K. (2002). Exercise status and sexual orientation as moderators of body image disturbance and eating disorders in males. *International Journal of Eating Disorders*, 31(3), 307-311.

5. Conner, M., Johnson, C., & Grogan, S. (2004). Gender, sexuality, body image and eating behaviours. *Journal of Health Psychology*, 9(4), 505-515.

6. Diemer, E. W., Grant, J. D., Munn-Chernoff, M. A., Patterson, D. A., & Duncan, A. E. (2015). Gender identity, sexual orientation, and eating-related pathology in a national sample of college students. *Journal of Adolescent Health*, 57(2), 144-149.

7. French, S. A., Story, M., Remafedi, G., Resnick, M. D., & Blum, R. W. (1996). Sexual orientation and prevalence of body dissatisfaction and eating disordered behaviors: A population-based study of adolescents. *International Journal of Eating Disorders*, 19(2), 119-126.

8. Garofalo, R., Wolf, R. C., Kessel, S., Palfrey, J., & DuRant, R. H. (1998). The association between health risk behaviors and sexual orientation among a school-based sample of adolescents. *Pediatrics*, 101(5), 895-902.

9. Hadland, S. E., Austin, S. B., Goodenow, C. S., & Calzo, J. P. (2014). Weight misperception and unhealthy weight control behaviors among sexual minorities in the general adolescent population. *Journal of Adolescent Health*, 54(3), 296-303.

10. Harvey, J. A., & Robinson, J. D. (2003). Eating disorders in men: Current considerations. Journal of Clinical *Psychology in Medical Settings*, 10(4), 297-306.

11. Hepp, U., & Milos, G. (2002). Gender identity disorder and eating disorders. *International Journal of Eating Disorders*, 32(4), 473-478.

12. Hospers, H. J., & Jansen, A. (2005). Why homosexuality is a risk factor for eating disorders in males. *Journal of Social and Clinical Psychology*, 24(8), 1188-1201.

13. Hudson, J. I., Hiripi, E., Pope, H. G., & Kessler, R. C. (2007). The prevalence and correlates of eating disorders in the National Comorbidity Survey Replication. *Biological Psychiatry*, 61(3), 348-358.

14. Johnson, J. G., Spitzer, R. L., & Williams, J. B. W. (2001). Health problems, impairment and illnesses associated with bulimia nervosa and binge eating disorder among primary care and obstetric gynaecology patients. *Psychological Medicine*, 31(8), 1455-1466.

15. Kann et al (2016). Sexual Identity, Sex of Sexual Contacts, and Health-Related Behaviors among Students in Grades 9-12--United States and Selected Sites, 2015. Morbidity and Mortality Weekly Report. Surveillance Summaries. Volume 65, Number 9. *Centers for Disease Control and Prevention.*

16. Link, B. G. (1987). Understanding labeling effects in the area of mental disorders: An assessment of the effects of expectations of rejection. *American Sociological Review*, 52, 96–112.

17. Matthews-Ewald, M. R., Zullig, K. J., & Ward, R. M. (2014). Sexual orientation and disordered eating behaviors among self-identified male and female college students. *Eating Behaviors*, 15(3), 441-444.

18. Merikangas, K. R., He, J. P., Burstein, M., Swanson, S. A., Avenevoli, S., Cui, L., Benjet, C., Georgiades, K., & Swendsen, J. (2010). Lifetime prevalence of mental disorders in US adolescents: results from the National Comorbidity Survey Replication–Adolescent Supplement (NCS-A). *Journal of the American Academy of Child & Adolescent Psychiatry*, 49(10), 980-989.

19. Meyer, I. H. (2003). Prejudice, social stress, and mental health in lesbian, gay, and bisexual populations: conceptual issues and research evidence. *Psychological Bulletin*, 129(5), 674.

20. Mine, S., Tashiro, K., & Shimada, H. (2018). Recent issues and future prospects of programs for preventing eating disorders in adolescent girls. *Journal of Health Psychology Research*, 30(Special_issue), 187-194.

21. Mitchison, D., & Mond, J. (2015). Epidemiology of eating disorders, eating disordered behaviour, and body image disturbance in males: a narrative review. *Journal of Eating Disorders*, 3(1), 20.

22. O'Dea, J. A., & Abraham, S. (2000). Improving the body image, eating attitudes, and behaviors of young male and female adolescents: A new educational approach that focuses on self-esteem. *International Journal of Eating Disorders*, 28(1), 43-57.

23. Russell, C. J., & Keel, P. K. (2002). Homosexuality as a specific risk factor for eating disorders in men. International Journal of Eating Disorders, 31(3), 300-306.

24. Safer, J. D., Coleman, E., Feldman, J., Garofalo, R., Hembree, W., Radix, A., & Sevelius, J. (2016). Barriers to health care for transgender

individuals. *Current Opinion in Endocrinology, Diabetes, and Obesity,* 23(2), 168.

25. Smart, L., & Wegner, D. M. (2000). The hidden costs of hidden stigma. *The Social Psychology of Stigma,* 220-242.

26. Stice, E., Shaw, H., Becker, C. B., & Rohde, P. (2008). Dissonance-based Interventions for the Prevention of Eating Disorders: Using Persuasion Principles to Promote Health. *Prevention Science,* 9(2), 114-128.

27. Williamson, I. (2000). Internalized homophobia and health issues affecting lesbians and gay men. *Health Education Research,* 15, 97–107.

28. Yelland, C., & Tiggemann, M. (2003). Muscularity and the gay ideal: Body dissatisfaction and disordered eating in homosexual men. *Eating Behaviors,* 4(2), 107-116.

29. Young, R. M., & Meyer, I. H. (2005). The trouble with "MSM" and "WSW": Erasure of the sexual-minority person in public health discourse. *American Journal of Public Health,* 95(7), 1144-1149.

Special Considerations for Routine Health Maintenance for Lesbian, Bisexual, and Transgender Patients

Anonymous

Abstract

While lesbian, bisexual, and transgender individuals comprise a small but significant sample of our population, high quality scientific literature regarding these individuals has only recently begun to blossom. Despite the paucity of research, that which does exist suggests that these women are disproportionately affected by obesity, substance abuse, intimate partner violence and certain behaviors put them at higher risk for certain disease processes. Due to past stigmatization and fear of harassment and judgement, many of these patients do not reveal their sexuality to their healthcare providers, making it more difficult for the provider to optimize and personalize the care for them. Most physicians and medical students do not receive adequate training on how to care for this population and thus same feel they are not equipped to provide the care effectively. This paper will investigate some of the major health concerns for the LGBTQIA population and hopefully shed light on the fact that even with little extra training, if a primary care physician creates a welcoming safe environment for their patients to reveal their sexuality and behaviors they can address many of these concerns with good screening and intake questions and recommendations for appropriate routine health maintenance tests.

Introduction

The 2013 United States National Health Interview Survey, an annual survey of over 34,500 adults aged 18 years and older, reported that 96.6 percent of adults identified as heterosexual, 1.6 percent identified as gay or lesbian, 0.7 percent identified as bisexual, and 1.1 percent were not identified (i.e., responded as "something else," "I don't know," or declined to answer) (National Health Interview Survey, 2014). While this shows that lesbian, gay, bisexual and transgender (LGBT) individuals represent a significant proportion of our population, it is only recently that the healthcare and scientific community have begun to recognize them as such. During the AIDS epidemic of the 1970-80s which disproportionately affected men who had sex with men (MSM), this became realized and the scientific literature on the topic blossomed. Peer reviewed literature for other sexual minorities such as lesbian, bisexual, and transgender women, or sexual minority women (SMW) has absolutely lagged behind. It is encouraging that we are seeing more studies each year which has begun to elucidate many health disparities that lesbian and bisexual women face compared to heterosexual women. These consist of disproportionate rates of obesity, intimate partner violence, substance abuse, increased risk factors for many diseases, mental health care, and barriers to healthcare in general. This paucity of research is referenced in numerous peer reviewed article introductions that call for more high-quality research, as many of the current studies rely on self-reported sexual orientation, small sample size, and low-quality research which lacks generalizability. Another issue with the literature is that sexual behavior is fluid and individuals may not identify their sexuality as their behavior and activities suggest. The current literature is limited only to those women who "are out." The terminology "are out" means declaring their sexual orientation to everyone. There are no known biological differences between lesbians and heterosexual women that could increase or decrease the risk of chronic disease (Aaron et al, 2001). Thus, any hypothesized differences in risk for chronic disease are due to differences in behavioral and environmental factors, which have the potential to influence health. The health care needs of lesbians and bisexual women are similar to those of all women, however, many experience additional risk factors and barriers to care that can impact their health status. This paper will attempt to review and synthesize the existing literature on common health disparities and risk factors experienced by SMW as it pertains to a primary health care setting and serve as a reminder on how to best deliver quality care to these patients.

Barriers

Any discussion of sexual minority women in the context of primary care must begin with the barriers that they face. There are three major barriers to receiving quality health care that lesbian and bisexual women face: (1) hesitancy of physicians to inquire about sexual orientation; (2) hesitancy of lesbians and bisexual women to disclose their sexual behavior; and (3) lack of knowledge, comfort, and research regarding health issues specific to lesbians and bisexual women (Aaron et al, 2001). It is important to remember the homophobia and stigmatization (or fear of such) that patients may have experienced in the past which may account for the fact that lesbian and bisexual women have 30% lower odds of routine annual healthcare compared to heterosexual women (Blosnich et al, 2014). In addition, 45% of lesbian and bisexual women surveyed said they are not out to their provider. In order to maximize the quality of the healthcare and reduce the risk factors and disparities listed below it is essential to have a welcoming practice that seeks to identify sexual orientation from the first visit. This is not enough though as orientation should not be assumed to correlate with behavior and so further early screening is necessary for sexual behavior.

Obesity

Lesbian and bisexual women typically have higher rates of obesity than their heterosexual counterparts (Aaron et al, 2001). This trend, apparent even among college aged women, highlights that this is a pervasive issue within the community across generations (Struble, 2010). Obesity, as we know puts women at risk for a variety of health related complications (Hu, 2004). Obese women are more susceptible to developing Type II diabetes a risk factor for heart disease, hypertension, stroke, sleep apnea, osteoarthritis, and kidney disease. Obesity is also a risk factor for major cancers for women including breast (after menopause), endometrial, colorectal, gallbladder and kidney (American Cancer Society, 2017). For those women who desire to have children, their fertility is jeopardized by body mass indicies (BMI) above 30 kg/m3 which can lead to the development of irregular menstrual cycles, chronic anovulation, and Polycystic Ovarian Syndrome. If a woman does become pregnant, her risk of miscarriage is elevated, along with risk for gestational diabetes, pre-eclampsia, and Caesarean section. These risks are passed on to the fetus of an obese mother who is more likely to experience antenatal stillbirth, have macrosomia, and grow to become obese themselves (Yu, Teoh, and Robinson, 2006). Higher BMI is associated with sub-optimal success with assisted reproduction techniques as well (Maheshwari, Stofberg, Bhattacharya, 2007).

Why are women that identify as lesbian more likely to be obese? This could be due to the cultural norms within the community which may differ from the mainstream notions of ideal beauty and thinness (VanKim et al 2016)..

Though these findings do not necessarily indicate sexual orientation as a risk factor, the physician must be aware of the trend and watch for it, or even better, prevent it by reminding and educating the patient at each visit about the benefits of a healthy weight and how achieving and maintaining a healthy weight is in line with their health goals.

Substance use

Studies show that those within the LGBT community abuse substances at higher rates than the population in general (Green & Feinstein, 2012). This is particularly true for lesbian and bisexual women, who use tobacco, alcohol, and all illegal drugs at higher rates than heterosexual women (Kerr, 2014). While there are immediate dangers and risks concomitant with alcohol (binge drinking and drunk driving are increased in lesbian and bisexual women), tobacco, and drug abuse, long term effects of each such as cirrhosis of the liver, COPD, hypertension, heart disease, cancer etc. will have to be screened for and managed (Blosnich et al 2014). Bisexual women also report more "behaviors related to HIV risk" (i.e., intravenous drug use, being treated for a sexually transmitted or venereal disease, given or received money or drugs in exchange for sex, or had anal sex without a condom).

Nulliparity/low parity.

Although the trend is changing, many lesbian women choose not to have children or have fewer children. Along with obesity mentioned above, lesbian women remain at a higher risk for reproductive cancers including breast, endometrial, and ovarian (Zaritsky, Dibble 2010). Those who remain nulliparous or begin having children later in life, are at increased risk for breast and endometrial cancer due to increased estrogen exposure. Breastfeeding confers a protective advantage for ovarian and breast cancer as estrogen levels are reduced during this time. Additional risk factors for breast cancer are smoking and alcohol use which are increased in this population as described above. This is compounded if they are obese as this also increases exposure to estrogen, due to increased peripheral conversion of androgens. Some of the increased risk for endometrial and ovarian cancer can be decreased by oral contraceptive pills, but at the expense of increased risk of cervical and breast cancer.

Intimate partner violence

Many people identify intimate partner violence as perpetrated by a man against a woman. One particular aspect of lesbian and bisexual health that may be overlooked due to incorrect assumptions about the community is intimate partner violence. The CDC's 2010 National Intimate Partner and Sexual Violence Survey reported that 44% of lesbian women, 61% of bisexual women, and 34% of heterosexual women were victims of rape, physical violence, or stalking by an intimate partner in their life (CDC, 2010). Physical abuse by family members is also widely prevalent among younger patients and should be screened for.

<u>Transgender issues</u>

Transgender studies is an even newer field and significantly lacks quality research at this point. Despite this, a number of healthcare disparities seem to exist and primary care health providers have the opportunity to meet the needs of this population. Similar barriers to health care described above exist for transgender individuals in terms of fear of stigma and homophobia in the healthcare setting that a practitioner can begin to ameliorate with awareness and training. A disproportionate number of transgender individuals are homeless. Many are denied by shelters due to lack of appropriate gender-neutral quarters or choose not to go to shelters due to harassment experienced in shelters. Thus, many live on the streets and turn to "survival sex", or sex in exchange for food, shelter, or money. This puts them at significantly greater risk for sexually transmitted diseases (STDs) and violence and thus these should be screened for.

A lack of access to expert physicians in caring for transgender patients due to the scarcity of trained experts and the financial expense, causes many of those who are transgender to obtain and use hormones illegally and also attempt to modify their physical features by injecting silicone in their bodies. Both practices are obviously dangerous due to lack of supervision in a non sterile environment and have led to serious injury, illness, and death. The American College of Obstetricians and Gynecologists (ACOG) recommends age appropriate screening for breast and cervical cancer in female to male transgender patients unless they have had a mastectomy or hysterectomy (ACOG, 2011). There may also be an increase in endometrial cancer in patients taking androgens (Moore, Wisniewski, Dobs, 2003). For male to female transgender, it is necessary to remember that patients may still have their prostates that will require age specific screenings. Also, if there has been gender reassignment surgery the neovagina and neocervix must be screened for STDs and HPV. The glans penis is usually used to create the neocervix and is more prone to cancerous changes than penile shaft skin (Lawrence, 2001). Breast cancer screening is also necessary if taking hormones.

Discussion

A quote from Dr. MG, one of the physicians I interviewed for this paper, made a very good point, "Sometimes we can focus too much on the sexuality" (Personal communication, 2017). At this time, in the advent of increased concern for the healthcare of the LGBT community, it is important not to become overwhelmed as a physician. As mentioned above, from our current understanding, women who have sex with women do not differ biologically from heterosexual women. For transgender, their physiologic differences result from gender affirming surgery, cosmetic surgery, and hormone use. I believe the main concern from a health care stand point for both of these populations is fostering an environment that is welcoming, comfortable, and safe in the clinics. The patient must feel at ease both within the healthcare setting and with the physician so that they share their sexual identity and behaviors. Once this information is elicited in a non-judgmental way and the trusting therapeutic relationship begins, the physician can elucidate the patient's risks and health care needs. ACOG has also written in numerous bulletins that an OB/GYN should be prepared to refer their transgender patients to an expert. However, very few of these experts are accessible to patients because of the cost creating a major barrier to care. I believe a way to ameliorate this issue is to increase the education on transgender specific concerns during OB/GYN residency training and prepare the doctors to work with this population and be able to manage their medical issues, thus increasing the number of providers who are needed to care for this population.

In a highly cited paper from 2011 published in the JAMA, researchers found that in 176 medical schools surveyed, the average time dedicated to LGBT education was 5 hours (Obedin, 2011). In order to decrease health disparities medical students must first be taught to understand and appreciate that there are disparities and then how to approach them. The AAMC Advisory Committee on Sexual Orientation, Gender Identity, and Sex Development developed a publication that stated many of the health disparities the community faces, discussed recommendations on how medical schools can integrate the LGBT content into their curriculum, and provided a framework for assessing adeptness in the area at an individual and institutional level. While nearly every professional medical organization has called for increased education and training in caring for the LGBTQIA populations, no mandatory requirements are currently in place in medical schools or residency training. While it seems inevitable that this will change in coming years, at this point it is on individual institutions to make these changes.

Conclusion

Hopefully this paper has been informative in revealing some of the major health disparities that lesbian, bisexual, and transgender women face, particularly regarding obesity, substance abuse, intimate partner violence and the risk factors for disease that they experience at higher rates than heterosexual women. A physician who wants to better the healthcare of this population does not need necessarily extra medical training to decrease these disparities and take care of many of these issues. Obtaining a thorough history, complete with screening questions for substance abuse, intimate partner violence, depression, along with age appropriate screening tests (which should be done for every patient anyway) can go a long way in reducing these health care disparities. Further scientific investigation with higher quality studies that begin with broader self-identification of sexual identity in large healthcare databases will lead to better understanding of the needs of the LGBTQIA community and the health risks they face. Finally, mandatory educational requirements for accreditation for both medical schools and residency programs regarding education on LGBT concerns will ensure that each future generation of physician is prepared to meet the unique needs of all their patients in the community.

References

1. Aaron D.J., Markovic N., Danielson M.E., Honnold J.A., Janosky J.E., Schmidt N.J. (2001). Behavioral risk factors for disease and preventive health practices among lesbians. *American Journal of Public Health.* 91:972–5.

2. American Cancer Society. (2017). Cancer Facts for Lesbian and Bisexual Women. https://www.cancer.org/healthy/find-cancer-early/womens-health/cancer-facts-for-lesbians-and-bisexual-women.html#references. Accessed 2 Nov 2017.

3. American College of Obstretricians and Gynecologists. (2011). Committee Opinion: Healthcare of Lesbian and Bisexual Women. No. 511. https://www.acog.org/Resources-And-Publications/Committee-Opinions/Committee-on-Health-Care-for-Underserved-Women/Health-Care-for-Transgender-Individuals. Accessed 2 Nov 2017.

4. Blosnich J.R., Farmer G.W., Lee J.G.L., Silenzio V.M.B., Bowen D.J. (2014). Health Inequalities Among Sexual Minority Adults: Evidence from Ten U.S. States, 2010. *American Journal of Preventive Medicine. 46(4), 337-349.*

5. Center for Disease Control. (2013). National Health Interview Survey 2013. https://stacks.cdc.gov/view/cdc/24087. Accessed 2 Nov 2017.

6. Center for Disease Control. (2010). National Intimate Partner and Violence Survey: An Overview of 2010 Findings on Victimization by Sexual Orientation. https://www.cdc.gov/violenceprevention/pdf/cdc_nisvs_victimization_final-a.pdf. Accessed 2 Nov 2017.

7. Hu F.B. (2004). Overweight and Obesity: Health Risks and Consequences. *Journal of Women's Health. 12(2):163-172.*

8. Kerr D., Ding K., Burke A., Ott-Walter K. (2014). An Alcohol, Tobacco, and Other Drug Use Comparison of Lesbian, Bisexual, and Heterosexual Women. *Substance Use and Misuse. 50(3):340-9.*

9. Lawrence A.A., (2001) Vaginal Neoplasia in a Male-to-Female Transsexual: Case Report, Review of the Literature, and Recommendations for Cytological Screening. *International Journal for Transgender. 5(1).*

10. Maheshwari, A., Stofberg, L., Bhattacharya, S. (2007). Effect of Overweight and Obesity on Assisted Reproductive Technology – A Systematic Review. *Human Reproduction Update, 13(5), 433-444*

11. Moore E., Wisniewski A., Dobs A. (2003). Endocrine treatment for transsexual people: A Review of Treatment Regimens, Outcomes, and Adverse Effects. *Journal of Clinical Endocrinology and Metabolism. 88, 3467-73.*

12. Mravcak, S.A. (2006). Primary Care for Lesbians and Bisexual Women. *American Family Physician. 74(2), 279-286.*

13. Obedin-Maliver J., Goldsmith E.S., Stewart L., White W., Tran E., Brenmen S., Wells M., Fetterman D.M., Garcia G., Lunn M.R. (2011). Lesbian, Gay, Bisexual, and Transgender-Related Content in Undergraduate Medical Education. *Journal of the American Medical Association. 306(9):971-7.*

14. Pasquali, R., Patton, L., Gambineri, A. (2007). Obesity and Infertility. *Current Opinion in Endocrinology, Diabetes, and Obesity, 14, 482-487.*

15. Struble C.B., Lindley L.L., Montgomery K., Hardin J., Burcin M. (2010). Overweight and Obesity in Lesbian and Bisexual College Women. *Journal of American College Health. 59(1):51-6.*

16. VanKim N.A., Porta C.M., Eisenberg M.E., Neumark-Sztainer D., Laska M.N. (2016). Lesbian, Gay and Bisexual College Student Perspectives on Disparities in Weight-Related Behaviours and Body Image: A Qualitative Analysis. *Journal of Clinical Nursing. 25(23-24), 3676-3686.*

17. Yu C.K.H., Teoh T.G., Robinson S. (2006). Review Article: Obesity in Pregnancy. *British Journal of Obstetrics and Gynaecology. 113(10), 1117-1125.*

18. Zaritsky, E., Dibble, S.L. (2010). Risk Factors for Reproductive and Breast Cancers Among Older Lesbians. *Journal of Women's Health, 19(1),* 125-131.

Suicide Among Transgender Adolescents

Anonymous

Introduction

Suicide is a devastating public health problem among adolescents. It results in the loss of approximately 4,600 lives between the ages of 10-24 every year.[1] According to the national Youth Risk Behavior Survey (YRBS), 17.2% of adolescents have seriously considered attempting suicide within the last twelve months and 7.4% have attempted suicide in the past twelve months they were surveyed.[2] It is especially troubling that transgender adolescents experience suicidal ideation and suicide attempts at an alarming rate when compared to their non-transgender peers.

Background

In order to adequately address this topic, it is essential to define what is meant by the term transgender. According to the CDC, "*Transgender* is an umbrella term for persons whose gender identity or expression (masculine, feminine, other) is different from their sex (male, female) at birth."[3] Gender identity and sexual identity are not synonymous. Transgender individuals can have different sexual identities, including heterosexual, homosexual, bisexual, or asexual. There is a multitude of additional gender and transgender terms that are important to be aware of as a health care practitioner in order to better serve patients, but will not be further explored in this discussion.

Transgender adolescents experience health disparities, including both general and mental health disparities. Evidence exists that transgender and gender non-conforming youth may experience poorer health, receive fewer health checkups, and more school nurse office visits than their peers who identify as cisgender.[5] The American Academy of Pediatrics (AAP) made their first policy statement in 1983 on sexual minority teenagers. With increasing acceptance of non-conforming gender and sexual identities, new research on these groups has shed light on the health disparities they face.[4] The AAP concisely describe how to approach LGBTQIA youth health disparities in a recent policy statement that reads,

"Being a member of this group of teenagers is not, in itself, a risk behavior and many sexual minority youth are quite resilient; sexual minority youth should not be considered abnormal. However, the presence of stigma from homophobia and heterosexism often leads to psychological distress, which may be accompanied by an increase in risk behaviors. Health disparities exist in mental health, substance abuse, and sexually transmitted infection (STI)/HIV."[4]

Therefore, we should not assume the transgender adolescent in our office is struggling with a mental health problem, but we should have a lower threshold for looking for it. Addressing mental health difficulties among these adolescents should be a priority for health care providers.

As acceptance of gender non-conformity has increased over the years, there has been a need for medical centers geared toward managing their gender issues. These centers often administer mental health scales to parents and their children which have reflected the problems that these adolescents face, particularly suicide and self-harm. Transgender girls have been found to self-report more "worry" than transgender boys, and older transgender patients experienced more of the following compared to their younger peers: poor self-competence, higher levels of anxiety, decreased happiness, and satisfaction.[6] It is concerning that these children and adolescents experience high rates of negative emotions despite that the parents in this study were likely more accepting of their gender identities as they consented for their children to receive treatment, such as puberty blockades or hormone therapy. In addition, the parents and children were found to have similar scores about the child's mental health, except that parents tended underestimate suicidal ideation.[6] Despite these parents' fairly accurate assessments of their children's feelings, the underestimation of suicidal ideation gives further evidence to healthcare practitioners having a lower threshold for asking transgender adolescents about suicide.

Epidemiology & Global Perspective

Multiple studies have reported different rates of suicidal ideation or attempts among transgender adolescents. One large study, that surveyed students in California, found that transgender students self-reported suicidal ideation in the past 12 months at a rate of 33.73% compared to the only 18.85% of their non-transgender peers.[7] These authors acknowledge two points about previous data on transgender youth suicidal ideation. First, it was only recently that a shift has been made to avoid aggregating gender and sexual minority youth into one category so that independent trends can be more well delineated among these groups. Second, much of the data we have is from community or clinic-based recruitment and therefore may not be generalizable.[7] Transgender youth have also self-reported higher rates of long-term mental health difficulties (59.3%) than their cisgender peers (17.4%).[5]

Public Health Impact

Multiple factors can contribute to transgender adolescents' mental health including victimization, body dissatisfaction, and age at which acknowledgement and treatment are initiated. Both general risk factors such as social support, major depressive disorder symptoms, and feelings of hopelessness, and LGBT-specific risk factors such as victimization, can influence suicide.[8] One study reported that transgender youth they surveyed reported more depressive symptoms and school-based victimization, but these two factors only account for 14-17% of the association between gender identity and suicidal ideation.[7] It is therefore reasonable to assume additional factors exist that account for this association, and further exploration in research should continue.

Another factor that could play a role in transgender youth suicide is body dissatisfaction. In a study conducted by Peterson et al., transgender youth at a clinic were surveyed and results reflected that 30.3% had attempted suicide and 41.8% had performed self-injurious behaviors.[9] They found that a significant relationship exists between a drive for weight change and history of suicide attempts among transgender youth. Forty-one percent of the transgender youth who indicated they had an interest in weight loss or gain, also had a history of a suicide attempt compared to the only 20% who indicated no weight change was desired and had a suicide attempt.[9] Comorbid mental health difficulties could influence suicidality among transgender youth.

Age at which medical treatment is initiated is another aspect of the transgender experience that could impact suicidality. If a transgender adolescent presents at a later stage of development (Tanner stage 4-5), it would be too late for pubertal suppressive therapy and the option would be to begin cross-sex hormone therapy. Of transgender patients who presented for medical treatment, one sample study found that 44.3% of patients had a significant psychiatric history, 21.6% had history of self-injurious behavior, and 9.3% had previous suicide attempts. They observed that with medical treatment, psychiatric functioning improved. [10] One study has found that among socially transitioned transgender children (meaning they live openly as their identified gender) had average rates of depression and slightly higher rates of anxiety than their non-transgender peers and this trend is argued to extrapolate into allowing children to socially transition and family support can decrease the high rates of depression in this group.[14] If family support is not present, it could be beneficial to engage in family therapy. The uncomfortable unknown can force adults to have unsupportive attitudes, and family therapy could help target both family stressors and parental coping.

Prevention

Solutions to address suicidality among transgender youth include: further research, addressing stigma, safe school environments, and continued education for healthcare providers. Shortcomings exist within transgender health research. While mental health is the most common research topic in transgender health, most of investigations are prevalence studies and there is a paucity of studies focused on risk factors, PTSD, and eating disorders.[11] In addition, more studies are needed that include a measured intervention, a focus on social and economic exclusion, and legal issues faced by transgender individuals.[11] More population-based studies and studies that do not just classify participants as binary male or female are needed.[5, 11]

Although there has been a gradual and general trend of acceptance for gender non-conformity, significant stigma continues to exist and hinder minority populations. Change is a hallmark of adolescence for most teenagers, and transgender or gender non-conforming adolescents may experience more stress than the average teenager. Transgender adults have been found to be less likely to attempt suicide if there is less structural stigma in place that includes societal conditions, policies and practices, and culture norms.[12] It is argued that future studies should include structural stigma such as hate crime policies, changing birth certificates, and general attitudes concerning transgender rights and legal protections. Changing structural stigma could impact the rate of transgender suicide attempts.[12]

Another arm of the solution exists at school. Transgender students who perceive they are in a more supportive school environment tend to also report that they have fewer depressive symptoms and suicidality.[13] Preventing victimization could decrease hopelessness and depression to ultimately prevent suicide attempts.[8] Increased efforts and attention should be given to transgender youth who have made a prior attempt, this was the strongest predictor for future attempts, and those who have an early same-sex attraction.[8]

My Personal Interview

An important aspect of attempting to understand a health disparity is to interact with the people who are affected by it or have a greater knowledge base. One such person is a woman who dedicates her time to answering a LGBTQIA helpline. Her interest in volunteering stems from having a both a gay and transgender grandchild. When speaking with her, she echoed the theme of the importance of family support that is easily reflected in the literature. This was especially important for her grandchild, whose identified gender made school officials uncomfortable to the point that she was asked to no longer attend their school. Her granddaughter's healthcare experience was positive in that her mother was her advocate, and explained the appropriate name, pronouns, etc. to staff and the physician. However, it was not indicated in the medical chart that she was transgender, and this caused confusion when another healthcare provider, who did not know her, took over her care for an acute sick visit. Overall, the most important thing a pediatrician can do is to listen to what a child is saying they feel about themselves, and to not discount it if we do not understand it.

Recommendation

As healthcare providers, we should strive to be compassionate and open to continuing education when caring for transgender patients. It is important to be open to caring for these patients because not only do they deserve the same dignity and respect that we afford our other patient populations, but it is our duty as physicians to look out for our vulnerable patients.

Not all healthcare providers have the experience or comfort of caring for transgender patients, but by continuing our own education about this marginalized and at-risk group, we can better serve them. The Gay and Lesbian Medical Association (GLMA) has published "Ten Things Transgender Persons Should Discuss with their Health Care Providers."[15] These recommendations are geared toward adults and include access to healthcare, health history, hormones, cardiovascular health, cancer, sexually transmitted diseases and safe sex, alcohol and tobacco, depression, injectable silicone, and fitness. While a subset of these topics is applicable to adolescents, it could benefit health care providers to have an adolescent-specific list to ensure they are addressing the main problems that face transgender adolescents.

Simple changes can be made in a primary care office to honor transgender patients' dignity and foster a more trusting environment. The National LGBT Health Education Center has published educational materials to support healthcare practitioners achieve this. Examples of recommendations include patient intake forms can include more options than binary man or woman; front line staff, nurses, medical aids, and providers can be trained to ask politely and respectfully about preferred pronouns and names, and to politely apologize if a mistake is made; non-discrimination policies including the terms "Gender identity and expression" can be displayed.[16]

Conclusion

Overall, it is clear that transgender adolescents experience higher rates of suicidality – this includes both suicidal ideation and suicidal acts. Victimization, body dissatisfaction, and age at which acknowledgement and treatment are initiated are just three factors that can influence suicidality among these adolescents. Further research, addressing stigma, safe school environments, and continued education for healthcare providers should be made priorities to address this public health concern.

References

1. "Suicide Among Youth" (2017). Centers for Disease Control and Prevention. Retrieved from https://www.cdc.gov/healthcommunication/toolstemplates/entertainmented/tips/SuicideYouth.html

2. "Trends in the Prevalence of Suicide – Related Behaviors. National YRBS: 1991-2017" (2017). CDC, Division of Adolescent and School Health.

3. "Transgender Persons" (2017). CDC: Lesbian, Gay, Bisexual, and Transgender Health. Retrieved from https://www.cdc.gov/lgbthealth/transgender.htm

4. Committee on Adolescence. (2013). Office-Based Care for Lesbian, Gay, Bisexual, Transgender, and Questioning Youth. Committee on Adolescence. *Pediatrics, 132,* 198-203. doi: 10.1542/peds.2013-1282

5. Rider, G.N., McMorris, B.J., Gower, A.L., Coleman, E., & Eisenberg, M.E. (2018). Health and Care Utilization of Transgender and Gender Nonconforming Youth: A population based study. *Pediatrics, 141.* doi: https://doi.org/10.1542/peds.2017-1683

6. Edwards-Leeper, L., Feldman, H.A., Lash, B.R., Shumer, D.E., & Tishelman, A.C. (2017). Psychological Profile of the First Sample of Transgender Youth Presenting for Medical Intervention in a U.S. Pediatric Gender Center. *Psychology of Sexual Orietnation and Gender Diversity, 4,* 374-382. doi: 10.1037/sgd0000239

7. Perez-Brumer, A, Day, J.K., Russel, S.T., Hatzenbuehler, M.L. (2017). Prevalence and Correlates of Suicidal Ideation Among Transgender Youth in California: Findings from a Representative, Population Based Sample of High School Students. *Journal of American Academy of Child and Adolescent Psychiatry, 56(9),* 739-746.

8. Mustanski, B. & Liu, R.T. (2013). A Longitudinal Study of Predictors of Suicide in Lesbian, Gay, Bisexual, and Transgender Youth. *Archives of Sexual Behavior, 42,* 437-448. doi: 10.1007/s10508-012-0013-9

9. Peterson, C.M., Matthews, A., Copps-Smith, E., Conrad, L.A. (2016). Suicidality, Self-Harm, and Body Dissatisfaction in Transgender Adolescents and Emerging Adults with Gender Dysphoria. *Suicide and Life-Threatening Behavior, 47(4).* doi: 10.1111/sltb.12289

10. Spack, N.P., Edwards-Leeper, L., Feldman, H.A., Leibowitz, S., Mandel, F., Diamond, D.A., Vance, S.R. (2012). Children and Adolescents with Gender Identity Disorder Referred to a Pediatric Medical Center. *Pediatrics, 129(3),* 418-425. doi:10.1542/peds.2011-0907

11. Reisner, S.L., Poteat, T., Keatley, J., Cabral, M., Mothopeng, T., Dunham, E., Holland, C.E., Max, R., Baral, S.D. (2016). Global Health Burden and

Needs of Transgender populations: a review. *The Lancet, 388,* 412-436. doi: http://dx.doi.org/10.1016/S0140-6736(16)00684-X

12. Perez-Brumer, A., Hatzenbuehler, M.L., Oldenburg, C.E., & Bockting, W. (2015). Individual- and Structural-Level Risk Factors for Suicide Attempts Among Transgender Adult. *Behavioral Medicine, 41(3),* 164-171. doi: 10.1080/08964289.2015.1028322

13. Denny, S., Lucassen, M.F.G., Stuart, J., Fleming, T., Bullen, P., Peiris-John, R., Rossen, F.V., & Utter, J. (2016). The association between supportive high school environments and depressive symptoms and suicidality among sexual minority students. *Journal of Clinical Child & Adolescent Psychology, 45(3),* 248-261. doi: 10.1080/15374416.2014.958842

14. Olson, R.K., Durwood. L., DeMeules, M., McLaughlin, K.A. (2016). *Pediatrics, 137(3).*):e20153223

15. Allison, R.A. (2012). "Ten Things Transgender Persons Should Discuss with their Health Care Providers" Gay and Lesbian Medical Association. Retrieved from http://www.glma.org/index.cfm?fuseaction=Page. viewPage&pageID=692

16. Reisner, S. *Meeting the Health Care Needs of Transgender People* [PowerPoint slides]. Retrieved from http://www.lgbthealtheducation. org/wp-content/uploads/Sari-slides_final1.pdf

PrEP for HIV Prevention and the Rise of Other STIs: LGBT Health Provision for Primary Care Providers

Anonymous

Background

Men who have sex with men (MSM), typically those who identify as bisexual or gay men, have long presented a challenging health care population for the general primary care provider. Nationally, MSM are estimated to be about 4% of the population (Purcell et al, 2012). The human immunodeficiency virus (HIV) that leads to acquired immune deficiency syndrome (AIDS) exploding in the 1980s ignited growing concern for medical provision that addressed the unique features of sexual activity in the lesbian, gay, bisexual, and transgender (LGBT) population that fostered HIV. Other sexually transmitted infections (STIs) were also of concern. Historically, efforts were made to reduce the frequency of sexual contact and improve safer sex practices for MSM.

Note: This paper does not attempt to differentiate between biological sex and gender identity, and accepts that some terminology in this paper may seem exclusive of transgender men, those born as female and later transitioning to identify on the masculine spectrum and who also have sex with other men. Transgender MSM are well within the spectrum of this conversation regarding HIV and STIs and may require additional considerations such as penetrative vaginal sex, decreased power or availability of selection in negotiating a sexual interchange, and risk for cervical cancer in the absence of a total hysterectomy.

Examples of safer sex practices include increasing barrier use with condoms for penetrative anal sex and dental dams for the practice known as "rimming," in which one man applies oral contact to another man's anus, biannual or quarterly HIV screening, and closing men's bathhouses where there were high rates of bareback (unprotected) sexual activity. With the advent of *highly active antiretroviral therapy* (HAART), HIV became less of a burden. Currently HIV is generally well controlled on a triple drug HAART regimen, leading to lower rates of HIV transmission among HIV positive men. These interventions represent a multipronged public health approach including primary, secondary, and tertiary prevention as well as individual and community level interventions. Now the newest generation of MSM is coming to age of identity development and sexual activity without a communal memory of AIDS-related losses and safer sex practices.

PrEP (Pre-exposure prophylaxis)

Previously, interventions mainly relied on the willingness to be active in identifying oneself as either negative or positive or assuming that the use of barriers is mandatory for sexual activity. However, U.S. epidemiological data from 2008 to 2011 demonstrated that the rate of new infections annually was staying steady at 15-16/100,000 despite interventions (Centers for Disease Control and Prevention, 2013). While there is a 72-hour window in which someone can take post-exposure prophylaxis using a high dose three-drug HAART regimen, availability is limited. The development of *pre-exposure prophylaxis* (PrEP), where two HAART medications can be taken on a daily basis, is an enormous tool to lower HIV transmission risk. According to the U.S. Public Health Service clinical practice guidelines for PrEP (2014), typically PrEP is prescribed as a single pill called Truvada (Gilead), a combination of emtricitabine and tenofovir. Taken daily, PrEP is more effective than condom use; the CDC Vital Signs report (*MMWR*, 2015) cites studies showing risk reduction of 92% for MSM, and that this rate translates to real life practice.

PrEP use requires screening beforehand to ensure that a person is HIV negative and liver function tests are normal. If unknowingly HIV positive, PrEP could encourage the development of a drug resistant viral strain. For this reason, initial and quarterly HIV screening is mandatory. Many patients volunteer to have comprehensive STI screening (primarily gonorrhea, chlamydia, and syphilis) in conjunction with the quarterly HIV screen. PrEP also requires daily adherence, though studies show that if taken "on demand" before and after sexual activity, its effectiveness seems to be similar (Molina, et al., 2015).

PrEP empowers HIV negative men with the ability to reduce risk of seroconversion, or the transition from HIV negative to HIV positive. PrEP is also a powerful agent in reducing the stigma surrounding HIV, and many HIV negative MSM anecdotally ascribe PrEP with their growing willingness to sexually and romantically interact with HIV positive men (Peterson, 2014; anonymous, personal communications, multiple, 2015).

However, as Peterson also mentions, the introduction of PrEP has not come without its criticisms. The largest is that PrEP is negatively viewed as the liberty to "bareback" or "whore around" (increased number of sexual partners) – in other words, the ability to control one's own risk regardless of sexual partner choice or drug use bestows the freedom to have unhindered sexual activity and unsafe activity. Therefore, even if HIV transmission alone is effectively reduced, other STIs or unsafe behaviors may increase. Therefore, some see PrEP as a potentially double-edged sword.

Epidemiology

However disturbing trends have emerged from the Centers for Disease Control and Prevention (CDC) STI surveillance data. In 2015, the CDC published a report on syphilis announcing a 15% increase in newly reported primary and secondary syphilis cases, ascribing 83% of those to a partner who is MSM. Kaiser Permanente in San Francisco (2015) also released data showing that for MSM using PrEP, there were zero new infections in a study group of 388 person-years of observation (657 patients that started PrEP). Yet accompanying no new HIV infections were self-reported data showing in a subset population of 143 patients, 41% reported a decrease in using condoms and number of sexual partners increased in 11%. Kaiser did not have a control group, but 50% of PrEP users had at least one separate STI within 12 months, including 5.5% with syphilis. While this cannot be correlated with decreased condom use or increased number of partners, and also is a very small sample, it does attest to the vigilance of STI screening in MSM.

As Boston institution Fenway Health HIV/AIDS researcher Kevin Maloney states, his currently unpublished data demonstrate that local cases of syphilis in MSM have been previously well contained within the HIV positive population but has increased in HIV negative MSM concurrent with the increasing use of PrEP (personal communication, November 23, 2015). Fenway's observational research also reveals increased rectal and pharyngeal gonorrheal and chlamydial infections, indicative of sexual activity likely without barrier protection. However, establishing causation is difficult because, as Maloney explains, the increases in syphilis and rectal and pharyngeal gonorrhea likely predated the start of PrEP. PrEP also mandates increased frequency of STI screening, so increased incidence is expected, forming essentially lead time bias with asymptomatic infections and more likelihood for reinfection within the same time frame as previous testing frequencies were held. Unfortunately, Maloney sees no way to analyze the data that circumvents the increased screening frequency conundrum, but the data that shows the spread of syphilis outside of the HIV positive population is nonetheless a developing trend in Boston's MSM community. There is speculation, without evidence for correlation, that there may be more intermingling of HIV positive and HIV negative sexual partners, both with and without barrier protection.

These trends are not isolated to Boston; Dr. Mark Goodman, family physician specializing in HIV/AIDS and LGBT care for the metropolitan Omaha area, has also seen an increase of syphilis diagnoses in his office visits over the last two years (personal communication, November 25, 2015). In Omaha, gonorrhea and chlamydia are found primarily in heterosexual women, so he has not seen an accompanying rise of these infections among his MSM patients. The Douglas County Health Department STDs Report (2015) shows, however, that cases of syphilis remained 10 or less until 2013, when suddenly cases rose to 30 and continued to rise to 37 in 2014; the report does not offer a gender other demographic breakdown, but Dr. Goodman states his cases have almost exclusively been among MSM or persons who have sex with MSM.

Impact on Health Care

The impact on primary care providers and allied health providers is tangible. We are still struggling as a generation of physicians on how to integrate LGBT identity into our clinical practices. Medical school merely teaches us how to inquire about sexual partners and the gender of sexual partners; very little, if any, time is spent educating us on PrEP, current STI trends, or special health care issues relevant to LGBT individuals. Furthermore, as Manning (2014) describes, MSM often view sexual health discussions with their primary care providers negatively as being HIV-centric and neglecting their full identity as a gay or bisexual man, including the romantic aspects of dating, the psychological well-being under heterosexism/homophobia, and the continuous coming out process.

It is time for primary care providers to push beyond merely accepting the diversity of patients presenting to our offices but to become acutely aware of trends affecting these populations. For our gay and bisexual men who are sexually active, current developments are the use of PrEP as well as the recent rises in syphilis nationally, as well as other infections. The CDC (2015) is concerned that syphilis infection is often associated with HIV coinfection, given the ulceration (this increased risk of HIV infection is also found with herpes, secondary to the ulcerative rash that develops in the genitals). The other concern is whether persons becoming infected with syphilis are also conducting higher risk behaviors, regardless of whether one is taking PrEP or not. An answer to this is to offer and explain, without judgment, the need for STI testing in a way that does not automatically assume that any patient in the office is promiscuous or engaging in riskier sexual behaviors. A possible way to encroach this topic is to explain the reality that syphilis is often confused as an innocuous sore, such as a ingrown hair. Providers, similarly, need to educate ourselves on anal pap smears and pharyngeal cultures to assess for rectal HPV, gonorrhea, and chlamydia.

Research on PrEP-like interventions for other STIs is also underway; Bolan et al (2015) conducted a small sample study of MSM showing that doxycycline taken daily as a prophylactic reduced STI infections by 73% compared to a control group. However, the authors detail concerns about developing antibiotic resistant strains of syphilis, gonorrhea, and chlamydia, as well as the feasibility of financing on a larger scale. Yet, these may become tools in providers' pockets over the next decade. Other questions remain regarding the use of PrEP and these interventions, such as their cost of provision versus costs saved and systemic oppression of LGBT and HIV positive persons. These issues require considerable thought beyond the narrow scope of STIs concurrent with PrEP administration.

Conclusion

Eugene McCray and Jonathan Mermin, directors under the CDC HIV/AIDS Division concluded in a memorandum on November 24, 2015 that PrEP is an underutilized parcel of a comprehensive HIV/AIDS prevention and risk reduction package, and does not represent a deviation away from barrier use, reducing intravenous drug needle sharing, and effective HAART. They note that primary care providers remain undereducated about PrEP. Yet, the data shows that regardless of other STI rates rising, PrEP is absolutely integral to reducing new annual cases of HIV for MSM, as well as relevant in intravenous drug users and some very high-risk heterosexual individuals. However, for primary care providers the use of PrEP should only imply that we need to shift from simply integrating LGBT identities as a set of formulaic questions regarding gender of sexual partners, HIV testing, and whether one needs birth control. Instead, providers need to educate themselves about PrEP, their local community trends of STIs, and understand that PrEP is undoing several decades' internalized stigma regarding being HIV positive. Yet, with this comes a very real need to have open dialogues with MSM patients about their sexual practices and the risks of having other STIs despite their less fatal consequences. We must move away from the discourse that MSM are inherently promiscuous or should fear HIV but envision a future that is, hopefully, free from new HIV infections but also free from the fear of discussing sexual health topics engagingly with primary care providers.

There are many resources available for educating oneself on LGBT health issues and PrEP, listed at the end of this article. Local Omaha pharmacies are well educated on the nuances of PrEP therapy; their numbers are also listed. At this time, provider education is largely self-initiated or at the behest of larger employers and medical school curriculum developers through medical education courses, but the conversation is growing.

References

1. Bolan, R.K., Beymer, M.R., Weiss, R.E., Flynn, R.P., Leibowitz, A.A., & Klausner, J.D. (2015). Doxycycline Prophylaxis to Reduce Incident Syphilis among HIV-Infected Men Who Have Sex With Men Who Continue to Engage in High-Risk Sex. *Sexually Transmitted Diseases*, 42(2), 98-103. http://dx.doi.org/10.1097/olq.0000000000000216

2. Centers for Disease Control and Prevention. (2013, February). *HIV Surveillance Report, 2011*; vol. 23. Retrieved November 25, 2015 from http://www.cdc.gov/hiv/topics/surveillance/ resources/reports

3. Centers for Disease Control and Prevention. (2015, November 9). *Syphilis and MSM (Men Who Have Sex With Men) – CDC Fact Sheet*. Retrieved November 27, 2015 from www.cdc.gov/std/syphilis/stdfact-msm-syphilis. htm

4. Douglas County Health Department. (2015, July 06). *STDs in Douglas County*. Retrieved November 27 ,2015 from http://www. douglascountyhealth.com/images/stories/stats/ morbidity/STD2014_ short_final_2014PopEst.pdf

5. Kaiser Permanente. (2015, September 1). Press Release: Large Study of PrEP Use in Clinical Practice Shows No New HIV Infections. Retrieved

November 25, 2015, from http://share.kaiserpermanente.org/article/large-study-of-prep-use-in-clinical-practice-shows-no-new-hiv-infections/

6. Manning, J. (2014). Coming Out Conversations and Gay/Bisexual Health: A Constitutive Model Study. In V. Harvey & T. Heinz Hounsel, *Health Care Disparities and the LGBT Population* (1st ed., pp. 27-54). Lanham, CT: Lexington Books.

7. McCray, E. & Mermin, J.H. (2015, November 24). Dear Colleague: November 24, 2015 (Centers for Disease Control and Prevention) Retrieved November 24, 2015, from http://www.cdc.gov/hiv/dhap/ new/ dcl/112415.html

8. Molina, J., Capitant, C., Spire, B., Pialoux, G., Chidiac, C., Charreau, I.,. . . Delfraissy J. (2015). On Demand PrEP with Oral TDF-FTC in MSM: Results of the ARNS Ipergay Trial. [Abstract] Retrieved November 25, 2015 from http://www.croiconference.org/ sessions/demand-prep-oral-tdf-ftc-msm-results-anrs-ipergay-trial

9. Peterson, E. (2014, November 12). The Case for PrEP, or How I Learned to Stop Worrying and Love HIV-Positive Guys. Retrieved November 25, 2015, from http://www.thestranger. Com/seattle/the-case-for-prep-or-how-i-learned-to-stop-worrying-and-love-hiv-positive-guys/ Content?oid=20991643

10. Purcell, D.W., Johnson, C.H., Lansky, A., Prejean, J., Stein, R., Denning, P., . . . Crepaz, N. (2012). Estimating the Population Size of Men Who Have Sex with Men in the United States to Obtain HIV and Syphilis Rates. *The Open AIDS Journal, 6*(1), 98-107. DOI: 10.2174/1874613601206010098

11. Smith, D., Van Handel, M., Wolitski, R., Stryker, J., Hall, H., Prejean, J., . . . Valleroy, L. (2015, November 24:64(Early release);1-6). Vital Signs: Estimated Percentages and Numbers of Adults with Indications for Preexposure Prophylaxis to Prevent HIV Acquisition — United States, 2015. Centers for Disease Control and Prevention. Retrieved November 24, 2015, from http://www.cdc.gov/mmwr/preview/mmwr html/ mm64e1124a1.htm?s_cid=mm64e1124a1_w

12. US Public Health Service. (2014). Preexposure Prophylaxis for the Prevention of HIV Infection in the United States—2014: A Clinical Practice Guideline. Retrieved November 25, 2015, from http://www.cdc.gov/hiv/pdf/guidelines/PrEPguidelines2014.pdf

Resources

US Public Health Service PrEP Clinical Guidlelines:

- http://www.cdc.gov/hiv/pdf/guidelines/PrEPguidelines2014.pdf

Centers for Disease Control and Prevention HIV/AIDS: http://www.cdc.gov/hiv

- PrEP resources, informatics, fact sheets (http://www.cdc.gov/hiv/risk/prep/index.html)
- Bulletins regarding ongoing and new studies
- Epidemiology
- Resources on funding

GLMA (Health Professionals Advancing LGBT Equality): http://www.glma.org

- Patient and provider resources
- Several webinars on LGB and Transgender health
- Annual conference

National LGBT Health Education Center (Fenway Health, Boston): http://www.lgbthealtheducation.org

- Premier research center
- Learning modules
- Monthly webinars, including several on real life practice and outcomes of PrEP

- Publishes textbook on LGBT health

Association of American Medical Colleges:

- https://www.aamc.org/initiatives/diversity/portfolios/330894/lgbt-patientcare-project.html

- Advisory Committee on Sexual Orientation, Gender Identity, and Sex Development

Specialized Pharmacies in Omaha:

- Walgreens

  · 240 S 77th, Omaha, NE 68114

  · (402) 397-5906

- Kohll's:

  · Matthew Feerhusen – Specialized Medicine Advisor

  · mfeerhusen@kohlls.com

  · (402) 218-6926

Sexual Health and STIs among Sexual Minority Women

Anonymous

Introduction

The purpose of this paper is to investigate differences in sexual health between heterosexual and sexual minority women.

Sexual orientation identity and sexual behavior are important aspects of a patient's history, because differences in these aspects of sexuality predispose individuals to different risks. Both are important because the sexual behavior of an individual may not strictly align with her or his (or a different preferred pronoun) sexual preferences.

Sexual Behavior

A study in the United Kingdom investigated the sexual health of 708 lesbian and bisexual women (92% and 7% of the studied population, respectively) between 1992 and 1995 (Bailey et al., 2004). Although 92% of the women studied had a sexual preference for women, 82% of the total study population reported having a lifetime sexual history with men but 6.7% had sex with men in the past year. Bailey et al. did not include a breakdown of the demographics of their study population, so the sexual identity of those women who had sex with men in the past year is unclear (Bailey, 2004). Thus, their study investigates women's sexual practices based on those women who have sex with women (WSW) and women who have sex with men and women

(WSMW). The goal of their research was not to identify women's sexual practices and how they compare with sexual orientation and preference, but to look at how sexual practice affected sexually transmitted infection (STI) risk.

Chlamydia, gonorrhea, and pelvic inflammatory disease (PID) were diagnosed only in women with a history of sex with men, indicating that spread of these infections may require male sexual contact. However, there were not enough cases of these diseases and study participants to reach statistical significance. Three women who had never been sexually active with men were diagnosed with genital warts, primary genital herpes, or trichomoniasis. This suggests sexual transmission of these is possible between women. Bailey et al. did not inquire into specific sexual acts, so there is not data as to whether specific practices within female to female sexual contact are riskier than others in terms of STI risks (Bailey, 2004). Two women were diagnosed with hepatitis C, both of whom had a history of injection drug use, and are thus not protected from blood-borne acquisition of diseases. Smoking was also associated with a higher risk of having an STI; perhaps this is due to a propensity for riskier behavior.

Clearly, a larger volume of patients is needed. From the data Bailey et al. were able to gather, it appears that there is likely a difference in STI risk among women based on sexual behavior. It is important when collecting a sexual history to cover sexual practices, as well as other behavioral practices, as WSW can still transmit blood-borne diseases through injection drug use.

Sexual Orientation Identity

While it is important to look at sexual behavior to know what risks a patient faces, identity is also a crucial factor to consider. Everett investigated the differences in STI risk between behavior and identity and conclude that behavior and identity are neither interchangeable categories, nor does one perspective alone categorize the risks which patients face (Everett, 2013). Private sexual acts may facilitate transmission of disease based on tissue and fluid contact, but public sexual identity affects an individual's social behavior and how others perceive them. Sexual minorities—a broad description which refers to those who are not strictly heterosexual—face multiple issues. Additionally, behavior and identity do not perfectly align. Everett identified the range of women's sexual behavior separately from women's range of sexual orientation (Everett, 2013). In that study population, there were heterosexual women who have sex with men (WSM), heterosexual WSMW, bisexual WSMW, bisexual WSW, bisexual WSM, gay WSW, and gay WSMW.

When compared to heterosexual WSM (46.6%), gay WSMW (32.0%) have a lower STI risk, whereas heterosexual WSMW (58.1%) and bisexual WSM (51.1%) and bisexual WSMW (64.1%) have higher risks for contracting an STI (Everett, 2013). Not all sexual minority women need to be labeled as "high risk" in terms of STIs. What is important to consider are the social implications of being a sexual minority. Many sexual minorities face other challenges in their lives which accounts for some of the differences in STI risk. Everett reported that sexual minorities face "elevated levels of victimization, fewer political or interpersonal resources, as well as decreased access to social support systems and accurate sexual health information (Everett, 2013)." Heterosexual WSM faced the least amounts of victimization at 25% of that population, compared to 29.7% of bisexual WSM, 34.6% of gay WSMW, and 44.2% of bisexual WSMW. Being a sexual minority has the potential to "flag" an individual for victimization. Everett found this difference did account for much of the difference in STI risk between heterosexual WSM and sexual minorities (Everett, 2013). The rest of that difference in STI risk was accounted for by an increase in lifetime sexual partners and practice of anal sex by female sexual minorities. Other literature cited by Everett indicates "WSW/WSMW have higher rates of STI diagnosis and higher rates of engagement in several STI risk indicators, including intravenous drug use, exchanging sex for money, more lifetime sexual partners, and unprotected opposite-sex relationships, compared to WSM."

Dr. MG is a family practitioner who treats a large LGBTQIA patient base. In an interview, he noted observing these trends in STI risk among his female patients (Goodman, 2017). Regarding the increased STI risk among WSMW, he sees that often male partners of WSMW infect their female partners with STIs. Frequently, male partners of bisexual women are bisexual themselves. However, these men may remain closeted about attraction towards the same sex and feel shameful. This can lead to a hesitance to approach same-sex encounters with a clear head, and patients often "dive in" to situations, use alcohol or drugs to mask discomfort, and do not consider safe sexual practices. Not wanting to admit a same-sex sexual encounter to their female partner afterwards, they may continue to neglect use of safe sex practices to hide their actions, even if they have contracted an STI.

Sexual behavior does not necessarily line up with sexual orientation identity. Behavior is important, but it does not exist in a social vacuum. Identity differences may increase other social risks like victimization. While the medical field often uses sexual behavior to categorize patients based on risk for different diseases and conditions, there are differences in STI risks between orientation identity and sexual behavior which are important to consider.

HPV Screening

As a specific STI, human papilloma virus (HPV) is important due to its involvement in cervical cancer. Knowing sexual minority women are at higher risk of STIs in general, it is important to focus on HPV specifically because of the additional healthcare involved in screening for it and cervical cancer. Charlton et al. found that compared to completely heterosexual women, bisexual and mostly heterosexual women had a 30% lower odd of having a Papanicolaou (Pap) smear within the past year, but had a 29% increased odd of ever having a Pap smear (Charlton, 2011). This is in conjunction with lesbian identifying women, who had an 87% decreased odd of having a lifetime Pap smear and a 75% decreased odd of having a Pap smear within the year. Charlton et al. also found that the rate for an abnormal Pap smear was similar between sexual orientations at 20%, as was HPV diagnoses, at 66% (Charlton, 2011). This is important. Even though primary transmission of HPV is female to male, spread is also possible through between women, as also supported by Everett in 2013 (Charlton et al., 2011). As Everett pointed out, orientation does not always align perfectly with behavior (Everett, 2013). Charlton et al.

found that most of each sexual orientation had sexual contact with males, with lesbians at 65%, bisexuals at 96%, mostly heterosexuals at 97%, and completely heterosexuals at 90% (Charlton, 2011). Additionally, sexual minorities are at increased risk of cigarette smoking, which increases the risk of progression from an HPV infection to invasive carcinoma. Thus, lesbians and any WSW are at risk for HPV acquisition and development of cervical cancer, and need screening for these diseases.

Physician Use

Not only are sexual minority women not getting pap smears as frequently, but they are also going for fewer annual physicals. Charlton et al. found that while 59% of completely heterosexual females received a physical examination in the past year, 53% of mostly heterosexual, 54% of bisexual, and 47% lesbian females had an exam (Charlton, 2011).

There seem to be multiple reasons for this decreased usage of health services by female sexual minorities. One is the belief that orientation is a protective factor against STIs; by having sex with other women rather than men, young women believe they are unable to contract STIs (Ben-Natan et al., 2009). Goodman observed that many lesbians and WSW have a strong attitude of self-sufficiency with less reliance on the medical profession (Goodman, 2017). These women often also have a strong preference for a female provider for pelvic and breast exams, and may have a decreased perception of want and need for the same. Additionally, non-heterosexual and WSW may have less social support from family and friends, which can mean decreased external/social impetus for visiting a physician (Everett, 2013 & Charlton et al., 2011). Goodman disagrees with this, noting that many lesbian women and other sexual minority females work together to form a tight-knit, supportive community (Goodman, 2017). Adverse experiences with prior pap screens may also negatively impact the motivation for sexual minority women to seek care (Marrazzo et al., 2001). As well, since sex between women is not procreative, lesbians may not seek out birth control, and thus do not have the need to visit a doctor to renew contraceptive prescriptions or replace a long-acting reversible contraceptive (Charlton et al., 2011).

Physician Attitude

Related to women's negative prior experiences with pap testing, it is important to create an environment for women to be comfortable with their physicians early on in a woman's history of care. Fuzzell et al. investigates practitioners' interactions with female adolescent patients (Fuzzell, 2016). For sexual minority adolescents, inclusivity is a crucial factor to the interview, including openness and non-assumptive interviewing regarding pronouns, sexual behavior, and sexual orientation. These are important aspects for adolescent sexual health care overall, as adolescents are still forming their sexual identity and may not have established a sexual orientation. Ways to create this comfort with patients are to ask about attraction rather than orientation to be more indirect about sexuality, include signs identifying the office as a "Safe Zone," and to ask and inform about sexual topics at every visit (Fuzzell et al., 2016).

Conclusions

It is important when interviewing a patient to learn about sexual orientation as well as sexual behavior, and to do so inclusively and in an open manner. In treating sexual minority patients, STI screening is especially important in WSMW, and should not be neglected in WSW. HPV testing and Pap smears should also be included in regular treatment of WSW, and these patients should be encouraged to receive regular care by their provider.

References

1. Bailey JV, Farquhar C, Owen C, Mangtani P. Sexually transmitted infections in women who have sex with Women. Sex Transm Infect 2004;80:244-246.

2. Ben-Natan M, Adir O. Screening for cervical cancer among Israeli lesbian women. Int Nurs Rev 2009;56:433–41.

3. Charlton BM et al. Reproductive Health Screening Disparities and Sexual Orientation in a Cohort Study of U.S. Adolescent and Young Adult Females. Journal of Adolescent Health 2011;49:505–510.

4. Everett BG. Sexual Orientation Disparities in Sexually Transmitted Infections: Examining the Intersection Between Sexual Identity and Sexual Behavior. Arch Sex Behav 2013;42:225–236.Fuzzell L et al. "I just think that doctors need to ask more questions":

5. Sexual minority and majority adolescents' experiences talking about sexuality with healthcare providers. Patient Education and Counseling 2016;99:1467–1472.

6. Goodman, Mark. Interview, December 12, 2017.

7. Marrazzo JM, Koutsky LA, Kiviat NB, et al. Papanicolaou test screening and prevalence of genital human papillomavirus among women who have sex with women. Am J Public Health 2001;91:947–52.

The Rise of Gynecologic and Breast Cancer in the LGBT Community: Exploring the Barriers and Risk Factors among Lesbians and Transgender Men.

Anonymous

Introduction

There are many expert opinions in the health care community that guide practicing physicians using evidence-based medicine on the care for patients in disease prevention. Physicians look to the guidelines for cancer screenings from the United States Preventative Services Task Force (USPSTF), American Cancer Society, American Academy of Family Physicians, and the American College of Obstetrics and Gynecology to name a few. Each society puts out recommendations for patients in relation to gender, age, and risk factors. For example, in relation to breast cancer screening, USPSTF recommends a screening mammography every 1-2 years for women age 40 years and older (USPSTF A and B recommendations, July 2018). This recommendation and many others are created without consideration for the fact that not all patients who require certain preventative screening fit into the vague categories defined by the guidelines. Physicians look to these expert recommendations to guide their practice of medicine to screen patients for cancers for earlier detection and potential treatment. However, a patient that presents for an annual health care visit may not be a 45-year-old heterosexual woman who needs her annual mammogram, but a recently transgender female to male patient who has a cervix and breasts.

As a physician, an oath is taken to first *do no harm*. In order to abide by this oath physicians, strive to create and protect the physician-patient relationship. This relationship is important with all patients, but particularly important in the sensitive relationships of those individuals marginalized by the current health care system in the US. This paper will focus on the two groups of marginalized women: lesbian women and women who have transitioned to the male gender. These two groups are important for physicians to consider because of the increased risk of gynecologic and breast cancer compared to heterosexual women.

Background

In July 2014, The National Health Institute Survey reported that 3% of Americans identify as gay, lesbian, transgender (Gates, 2014). The Association of American Medical Colleges (AAMC) developed an advisory committee on sexual orientation, gender identity, and sex development that have defined terminology to improve health care for individuals who are of the sexual minority. The AAMC defines a lesbian as "a female person who identifies her primary romantic feelings, sexual attractions, and/or arousal patterns as being toward a person of the same gender or sex" (Association of American Medical Colleges, 2014). Lesbian women are considered to be in the sexual minority in regard to their health care and cancer prevention. Being in the sexual minority puts this group at increased risk for cancer. The National Cancer institute collects data on many factors relating to cancer, but it does not collect data regarding sexual orientation (Brown, 2008). Based on that fact alone, this group of females is being understudied and not considered in major data points relating to cancers with high morbidity and mortality. Additionally, this group of women is faced with certain risk factors that put that at an increased risk for certain cancers, in particular breast, ovarian, and endometrial. There are certain risk factors that are known to increase a women's risk of having breast, ovarian, and endometrial cancers. These include age, family history, exposure to estrogen, use of oral contraception pills, body weight, pregnancy, tobacco and alcohol use (McPherson, 2000). Lesbians are more likely to be nulliparous (4.7 times more likely), less likely to use oral contraceptive pills and have higher rates of obesity (Willes and Allen, 2014, p. 14; Brown, 2008). These risk factors are leading to higher incidence of female cancers in this group of women. Sadly, the most studied risk factors of the sexual minority are HIV and tobacco use (Burkhalter, 2010). In regard to cancer screening for women, mammography and Pap smears are important screening for the detection of breast and cervical cancers. Lesbians are 2.3 times more likely to never have had a Pap smear (Brown 2008) and 53% of lesbian women vs. 73% of heterosexual women are less likely to have biannual mammogram screening (Kerker, 2006). With the Pap smear being such a vital and effective screening test with a negative predictive value of higher than 99% and when combined with Human Papilloma Virus testing reached 100% sensitivity and a specificity of 92.5% for cervical cancer (Mayrand, 2007). It is detrimental to this group of women who are at risk to the Human Papilloma Virus. Interestingly, a study showed that lesbian women believe that they are less susceptible to cervical cancer than heterosexual women (Price, 1996).

The American Association of Medical Colleges (AAMC) defines transgender as "individuals who have gender identities that do not align with the gender labels they were assigned at birth" (Association of American Medical Colleges, 2014). Female to male transition are referred to transgender men, many of whom retain female organs such as breast tissue, ovaries, uterus, and cervix. This population is of the 3% of sexual minority with only 0.3% identifying as transgender (Gates, 2014). While this number is small, there is significance to the problem regarding health care screening for cancer prevention as many of the transgender population do not feel comfortable discussing this issue with their provider. The health disparities among the transgender population are extreme, the National Transgender Discrimination Survey found that 50% of participants had to educate their healthcare provider, 44% were denied treatment, and 28% postponed care due to stigmatization (Levitt, 2015). The lack of education for providers makes providing healthcare services even greater because not all transgender patients undergo gender-reaffirming surgeries. Transitioning can include hormone therapy, psychological therapy, and or surgery (Levitt, 2016). Therefore, a patient who appears as a male during the encounter based on appearance alone may still retain the organs of a female including a uterus and cervix warranting cervical cancer screening. An even larger barrier to healthcare for LGBT populations include insurance coverage. For example, gender specific services complications for transmen, legally changed genders from female to male could be denied coverage for a Pap smear. Pap smear is covered under women's wellness visit (Hartofelis, 2013). Even if transmen are receiving cancer preventative screening, it was found that they are 8.3 times more likely to have an inadequate Pap smear than non-transgender females (Peitzmeier, 2014). Additionally, transmen often tend to undergo virilization with testosterone administration. This puts transmen at an increased risk of cancer as androgens are metabolized to estradiol (Levitt, 2105). This increased estrogen increases the risk of breast cancer, ovarian cancers, endometrial, and cervical cancers. Long-term androgen treatment and testosterone therapy are linked to higher rates of Polycystic Ovarian Syndrome causing increased risk of endometrial, breast cancers and decreased fertility (Hartofelis, 2013).

Public Health

Health care disparities have largely focused on disparities in health and ethnicity, but health care disparities exist due to sexual orientation and gender. These disparities are finally starting to be recognized on a national level so that those affected can benefit from reductions in morbidity, mortality, and an improved quality of life. The Centers for Disease Control and Prevention's (CDC) Division of Cancer Prevention and Control has taken to idea of increasing research and data collection in regard to LGBT populations affect by certain cancers. The North American Association of Central Cancer Registries recently modified the sex categories to include: transgender, male; and transgender, female (Massetti, 2015). The CDC has additionally increased public health programs for evidence-based cancer screening interventions for underserved populations. These include the National Breast and Cervical Cancer Early Detection Program and the Colorectal Cancer Control Program. These both provide screening and diagnostic services to low-income, uninsured and underinsured women, and even better neither program has a gender eligibility requirement to increase the need in LGBT groups (Massetti, 2015).

The National Institute of Health (NIH) LGBT research coordinating committee has examined the lack of research in areas of the LGBT populations. The data showed that the largest percentages of NIH funded projects for the LGBT communities included behavioral and social sciences (82%), HIV/AIDS (81.5%), but projects relating to cancer were only 7.7% of projects (Burkhalter, 2016). To this effect, it appears that globally research and global preventative health efforts are largely focused on HIV and AIDS prevention in the LGBT communities.

Global Health

Globally, the LGBT populations face extensive discrimination. It is found in 2014, in 81 countries, (38 of the 81 in Africa), it is a criminal offense to engage in sexual practices between adults of the same sex. It is a capital offense in 5 countries (Scherdel, 2014). The United Nations Universal Declaration on Human Rights notes that this discrimination effects the health and overall wellbeing of LGBT populations (Scherdel, 2014). The impact the discrimination has on LGBT populations globally causing a barrier to health due to fear leading many LGBT people from gaining access to education, protection, preventative health care, and treatment for HIV and sexually transmitted infections (Nagata, 2017). In Uganda for example, there is a law in place for failure to report homosexual behavior is a crime causing health care workers treating LGBT populations punishment and puts barriers around research and clinical care (Nagata, 2017). This law further threatens the patient physician relationship because there is a standard of confidentiality in the care of a patient allowing patients to develop trust to disclosure their vulnerabilities relating to their health care.

The Williams Institute of UCLA School of Law started researching the global acceptance of LGBT populations. The report found that 80 countries experience increased acceptance of LGBT populations with Iceland, the Netherlands, Sweden, and Denmark being the most accepting and 46 countries experienced a decline in acceptance, those being Saudi Arabia and Ghana (Moreau, 2018). There is increase positive impact on LGBT physical and mental health, employment, and political participation when they are socially accepted by their respective communities (Moreau, 2018). The United Nations (UN) is doing its part in the work to break down barriers and increase inclusion and awareness to LGBT populations. In 2016, 12 UN agencies issued a statement on "combating violence and discrimination against LGBT people (Reid, 2016). This was the first statement of its kind put out by the UN for the universality of human rights for the LGBT populations. As great lengths are being undertaken to manage the disparities of LGBT populations globally, this community still faces heavy violence and discrimination calling for stronger efforts by world leaders.

Research (Interactions)

Obstetrics and Gynecology (OB-GYN) is a primary care specialty that is a point of entry of care for a lot of the LGBT populations. This specialty provides expertise on sexual and reproductive health and two OB-GYN's in the Omaha community were able to offer their perspective on caring for LGBT patients. Both Meaghan Shanahan, MD and Kristi NewMyer, MD are OB-GYNs in the community with passions for caring for LBGT populations and have experience with a diversity of LGBT patients. Each physician expresses the importance of creating a strong patient-physician relationship especially due to the longitudinal care of OB-GYN that cares for very intimate and sensitive areas of a patient's health. For Dr. Shanahan, she reassess gender and sexual orientation at every annual exam and is thinking about adding additional questions to intake forms regarding pronoun preference and gender identity to allow patients to feel more comfortable expressing their true identities to the physician. For Dr. NewMyer, she opens each encounter letting the patient know that her office is a safe environment and expresses the confidentiality of the relationship. Dr. NewMyer is very frank with her all her patients regardless of sexual orientation and gender identity, as well asking "how they identify", "are you sexually active, and what does that mean to you." It is noted that not all patients are having an intimate relationship and it is the job of a physician to ask very specific questions and not assume to show sensitivity to the topic.

Cancer screening and sexually transmitted infection screening and risks are very important in the field of OB-GYN for all patients including those that are LGBT. As OB-GYNs, Drs. S and NM discuss sexual risks including STI counseling, HIV, use of protection and contraception, and PreP with all their patients, regardless of gender and sexual orientation. Dr. NM expresses the importance of educating her patients who have multiple sexual partners or high-risk sexual activity the risk factors associated and that oral/pharyngeal infections are a possibility. For lesbian patients, she notes that many have had an "exploring stage", meaning have had sexual interactions with male partners, and there is risk of STIs and HPV associated. In relation to cancer screenings, each physician follows current cancer screening guidelines associated with the anatomy regardless of how a patient identifies. Both physicians note the importance of not classifying the cancer screenings associating with a particular gender. For example, in a transmale patient with breast tissue in place, refer to breast exams as "chest exams" and educate the patient that males also can develop breast cancer so there is a need to monitor for cancer. For female patients who have never had penetrative sex with a male, it is important to educate the patient of cervical, uterine, vulvar, and vaginal cancers to develop in the absence of exposure to HPV. Dr. NM educates patients who have had reconstructive genital surgery such as a neovagina that the tissue needs to be examined yearly as well because it is created from the penis and testicles leading to a chance of cancer.

Both physicians have encountered patients that have been victimized by past providers due to their gender and sexual identity. The LGBT populations have a difficult time finding providers for their health care because they feel they spend the visit educating the physician on what it means to be LGBT than about their health care issues. The physicians note the biggest barrier for LGBT health care is the lack of education for physicians, medical students, and residents. Additional awareness and education are needed to increase the amount of providers that the LGBT community will feel comfortable and received great health care. Dr. NM also notes that it is the job of the physician to simply ask the patient. She has encountered many patients who have gone 50+ years without physicians asking how they identify, and she was the first provider increasing their trust with her and the health care received.

A leader in both medicine as a Cardiologist and a Dean of medical education, Dr MW, offered a unique perspective on the physician patient relationship with the LGBT populations. As a Cardiologists, his patients suffer greatly after myocardial infarctions or due to congestive heart failure. He informs that in order to gain insight into the lives as a provider of his patients, he asks about their support networks. This is important from a medical standpoint because a patient's support network after a myocardial infarction greatly impacts their morbidity and mortality as explained by Dr. MW. More importantly, by asking about support networks and family life he is able to eloquently and compassionately discover a patients' sexual orientation and gender expression without making the patient feel discriminated against. When asked how a physician learns to have a comfortable dynamic with a patient from the LGBT community, Dr. White is frank and says "sensitivity to any patient, especially the LGBT is important. You need to have empathy and that is part of being a physician." It was further discussed that this may be hard for some physicians especially those who are specialist like Dr. MW who may not have the time or longitudinal care to form a deep patient physician relationship. He noted that is where our medical education system is failing providers. The current medical school curriculums are not designed to expose students to underserved and marginalized populations. As a leader and Dean of medical education, Dr. White sees the failure of the system and recommends that exposure is needed from the start in the first year of medical education. He does not feel a few lectures will provide the training for students to build sensitivity to their patients, but he recognizes the need of additional simulation modules. An example he describes is actors portraying an LGBT patient during the practice interviewing sessions. When students are able to make mistakes during their training, they feel more comfortable having those interactions in real practice. He believes the members of the LGBT community would be more than happy to assist medical education to further bridge the gap in physician training. Although Dr. MW, as a Cardiologist, does not have exposure to patients undergoing preventative cancer screens or exposure to gynecological cancers. He expresses that the LGBT populations are also at a high-risk in relation to their cardiovascular health. Providing an expert opinion that some of the HIV medications effect the cardiovascular system in a negative way, and the increase in obesity in the LGBT community puts them at a disadvantage from a cardiologists' point of view. He additionally points out that in all the cardiology research papers he has read; he has never seen a study that highlights the sexually marginalized or includes sexual orientation or gender identity data.

Recommendations

It is important to brainstorm how we can improve as physicians in decreasing the marginalization of the sexual minority and breaking down the health care barriers so that there is equal access and assessment in their health. In medical education, there is minimal effort in the curriculum at most institutions to teach future physicians how to approach the care of patients in the LGBT community. For lesbian patients, "clinicians often presume heterosexuality when taking a sexual history of a woman...and many feel uncomfortable reporting lesbian behavior" (Capriotti, 2016). Training during medical school needs to have more simulated patient encounters that highlight caring for an LGBT patient so that a foundation is set to provide care for this community in the future. It was noted previously that physical exams and screening tests for cancer such as a Pap smear are not performed as adequately as for a heterosexual, gender normative patient. Medical education is falling short if all patients are not treated equal in regard to history taking, physical exams, and testing creating an increased likelihood of missing ailments, especially cancer that could have been detected earlier. Medical school curricula need to allow students access to a more diverse patient population and integrate education that does not create marginalization.

The American College of Obstetrics and Gynecology (ACOG) has published opinions regarding serving the underserved LGBT populations. It is important for primary care organizations to be leaders as they are most often the first contact patients have to the health care system. In 2011, ACOG released an opinion paper noting the lack of awareness and knowledge leads the LGBT populations to have inadequate access and underutilization of health care (Hartofelis, 2013). It has been beneficial to see organizations making an effort to bridge the gap for underserved populations and this leads to increased policy change and an overall cultural change. More advocacy and awareness by leaders in various health care specialties, especially OB-GYN and other primary care organizations, because physicians look to these for guidance and education in the care of their patients.

As noted previously, more inclusion of sexual orientation and gender identity need to be included in research because the data collected often excludes LGBT populations. Burkhalter et al. notes that sexual orientation and gender identity are not collected by most cancer surveillance programs leading to a huge disparity for LGBT communities (2016). Physicians look to studies of evidence-based medicine to show the gold standards for care to patients. The LGBT communities deserve that same standard of care as all patients. Fortunately, there are efforts to start including these aspects as apart of data collection and research, but physicians need to also extrapolate current data and research to think how it has an impact on those not included. In parallel to our efforts on a national level, policy needs to change to allow coverage of screening tests regardless of gender. A female to male transgender patient who retains sexual organs and breast tissue should still be covered by insurance for a Pap smear and mammography to decrease the incidence and mortality of cervical, breast, and other gynecologic cancers in the sexual minority.

Conclusion

This paper addressed the barriers of the health of LGBT populations focusing on gynecologic and breast cancer in lesbian and transgender male patients. Bringing forth the data showing the risk factors lesbian and transgender patients face causing increased gynecologic and breast cancers, shows that this population is in need of an increased level of health care. Increasing awareness, education, and access to health care lends hope that the barriers to cancer screening, research, and the patient physician relationship will be bridged. Physicians are the leaders in helping underserved and marginalized communities access health care that is equal to the majority of patients. Current and future physicians need to do all they can to lead the world to recognize the failures in our current health care system and find solutions to allow better health care and well-being of all patients regardless of gender identity and sexual orientation.

References

1.   Brown, J. P., & Tracy, A. J. K. (2008). Lesbians and cancer: an overlooked health disparity. https://doi.org/10.1007/s10552-008-9176-z

2.   Burkhalter, J. E., Hay, J. L., Coups, E., Warren, B., Li, Y., Jamie, •, & Ostroff, S. (2010). Perceived risk for cancer in an urban sexual minority. https://doi.org/10.1007/s10865-010-9296-2

3.   Burkhalter, J. E., Margolies, L., Oli Sigurdsson, H., Walland, J., Radix, A., Rice, D., ... Maingi, S. (2016). The National LGBT Cancer Action Plan: A White Paper of the 2014 National Summit on Cancer in the LGBT Communities, 3(1). https://doi.org/10.1089/lgbt.2015.0118

4.   Capriotti, Theresa ; Gillespie, A. (2016). Healthcare issues in the LGBT community. *The Clinical Advisor: For Nurse Practitioners* , 19(8), 22–43. Retrieved from www.ClinicalAdvisor.com

5.   Gates, GJ. 2014. LGB/T Demographics: Comparisons among population-based surveys. Williams Institute, UCLA School of Law.11

6. Hartofelis, E. C., & Manchikanti Gomez, A. (2013). Expanding the Boundaries of Sexual & Reproductive Health Care. Retrieved from http://content.ebscohost.com/ContentServer.asp?T=P&P=AN&K=107 995115&S=R&D=ccm&EbscoContent=dGJyMNLe80Sep7c4yOvqOLC mr1Cep65Ss6i4SK6WxWXS&ContentCustomer=dGJyMOHo44Hl3vJ T69fnhrnb5ofx6gAA

7. Kerker BD, Mostashari F, Thrope L (2006). Health care access and utilization among women who have sex with women: sexual behavior and identity. *J Urban Health.* 83(5):970-979.

8. Levitt, N., Carr, E. R., & Editor, -Associate. (2015). Clinical Nursing Care for Transgender Patients With Cancer Oncology Essentials. *Clinical Journal of Oncology Nursing, 19*(3). https://doi.org/10.1188/15.CJON.362-366

9. Massetti, G. M., Ragan, K. R., Thomas, C. C., & Ryerson, A. B. (2015). Public Health Opportunities for Promoting Health Equity in Cancer Prevention and Control in LGBT Populations. Retrieved from https://www.ncbi.nlm.nih.gov/pmc/articles/PMC4639460/pdf/nihms-733990.pdf

10. Mayrand, M.-H., Duarte-Franco, E., Rodrigues, I., Walter, S. D., Hanley, J., Ferenczy, A., … Franco, E. L. (2007). Human Papillomavirus DNA versus Papanicolaou Screening Tests for Cervical Cancer. *New England Journal of Medicine, 357*(16), 1579–1588. https://doi.org/10.1056/NEJMoa071430

11. McPherson, K., Steel, C. M., & Dixon, J. M. (2000). Breast cancer—epidemiology, risk factors, and genetics. *BMJ : British Medical Journal, 321*(7261), 624–628.

12. Moreau, J. (2018). Global LGBTQ acceptance more polarized, new research finds. Retrieved July 29, 2018, from https://www.nbcnews.com/feature/nbc-out/global-lgbtq-acceptance-more-polarized-new-research-finds-n871106

13. Nagata, J. M. (2017). Challenges, health implications, and advocacy opportunities for lesbian, gay, bisexual, and transgender global health providers. *Global Health Promotion*, 175797591667750. https://doi.org/10.1177/1757975916677504

14. Peitzmeier, S. M., Reisner, S. L., Harigopal, P., & Potter, J. (2014). Female-to-Male Patients Have High Prevalence of Unsatisfactory Paps Compared to Non-Transgender Females: Implications for Cervical Cancer Screening. *J Gen Intern Med*, 29(5), 778–84. https://doi.org/10.1007/s11606-013-2753-1

15. Price JH, Easton AN, Telljohann SK, Wallace PB. Perceptions of cervical cancer and pap smear screening behavior by women's sexual orientation. *J Community Health*. 1996;21(2):89-105.

16. Reid, G. (2016). Equality to brutality: global trends in LGBT rights | Human Rights Watch. Retrieved July 29, 2018, from https://www.hrw.org/news/2016/01/07/equality-brutality-global-trends-lgbt-rights

17. Scherdel, L., Martin, A., Deivanayagam, A., Adams, E., & Shanahan, T. (2014). *The search for international consensus on LGBT health*. https://doi.org/10.1016/S2214-109X(13)70169-4

18. *USPSTF A and B Recommendations*. U.S. Preventive Services Task Force. July 2018. https://www.uspreventiveservicestaskforce.org/Page/Name/uspstf-a-and-b-recommendations/

19. Willes, K & Allen, M. The importance of sexual orientation disclosure to physicians for women who have sex with women. *Health Care Disparities and the LGBT Population*. (2014). Lanham, CT: Lexington Books. 9-25.

Preventative Care for Lesbian Women

Anonymous

Introduction

The current national dialogue on health care places its focus on health insurance and access to preventative care as the primary problems with the system. These factors are often discussed from a population level with focus on race, ethnicity, or socioeconomic status, but rarely does sexual orientation enter the discussion of health care disparities. A health care disparity is defined as a difference between population groups in "health coverage, access to care, and quality of care" ("Disparities in Health and Health Care", 2012). These differences go beyond variations in the health needs of the population group and are rooted much more deeply in the societal fabric ("Disparities in Health and Health Care", 2012). The health care disparities that can occur due to sexual orientation are rarely discussed, but an understanding that these disparities do occur and a discussion of why that may be the case is critical to finding solutions. One such disparity is the lower rate of Pap smear tests and Human Papilloma Virus (HPV) vaccinations in lesbian women, which may be placing these women at a higher risk for advanced cervical cancer.

To fully understand the population group at risk, a definition of what is meant by the term lesbian is necessary. Anywhere from 3% to 11% of females in the United States may be identified as lesbians (Waterman, Voss, 2015, p. 46). The variation in the percentage may be accounted for in the difficulties of the terminology. It is difficult to define the group as not all women who have a primary sexual or romantic relationship with a woman identify as a lesbian. Moreover, sexual identity does not reflect past sexual behaviors or attractions, and many women who self-identify as lesbians may have had male partners in the past or even have current male partners (Waterman, Voss, 2015, p. 49). The term "women who have sex with women" relates entirely to sexual behavior, while "lesbian" relates to sexual identity. (Polek, Hardie, 2010, p. E191). Not all women may accept the term lesbian, regardless of their sexual behavior. However, for the purposes of this paper, lesbian will be used loosely to describe both sexual behavior and sexual identity, but it should be mentioned that not all women described in the data would self-identify as lesbian.

Epidemiology

Lesbians experience many risk factors for HPV infection, making preventative tests such as Pap smears and HPV vaccines essential. HPV is the most common sexuality transmitted infection (STI) in the United States with an 80% lifetime incidence (Charlton, Corliss, Missmer, Frazier, Rosario, Kahn, Austin, 2011, p. 505). Nearly all cases of cervical cancer are caused by HPV, and incidence of new cervical cancer diagnosis is 7.8 cases per 100,000 women. There were 12,360 new cases of cervical cancer in 2014 with 4,020 associated deaths (McIntrye, Szewchuk, Munro, 2010, p. 886). Since introduction of Pap smears in 1950s, incidence of cervical cancer and cervical cancer deaths have decreased by more than 60%. However, lesbians continue to experience later detection of cervical cancer, which places them at higher stages with a worse prognosis (McIntrye, Szewchuk, Munro, 2010 p. 886). A primary risk factor for HPV infection is sexual contact with men and in woman who identify as lesbians, an average of 77% reported sex with men in their lifetime and an average of 17% reported sex with men in the previous year (Waterman, Voss, 2015, p. 49). When a patient identifies as lesbian, a physician may not realize that a sexual history with men may still be relevant to her preventative care.

Additionally, lesbians are placed at risk for HPV infection by their female partners. HPV transmission occurs via skin-to-skin contact (Waterman, Voss, 2015 p. 48). This includes genital-to-genital contact, oral-genital contact, and digital-genital contact, and many lesbians engage in these activities. It has also been shown that HPV DNA can exist on fomites that survive on hard surfaces such as fingers or sex toys, another way that HPV can be transmitted female-to-female (Waterman, Voss, 2015, p. 48). HPV can also colonize the oropharynx and be transmitted via oral-genital contact (Henderson, 2009, p. 43). The prevalence of HPV infection is similar among lesbians as compared to their heterosexual counterparts (Agénor, Peitzmeirer, Gordon, Haneuse, Potter, Austin, 2015, p. 99). Bailey, Kavanagh, Owen, McLean, and Skinner (2000), examined at cervical exams of 606 women in a London lesbian sexual health clinic. While they found that cervical abnormalities were more common in women reporting prior sex with men, they also found HPV-attributed cervical abnormalities in two patients who reported their sexual experiences to be exclusively with female partners (p. 482). Although this is self-reported data, it strongly suggests female-to-female HPV transmission.

It is clear that lesbians are exposed to HPV from both male and female partners. Once they have HPV, there are certain risk factors that lesbians experience as a population group that places them at an even greater risk of developing cervical cancer from that virus. Lesbians have been shown to have higher rates of cigarette smoking and higher obesity rates than their heterosexual counterparts, both of which are risk factors for the development of cervical cancer (Agénor, et al., 2015, p. 100). Lesbians may also have more alcohol use, another risk factor (Waterman, Voss, 2015, p. 50). These risk factors make Pap smear testing and HPV vaccination imperative in this population group.

Consistent evidence shows that lesbians have lower rates of Pap smears than heterosexual women. A literature review by Waterman and Voss (2015) showed that lesbians experience Pap smear screening at a rate of 5% to 18% lower than heterosexual women. While an average of 78% to 81% of heterosexual women report recent Pap smears, only 68.1% of lesbians report recent Pap smears (p. 48). Similar results were found by Charlton, et al. (2011) in their examination of a 2005 questionnaire with data from 4,225 adolescent females. They found that compared to heterosexuals, adolescent lesbians had lower odds of both having had a Pap smear in their lifetime and having had a Pap smear in the past year. This remained true even when controlling for sociodemographic factors (p. 508). Henderson (2009) looked at post-menopausal women and found that the women in that group who had never had a Pap smear were 2.33 times more likely to be lesbian or bisexual (p. 44). Similar preventative care disparities exist in regard to the HPV vaccination. Agénor, et al. (2015) focused on 2006-2010 survey data from 3,253 women ages 15 to 25 who were asked about the HPV vaccine. Of women who had heard of the vaccine, 8.4% of lesbians had initiated being administered the vaccine, compared to 28.5% of heterosexual women and 32.2% of bisexual women. The difference remained statistically significant when adjusted for sociodemographic factors and makers of health care access. The lower rates of preventative care measure in lesbian women show that a health care disparity exists; there are many possible reasons why lesbian women may have less utilization of these services.

Barriers to Care

One possible reason that lesbians may have lower rates of preventative services is that they feel uncomfortable discussing their sexual preferences with a health care provider. In many cases lesbians report a previous negative experience with a health care provider when discussing their sexual identity (Polek, Hardie E194). Sometimes these experiences can simply be created by heteronormative assumptions by health care providers that lead to uncomfortable conversations (Agénor, et al., 2015, p. 103). One woman reports her experience with these assumptions:

This seems to come up every time I go to the doctor now. A doctor or nurse asks me the routine questions, "Why am I there that day?", "What hurts?", "Am I on any medications?", "When was my last menstrual cycle?", etc. Slowly the questions get more and more personal, building the intensity in the room. When they ask if there is any chance that I am pregnant and I respond "No", they

ALWAYS respond with what I can only assume is a routine follow-up, catch-all question: "Have you had unprotected sex within the last nine months?" They usually look up from their chart when I respond with my simple "yes". They give the look of annoyance and ask how I am sure that I am not pregnant, forcing me to awkwardly defend myself. Yes, I have unprotected sex. How do I know I am not pregnant? Because I had it with my beautiful, intelligent, monogamous girlfriend.

—BR, 2015

In other cases, the discomfort comes when conversations of sexuality are simply never had, as reported in this case:

My doctor never asked me about my sexuality so I never told her. [She] just assumed I was straight. My sexuality is relevant to my health care not only physically but mentally as well.

—CW, 2015

These experiences reported show the discomfort that can occur with heteronormative assumptions by physicians and expose one possibility of why lesbian women may avoid routine preventative health care.

Another possible reason for the lower rates of preventative measures against cervical cancer in lesbian women comes from the lack of education that health care providers receive regarding female-to-female intercourse and the assumptions that this can create. Waterman and Voss (2015) found in their investigation that 9% to 10% of lesbian women were told by a health care provider that they did not need Pap smear screening since they were not sexually active with men (p. 52). McIntrye, Szewchuk, and Munro (2010) conducted a series of interviews with middle age lesbian women and some women reported to them that their physicians discouraged them from having a Pap smear because they were lesbians (p. 890). These same women felt that disclosing their sexuality to their physician only resulted in better care if their physician was knowledgeable about lesbian health needs and sexuality (p. 893).

It is not apparent how widespread the misconception that lesbians do not need HPV screening is within the health care field, but these cases demonstrate that there are women being affected by the lack of education physicians receive in lesbian healthcare.

The assumptions and misconceptions of lesbians is also a factor in the lower screening rates of lesbian women. Waterman and Voss (2015) found that Only 25% of women who have sex with women perceived themselves to be at HPV risk and even fewer believed that HPV can be spread female-to-female (p. 52). This belief is also shared in this experience:

> For some reason I thought my sexual identity also gave me a clean pass to whatever it was they were swabbing down that. After my last pap smear, I was told that I do not need to have one for another 3 years. At first I wasn't sure if that was because I was a girl who slept with girls and therefore was exempt or if it was a new medical practice to only have a pap every 3 years.
>
> —BR, 2015

In addition to the lack of full understanding about HPV in this statement, there is also an implied discomfort about asking the physician about the recommendations. Some women in the interviews conducted by McIntrye, Szewchuk, and Munro (2010) further explained why lesbians may feel that they do not need Pap smears. Women in the study reported feeling that they were at lower risk of STIs such as HPV because of the mainstream safe sex education that characterizes the primary risk of sexual intercourse to come from penile penetration (p. 885). Power, McNair, and Carr (2009) conducted a similar series of interviews and the lesbians in that study reported that the limited fluid exchange in female-to-female intercourse made them feel that STIs were not a concern (p. 76). These assumptions likely also can be attributed to mainstream sexual health messages that do not provide a well-rounded picture of all sexual activities that can transmit HPV and other STIs.

A final reason that lesbians are less likely to receive preventative screening measures is simply that they present to the health care setting less frequently. Lesbians are less likely to use contraceptives which results in fewer visits to gynecologic providers (Polek, Hardie, 2010, p. E192). Without these yearly visits to discuss or refill their contraceptives, women are more likely to miss preventative tests such as Pap smears (Henderson, 2009, p. 42). This same logic can be extended to the initiation of the HPV vaccination series. When young women are not seen routinely in the health care setting, it is much easier for these tests to be missed. A further extension of this idea was seen in the interviews of McIntrye, Szewchuk, and Munro (2010) in which some women perceived Pap smears to be related to birth control and therefore not necessary for women who were not on birth control (p. 890). The fact the lesbian women may present less frequently for routine appointments makes it critical that preventative tests are discussed when they do present to the health care setting to make sure that they are up to date in their care.

Possible Solutions

There are many ways that this disparity in preventative care experienced by lesbian women can be combatted. The first is simply open communication and discussion between physician and patient. When doctors ask open-ended and non-presumptuous questions about sexual activity, this can make the patients experience much more positive.

> My doctor was the first "grown-up" I came out to. She went through the routine questions of sexual experience and made it natural for me to disclose my female partner. She did not act surprised by this disclosure and continued on with the exam as I assume she normally would. This made me feel very comfortable.
>
> —SR, 2015

When patients feel comfortable with their provider they will be much more likely to share pertinent history and return for follow-up care. Physicians need to take a role in communicating to lesbians patients their specific need for regular Pap smear screening and HPV vaccination. Agénor, et al. (2015) found that women of all sexualities are more likely to initiate the HPV vaccination series after discussing it with their provider (p. 101). Along with these open discussions, it is important that physicians not make assumptions about past sexual experiences when a woman identifies herself as a lesbian or reports a current female partner. Physicians must be aware of the diversity of experiences lesbians can have and ask careful, open-ended questions to get a full sexual history of all past partners and sexual experiences.

In addition to open communication, education of both patients and physicians is necessary for resolution of this health care disparity. Women need to be aware of the possibility of female-to-female spread of HPV and their risk for cervical cancer. This can be accomplished by including information about female-to-female sex in mainstream safe sex campaigns. The specific risk to lesbians of HPV and other STIs from both female and male partners needs to be addressed so that lesbians realize that they need Pap smears and HPV vaccination at the same rate as heterosexual women. Physicians also need to be made aware of the risk of female-to-female spread of HPV. Information on sexual health as it specifically relates to lesbians should be included in medical school curriculums so that future providers can enter the field prepared for informed discussions with their lesbian patients.

Conclusion

Though health care disparities regarding sexual orientation are not commonly discussed or included in medical school curriculums, they are still occurring and having a negative impact on the lives of patients. From the existing evidence, it is clear that lesbians are at risk for HPV due to female-to-female transmission and the possibility of previous male partners. Therefore, lesbians need both regular Pap smear screening and HPV vaccination at the same rate as heterosexual women. However, current evidence suggests that such preventatives care measures occur in lesbians at a lower rate than in their heterosexual counterparts. The barriers causing this health disparity include discomfort caused by physician assumptions, lack of knowledge about lesbian sexual health in both patients and physicians, and the lower rates of routine gynecologic care among lesbians. There is a need for open communication between patient and provider and the education of both patients and physicians in issues of lesbian sexual health. A more informed perspective from both sides will allow for open-communication in the clinic setting and an emphasis on the importance of cervical cancer prevention for all women.

References

1. Agénor, M., Peitzmeier, S., Gordon, A.R., Haneuse, S., Potter, J.E., & Austin, S.B. (2015). Sexual Orientation Identity Disparities in Awareness and Initiation of the Human Papillomavirus Vaccine Among U.S. Women and Girls. Annals of Internal Medicine, 163(2), 99 – 106.

2. Bailey, J.V., Kavanagh, J., Owen, C., McLean, K.A., & Skinner, C.J. (2000). Lesbians and cervical screening. British Journal of General Practice, 50, 481-482.

3. Charlton, B.M., Corliss, H.L., Missmer, S.A., Frazier, A.L., Rosario, M., Kahn, J.A., & Austin, S.B. (2011). Reproductive Health Screening Disparities and Sexual Orientation Study of U.S. Adolescent and Young Adult Females. Journal of Adolescent Health, 49, 505-510.

4. Disparities in Health and Health Care: Questions and Answers (2012, November 30). Retrieved from http://kff.org/disparities-policy/issue-brief/disparities-in-health-and-health-care-five-key questions-and-answers

5. Henderson, H.J. (2009). Why lesbians should be encouraged to have regular cervical screening. Journal of Family Planning and Reproductive Health Care, 35(1), 49-52.

6. McIntrye, L., Szewchuk, A., & Munro, J. (2010). Inclusion and exclusion in mid-life lesbians' experiences of the Pap test. Culture, Health & Sexuality, 12(8), 885-898.

7. Polek, C., & Hardie, T. (2010). Lesbian Women and Knowledge About Human Papillomavirus. Oncology Nursing Forum, 37(3), E191-E197.

8. Power, J., McNair, R., & Carr, S. (2009). Absent sexual scripts: lesbian and bisexual women's knowledge, attitudes and action regarding safer sex and sexual health information. Culture, Health & Sexuality, 11(1), 67-81.

9. Waterman, L., & Voss, J. (2015). HPV, cervical cancer risk, and barriers to care for lesbian women. The Nurse Practitioner, 40(1), 46-53.

Chapter 5.

Conclusion

Sade Kosoko-Lasaki, MD, MSPH, MBA

The Creighton University Medical School elective that transitioned into this book shows the dedication of professors in guiding students through addressing health disparities in the LGBTQIA community. The students have worked hard in their research of these health disparities and have made meaningful recommendations on how practitioners can be cognizant of how to minimize them. In the Latin phrase, *primum non nocere* that means, "first do no harm", this should remind all healthcare personnel to consider the possible harm that any interventions may do. As a result, we want our students to strive to take care of all their patients, including the LGBTQIA individuals, regardless of their personal bias. This subject is of tremendous importance in the education and training of our healthcare professionals and I hope that it becomes part of the curriculum and not an elective that only a few students get to select.

Thank you to my co-authors, Drs Goodman and White, also Dr Greene for his contribution to this book. I have enjoyed working with you all.

Mark Duane Goodman, MD

It has been an honor to work with this fine team in creating this book. We have the perspectives of tremendous thoughtful and brave learners: who ask important questions about how to build better relationships going forward. We have thoughtful introduction, and tremendous support from all of the editors: who help to build a more just and safer environment for health care.

Repeatedly, in my practice, I have found that curiosity (as brilliantly outlined by Dr. Greene) expressed as a greeting in my patients native tongue, a conversation about food "from back home" and inquiries about spouse and parents and kids and school can build bridges with people, even if our lives have been very different. Expressions of curiosity and respect, and continued work on being a good listener and a good advocate are the true practice builders.

In the Jewish tradition, at bar mitzvah/bat mitzvah, the young person coming of age takes on the challenge of "tikkun olam" which means "to repair the world". In the same fashion, it is our aspiration that this book advances the thoughtfulness, competency and maturation of learners, so that they may be able also to repair the world. For far too long medical caregivers have been lofty, and separate from their patients, and perhaps not as culturally adept. LGBTQ patients historically have been shunned and stung in the former environments of cultural ignorance and judgment. Going forward, it is our belief that best care, and best outcomes will happen in an environment of safety, cultural competency and compassion: envisioning a world where patients need not fear their health care providers, and providers need not fear their patients. Thank you for sharing in this conversation.

Michael White, MD, MBA

Information on individuals' treatment and medical care continue to accelerate at a rapid pace requiring dedication to lifelong learning. Sexual orientation and gender identity have not been historically well covered in the curricula of health professions education. To improve the quality of care for the LGBTQIA community, we need to shift attitudes towards sexual orientation and gender identity to facilitate learning about these specific health needs.

It has been a pleasure to work with my colleagues to develop an opportunity for medical students to deeply explore the information and literature to understand their patients' specific needs. Providing these experiences allows the development of skills that will enhance the process of lifelong learning and improve the quality of patient care. As a Jesuit institution, Creighton University promotes core charisms of which one is "women and men for and with others." Educating physicians through this lens illustrates that more than just giving and providing service to those in need, we must work alongside those we serve to promote solidarity. Critical understanding of the entire patient is essential for exceptional care, and by challenging students to grow in all areas, we will continue to transform healthcare delivery.

Index

Intimate partner violence 277

L

LGBTQIA Community
  asexual 32, 113, 284
  bisexual 16, 17, 18, 32, 44, 48, 56, 67,
    68, 70, 76, 77, 78, 79, 81, 83, 84, 88,
    89, 92, 100, 107, 113, 115, 116, 117,
    118, 140, 141, 143, 146, 147, 160, 172,
    201, 211, 212, 215, 226, 243, 244, 246,
    262, 264, 265, 273, 274, 275, 276, 277,
    280, 284, 293, 297, 303, 305, 306,
    307, 326
  gay 16, 17, 18, 19, 20, 32, 35, 44, 56,
    59, 63, 67, 68, 70, 76, 77, 78, 79, 80,
    81, 82, 83, 84, 88, 89, 92, 94, 97, 100,
    107, 113, 115, 116, 125, 126, 140, 141,
    142, 143, 146, 147, 160, 163, 180, 201,
    204, 206, 211, 212, 219, 223, 225, 226,
    243, 244, 249, 252, 253, 254, 255,
    256, 257, 258, 262, 264, 266, 267, 274,
    289, 293, 297, 305, 311
  Homosexual men 66, 69, 71
  intersex 32, 113, 220, 262
  lesbian 16, 17, 18, 32, 44, 47, 48, 76,
    77, 78, 79, 80, 81, 82, 83, 84, 86, 88,
    89, 92, 94, 97, 107, 113, 115, 116, 117,
    118, 119, 125, 126, 140, 141, 143, 146,
    147, 160, 163, 180, 188, 201, 203, 204,
    206, 211, 212, 215, 223, 226, 243, 244,
    246, 252, 253, 254, 255, 256, 257, 258,
    262, 264, 265, 273, 274, 275, 276, 277,
    280, 293, 303, 306, 307, 311, 312, 316,
    318, 320, 323, 324, 325, 326, 327, 328,
    329, 330, 331
  LGBT individuals 19, 109, 170, 171,
    173, 174, 175, 202, 207, 245, 297

LGBTQ 13, 17, 18, 20, 24, 25, 37, 44,
  55, 56, 59, 60, 62, 63, 120, 146, 151,
  152, 153, 154, 163, 164, 165, 186, 188,
  222, 223, 224, 225, 226, 227, 228,
  229, 334
LGBTQIA Adolescents. *See*
  Adolescents
LGBTQIA population 44, 45, 46,
  47, 48, 49, 50, 51, 118, 121, 273
LGBT youth 18, 19, 80, 81, 82, 83,
  84, 85, 86, 135, 181, 184
queer 17, 18, 32, 113, 139, 140, 141,
  142, 143, 146, 160, 214, 223, 232
queer adolescents 232
queer/questioning 17
sexual identity 19, 38, 49, 80, 84,
  113, 115, 125, 140, 160, 162, 168, 213,
  220, 223, 225, 228, 257, 265, 279, 280,
  284, 303, 304, 308, 316, 324, 326, 328
Sexual minority 116, 119, 127, 262
Sexual minority adolescents 119,
  127
sexual minority youth 19, 80, 113,
  119, 120, 126, 127, 267, 285, 286
transgender 16, 17, 18, 32, 44, 46,
  47, 55, 57, 58, 62, 67, 88, 89, 94, 95,
  96, 97, 98, 99, 100, 101, 102, 103, 104,
  105, 106, 107, 108, 109, 110, 113, 121,
  123, 130, 131, 132, 133, 134, 135, 136,
  137, 140, 142, 143, 146, 147, 148, 149,
  150, 151, 152, 153, 154, 155, 168, 169,
  170, 171, 172, 173, 175, 178, 180, 181,
  182, 183, 184, 185, 186, 187, 188, 201,
  204, 211, 212, 213, 215, 224, 225, 226,
  227, 243, 244, 246, 248, 262, 264,
  266, 267, 268, 273, 274, 278, 279, 280,
  284, 285, 286, 287, 288, 289, 290, 293,
  310, 311, 312, 313, 319, 320